ROAD TO SUSPICION

Sociology Series

John F. Cuber, Editor
Alfred C. Clarke, Associate Editor

Gunter W. Remmling

Southern Illinois University

ROAD TO SUSPICION

*A Study of Modern Mentality
and the Sociology of Knowledge*

New York

Appleton - Century - Crofts

DIVISION OF MEREDITH PUBLISHING COMPANY

121

R 28 r

ACKNOWLEDGMENTS

(Page numbers given are those of this volume.)

p. 8   From Harold Fallding, "Functional Analysis in Sociology," *American Sociological Review*, Vol. 28, No. 1 (February, 1963). Reprinted by permission.

p. 8   From *The Great Time-Killer*, by Harold Mehling. Copyright (C) 1962 by Harold Mehling, reprinted by permission of The Harold Matson Company, Inc., and The World Publishing Company.

p. 8   Reprinted from ORDEAL BY SLANDER, by Owen Lattimore. Copyright © 1950 by Owen Lattimore. Reprinted with permission of Atlantic-Little, Brown and Company.

p. 8   From "Robert Oppenheimer" by Gerald W. Johnson. Reprinted by permission of THE NEW REPUBLIC, © 1963, Harrison-Blaine of New Jersey, Inc.

p. 9   From *Freud and the Crisis of Our Culture*, by Lionel Trilling, Beacon Press, 1955. Reprinted by permission of the author.

p. 9   From Jeanne Hersch, *Die Ideologien und die Wirklichkeit: Versuch einer politischen Orientierung*, München: R. Piper, 1957. Reprinted by permission.

p. 9   From Werner Heisenberg, *Physics and Philosophy: The Revolution in Modern Science*, New York: Harper & Row, Publishers, 1962. Reprinted by permission.

p. 9   From Pitirim A. Sorokin, *The Crisis of Our Age*, New York: E. P. Dutton, 1957. Reprinted by permission.

p. 10   From "Methodological Consequences of the Sociology of Knowledge," by C. Wright Mills. *American Journal of Sociology*, Vol. XLVI, No. 3, November, 1940. Printed with the permission of the University of Chicago Press.

p. 10   From C. Wright Mills, *White Collar: The American Middle Classes*, New York: Oxford University Press, 1956. Reprinted by permission.

p. 13   From Émile Durkheim, *The Elementary Forms of the Religious Life*, London: George Allen & Unwin Ltd., 1954. Reprinted by permission.

p. 21   From Robert K. Merton, "The Sociology of Knowledge," in Georges Gurvitch and Wilbert E. Moore (editors), *Twentieth Century Sociology*, New York: The Philosophical Library, Inc., 1945. Reprinted by permission.

p. 32   From *Ideology and Utopia: An Introduction to the Sociology of Knowledge*, by Karl Mannheim. Published by Routledge & Kegan Paul Ltd. Published by Harcourt, Brace & World, Inc. Reprinted with permission.

p. 34 ff.   From Max Scheler, *Die Wissensformen und die Gesellschaft. Gesammelte Werke*, Vol. 8, Bern and München: Francke Verlag, 1960. Reprinted by permission.

p. 34 ff.   From Karl Mannheim, *Essays on the Sociology of Knowledge*, New York: Oxford University Press, 1952. Reprinted by permission.

p. 34   From Karl Mannheim, *Diagnosis of Our Time*, London: Routledge & Kegan Paul Ltd., 1943. Reprinted by permission.

p. 39   From THE PROBLEM OF HISTORICAL KNOWLEDGE, by Maurice Mandelbaum. By Permission of LIVERIGHT, Publishers, New York. Copyright (C) Renewed, 1966 by Maurice Mandelbaum.

p. 42   From Gunter W. Remmling, "Karl Mannheim: Revision of an Intellectual Portrait," *Social Forces*, Vol. 40, No. 1 (October, 1961). Reprinted by permission.

p. 46   From *The Image: Knowledge in Life and Society*, by Kenneth E. Boulding. Copyright C

ACKNOWLEDGMENTS

by The University of Michigan 1956. Reprinted by permission of The University of Michigan Press.

p. 57 ff.　From *Critique of Pure Reason*, by Immanuel Kant, 1956. Reprinted by permission of Macmillan & Co., Ltd.

p. 66 ff.　From Georg Wilhelm Friedrich Hegel: REASON IN HISTORY, edited by R. S. Hartman, copyright, 1953, by The Liberal Arts Press, Inc., reprinted by permission of The Liberal Arts Press Division of The Bobbs-Merrill Company, Inc.

p. 69 ff.　From G. W. F. Hegel, *Philosophy of Right*, 1953, by permission of the Clarendon Press, Oxford.

p. 73 ff.　From Wilhelm Dilthey, *Weltanschauungslehre: Abhandlungen zur Philosophie der Philosophie, Gesammelte Schriften*, Vol. VIII, Leipzig and Berlin: B. G. Teubner, 1931. Reprinted by permission.

p. 73 ff.　From Wilhelm Dilthey, *Die Geistige Welt: Einleitung in die Philosophie des Lebens, Gesammelte Schriften*, Vol. V, Leipzig and Berlin: B. G. Teubner, 1924. Reprinted by permission.

p. 74　From Wilhelm Dilthey, *Einleitung in die Geisteswissenschaften: Versuch einer Grundlegung der Gesellschaft und der Geschichte, Gesammelte Schriften*, Vol. I, Stuttgart: B. G. Teubner, 1923. Reprinted by permission.

p. 74 ff.　From Wilhelm Dilthey, *Der Aufbau der Geschichtlichen Welt in den Geisteswissenschaften, Gesammelte Schriften*, Vol. VII, Leipzig and Berlin: B. G. Teubner, 1927. Reprinted by permission.

p. 78　From Wilhelm Dilthey, *The Essence of Philosophy*, Chapel Hill: The University of North Carolina Press, 1954. Reprinted by permission.

p. 78　From William Kluback, *Wilhelm Dilthey's Philosophy of History*, New York: Columbia University Press, 1956. Reprinted by permission.

p. 81　From Wilhelm Dilthey, *Dilthey's Philosophy of Existence: Introduction to Weltanschauungslehre*, translated by Klubach and Weinbaum, New York: Bookman Associates, Inc., 1957. Reprinted by permission.

p. 85　From H. A. Hodges, *The Philosophy of Wilhelm Dilthey*, London: Routledge & Kegan Paul Ltd., 1952. Reprinted by permission.

p. 88　From Heinrich Rickert, *Der Gegenstand der Erkenntnis*, 2nd ed., Tübingen: J. C. B. Mohr, 1904. Reprinted by permission.

p. 91　From *Ideas: General Introduction to Pure Phenomenology*, by Edmund Husserl. Copyright 1952. Published by The Macmillan Company. Published by George Allen & Unwin Ltd. Reprinted by permission.

p. 92　From Alfred Schuetz, "Phenomenology and Social Sciences," in Marvin Farber (editor), *Philosophical Essays in Memory of Edmund Husserl*, Cambridge, Mass.: Harvard University Press, 1940. Reprinted by permission.

p. 99　From *Man in the Modern Age*, by Karl Jaspers. Reprinted by permission of Routledge & Kegan Paul Ltd.

p. 109　From *European Sociology and the American Self-Image*, by Ralf Dahrendorf. Reprinted from the European Journal of Sociology, II (1961), pp. 324–366.

p. 118 ff.　From Francis Bacon, *Advancement of Learning and Novum Organum*, New York: John Wiley & Sons, 1944. Reprinted by permission.

p. 122　From *An Introduction to Metaphysics*, by Martin Heidegger (translated by Ralph Manheim). Reprinted by permission of Yale University Press.

p. 125　From *Wahrheit und Ideologie*, by Hans Barth, 1961. 2. Auflage. Reprinted by permission of Eugen Rentsch Verlag A.-G. Erlenbach-Zürich.

p. 126　From *The Study of Sociology*, by Herbert Spencer, 1961. Reprinted by permission of The University of Michigan Press.

p. 129 ff.　From Peter Gay, *The Party of Humanity: Essays in the French Enlightenment*, New York: Alfred A. Knopf, 1964. Reprinted by permission.

p. 130　From *Selected Essays*, by Karl Marx, translated by H. J. Stenning, pp. 11, 12, and 191. By Permission of International Publishers Co. Inc.

p. 132　From Carl L. Becker, *The Heavenly City of the Eighteenth-Century Philosophers*, New Haven: Yale University Press, 1932. Reprinted by permission.

p. 132　Crane Brinton, "Comment on Gay," *American Historical Review*, Vol. LXVI, No. 3 (April, 1961). Reprinted by permission.

p. 133 ff.　From M. Roustan, *The Pioneers of the French Revolution*, Boston: Little, Brown and Company, 1926. Reprinted by permission of Ernest Benn Limited, London.

p. 137　From *The Philosophy of the Enlightenment*, by Ernst Cassirer. Copyright 1951 by Princeton University Press. London: Geoffrey Cumberlege, Oxford University Press. This is a translation of DIE PHILOSOPHIE DER AUFKLÄRUNG, the German edition of which was published by J. C. B. Mohr in Tübingen in 1932. All the translator's notes have been provided by Mr. Pettegrove, and unless otherwise specified, all French and Latin sources quoted have been translated by him. Printed in the U.S.A. by Princeton University Press. Reprinted by permission.

ACKNOWLEDGMENTS

p. 141   From Charles Hunter van Duzer, *Contribution of the Ideologues to French Revolutionary Thought*, Dissertation, Baltimore: The Johns Hopkins Press, 1935. Reprinted by permission.

p. 143   From J. E. Barker, *Diderot's Treatment of the Christian Religion in the Encyclopédie*, New York: King's Crown Press, 1941. Reprinted by permission.

p. 143   From RAMEAU'S NEPHEW AND OTHER WORKS by Denis Diderot, translated by Jacques Barzun and Ralph H. Bowen. Copyright (C) 1956 by Jacques Barzun and Ralph H. Bowen. Reprinted by permission of Doubleday & Company, Inc.

p. 146 ff.   From T. B. Bottomore and Maximilien Rubel, Introduction to Karl Marx, *Selected Writings in Sociology and Social Philosophy*, London: C. A. Watts & Co., 1961. Reprinted by permission.

p. 146 ff.   From Sidney Hook, *Towards the Understanding of Karl Marx: A Revolutionary Interpretation*, New York: The John Day Co., 1933. Reprinted by permission.

p. 148 ff.   From *The German Ideology*, by Karl Marx and Friederich Engels, edited by R. Pascal, pages 6, 22, 181, 64 and 65, 70. By Permission of International Publishers Co. Inc.

p. 148 ff.   From Karl Marx, *Nationalökonomie und Philosophie*, Köln and Berlin: Verlag Kiepenheuer & Witsch, 1950. Reprinted by permission.

p. 153 ff.   From Karl Marx, Friedrich Engels, *Die Heilige Familie*, Berlin: Dietz Verlag, 1953. Reprinted by permission.

p. 156 ff.   From Ryazanoff, D. (Ed.) THE COMMUNIST MANIFESTO OF KARL MARX AND FRIEDRICH ENGELS, [1930], New York: Russell & Russell, 1963. Reprinted by permission.

p. 156 ff.   From Karl Marx, Friedrich Engels, *Selected Works*, Vol. I, Moscow: Foreign Languages Publishing House, London: Lawrence and Wishart Ltd., 1950. Reprinted by permission.

p. 159   From Frederick Engels, *Anti-Dühring: Herr Eugen Dühring's Revolution in Science*, Moscow: Foreign Languages Publishing House, 1954, London: Lawrence and Wishart Ltd., 1955. Reprinted by permission.

p. 160   From Karl Marx, Friedrich Engels, *On Religion*, Moscow: Foreign Languages Publishing House, 1957. Reprinted by permission.

p. 165 ff.   From Friedrich Nietzsche, *Gesammelte Werke*, München: Musarion Verlag, 1920–1929. Excerpts from vols. XVIII and XIX, "Der Wille zur Macht," used by permission of Alfred Kröner Verlag, Stuttgart.

p. 167   From *Nietzsche: Philosopher, Psychologist, Antichrist*, by W. Kaufmann. Copyright 1950 by Princeton University Press. London: Geoffrey Cumberlege, Oxford University Press. Reprinted by permission.

p. 170   From Bertrand Russell, *History of Western Philosophy and Its Connection with Political and Social Circumstances from the Earliest Times to the Present Day*, London: George Allen & Unwin Ltd., 1955. Reprinted by permission.

p. 176   From *The Unadjusted Man: A New Hero for Americans* by Peter Viereck. Reprinted by permission of the Beacon Press, copyright © 1956 by the Beacon Press.

p. 181 ff.   From Alfred Seidel, *Bewusstsein als Verhängnis*, Bonn: Verlag Friedrich Cohen, 1927. Reprinted by permission.

p. 182 ff.   From Arthur Schopenhauer, *The World as Will and Idea*, Routledge & Kegan Paul Ltd., 1948. Reprinted by permission.

p. 183 ff.   From Philip Rieff, *Freud: The Mind of the Moralist*, New York: The Viking Press, Inc., 1959. Reprinted by permission.

p. 183 ff.   To Sigmund Freud Copyrights Ltd., Mr. James Strachey, and The Hogarth Press Ltd., to quote from Volumes 14, 18, 21, 22, and 23 of the Standard Edition, THE COMPLETE PSYCHOLOGICAL WORKS OF SIGMUND FREUD. "Thoughts for the Times on War and Death (1915)," from Volume IV of the COLLECTED PAPERS OF SIGMUND FREUD, Basic Books, Inc., Publishers, 1959. "Why War? (1932)," from Volume V of the COLLECTED PAPERS OF SIGMUND FREUD, Basic Books, Inc., Publishers, 1959. From CIVILIZATION AND ITS DISCONTENTS by Sigmund Freud. Newly translated from the German and Edited by James Strachey. W. W. Norton & Company, Inc., New York, N.Y. Copyright © 1961 by James Strachey. Reprinted by permission from the publisher. From: BEYOND THE PLEASURE PRINCIPLE, by Sigmund Freud. By Permission of LIVERIGHT, Publishers, N.Y. From: THE FUTURE OF AN ILLUSION, by Sigmund Freud. By Permission of LIVERIGHT, Publishers, N.Y. From AN OUTLINE OF PSYCHOANALYSIS by Sigmund Freud. Translated by James Strachey. Copyright, 1949, by W. W. Norton & Company, Inc., New York, N.Y. Reprinted by permission.

p. 185   From *An Enquiry Concerning Human Understanding*, 2nd ed., by David Hume, 1966. The Open Court Publishing Company, La Salle, Illinois. Reprinted by permission.

p. 188   From Sigmund Freud, *Moses and Monotheism*, translated by Katherine Jones, New York: Alfred A. Knopf, 1939. Reprinted by permission.

To
Elba and Charlotte
Anita and Marc

Preface

The people of Leipzig and the citizens of Munich still speak the same language, yet each day they understand each other less. The inhabitants of divided Germany have an expression to describe their dilemma: *aneinander vorbeireden*. They are not the only ones who talk at cross purposes—Koreans and Vietnamese have similar problems, and so does the rest of the world. Each passing historical moment deepens the darkness which the communication blackout casts over the globe. The denizens of the Western World applaud the same concepts that haunt the people in the other sphere of influence: peace, democracy, freedom, progress, social justice, prosperity. Yet they regard each other with fear, hostility, and, above all, suspicion. Fear, hostility, and suspicion not only dominate the relations between capitalist and Communist nations; these mental states leave their imprint also on the contacts between white and colored men, developed and developing societies, affluent and underprivileged groups, liberals and conservatives, pacifists and militarists, believers and sceptics. . . .

Fear and hostility grow out of the suspicion which each group forms of the other's motives and intentions. The common question does not ask "what are they doing?" The common question is "what are they up to?" The modern mentality is an intellectual stance succumbing to the corroding influence of total suspicion; I devised the concept "mental entropy" to call attention to this central dilemma of the modern mentality.

Language reflects thought. The failure of language to establish meaningful communication is, therefore, also an intellectual predicament. Despite considerable and prolonged philosophical propaganda to the contrary, men came to realize that thought, in turn, reflects the interests, the constitution, and the social position of the thinker. The Sophists knew this; so did Machiavelli and a few others. But it took the systematic efforts of intellectual gadflies like Francis Bacon, Holbach, Marx, Nietzsche, and Freud to bring down to earth the classical heaven of pure thought. The iconoclasts of modern philosophy gave stature to the suspicion that the mind is neither sovereign nor independent; the protagonists of the sociology of knowledge enthroned it as the modern research intention *par excellence*.

Part I of this book describes problematic dimensions of the modern mentality and their connections with the various schools making up the sociology of knowledge. Therefore, the first part also presents an overview of this field of sociological specialization from its inception to the immediate present. In Part II, I try to show how crises and changes in modern philosophy from Kant to Husserl revolutionized our mode of questioning until the sociologists' suspicious queries into the functioning of the mind and its connections with social reality became not only possible but inevitable. Part III provides specific, detailed analyses of key concepts such as historicism and ideology which explain both the emergence of the sociology of knowledge and the unavoidable, though often unrecognized or unwanted, ascendancy of the modern mentality.

Many of those who use the book will be students in sociology. But the range of subject matter explains why it is also addressed to students in the fields of history, philosophy, economics, political science, psychology, and the humanities. The breakdown of meaningful communication, suspicion, and other ramifications of modern thoughtways have caused anxieties besetting not only students, but all thinking men and women. Therefore, I felt an obligation to the general reading public as well.

Like most authors I have contracted intellectual and personal debts to practically all individuals who have engaged me in genuine discussion and controversy—these obligations can be acknowledged only in general. In Berlin I received significant stimulation and lasting intellectual support; special thanks are due to Professors Hans-Joachim Lieber and Otto Stammer of the *Freie Universität*. I shall always gratefully remember the encouragement and valuable help given by Professor Seymour Martin Lipset of Harvard University and by Professor Charles H. Page of the University of California. I owe immense gratitude to Professor John F. Cuber, Editor of the Appleton-Century-Crofts Sociology Series, and to Mr. Jack K. Burton, Sociology Editor of Appleton-Century-Crofts; without their support and assistance the crucial steps from manuscript to book would never have been taken. I am greatly indebted to the Social Sciences Division and to the Research Committee of the Graduate Council of Southern Illinois University for their encouragement and generous support.

G. W. R.

Contents

CONTENTS

. . . time, like a river, bears down to us that which is light and inflated, and sinks that which is heavy and solid. . . . All the signs, therefore, of the truth and soundness of the received systems of philosophy and the sciences are unpropitious, whether taken from their origin, their fruits, their progress, the confessions of their authors, or from unanimity.

FRANCIS BACON OF VERULAM

PART ONE

THE SOCIAL
DETERMINATION OF IDEAS

CHAPTER 1

Dimensions of the Modern Mentality

As the twentieth century moves into its final phase, mankind is confronted with a question which, in its *secular* form, represents a problem of complete and devastating novelty: Will there be a twenty-first century?

For the first time in human history the apocalyptic vision has left its ancient domain of crepuscular poetry to dwell in the broad daylight of everyday life: in the lightning of thermonuclear explosions one of our oldest, wildest, darkest fears has been transformed into a reasonable, sober possibility which constitutes part of the hourly calculations of a technically highly rational scientific and logistic expertise.

For modern men the starred heavens of lovers and poets of old have changed into infinite space that plagues our imagination with rockets and poisonous fallout.

At the dusk of mid-century the grim specter of death is refracted variously: we have to live with instant death by all-out war and this is our collective condition, as Norman Mailer declares in what may be called the manifesto of the conscious fringe. There is also relatively fast death by the state as *l'univers concentrationnaire*, and this is man's freshest and most shameful memory.

There is a creeping death by conformity that suffocates everything that is creative and rebellious, and this is our exorbitant price for social progress and the rising standard of living.[1]

The feeling of insecurity which this central problem of the present human condition generates is heightened by the coming of age of another veteran enemy of man's peace and well-being: *doubt* and *suspicion*. The violent social, economic, and politico-military eruptions of recent history have, undoubtedly, contributed much to the destruction of moral and intellectual unity and trust. More importantly, the course of present social, economic, and politico-military events is dangerously affected by the growth of doubt and suspicion—mental attitudes that have escalated the more critical aspects of domestic and international human relations

---

[1] Cf. Norman Mailer, "The White Negro," in Gene Feldman and Max Gartenberg (editors), *The Beat Generation and the Angry Young Men*, A Dell Book, New York: Dell Publishing Company, 1960, p. 372.

to the nerve-corroding heights of "brinkmanship" where a sense of historical vertigo remains as the last human sentiment that can still be communicated and shared to any meaningful degree.

Mental Entropy

So far we have described the general, most widely shared dimensions of the modern mentality; to probe further and to reveal its less obvious dimensions is the purpose of the following essay which rests upon a primary assumption and a series of related secondary assumptions. This is the primary assumption: the history of ideas reflects a slow but steady exhaustion of the intellectual attitude; the process is reminiscent of the loss of energy asserted by the Second Law of Thermodynamics and may be defined as *mental entropy*.

Intellectual hesitancy and scepticism are as old as "imperial philosophy" and in the beginning there were the Sophists of classical Greece. But the age was strong enough, young enough, dogmatic enough to stand up to the greatness, originality, and depth of original inquiry. Plato's and Aristotle's philosophical imperialism vanquished the premature modernism of the Sophists and for centuries determined the mood of philosophical work.

In almost unbroken succession philosophers sustained a view of mind that makes it sovereign, self-sustaining, complete and capable of apprehending truth. The confidence and strength of the intellectual attitude which Plato inspired derived from the decision to degrade appearance —the empirical world—to mere appearance and to exalt true reality, as idea, to an eternal suprasensory realm.

Plato's decision was in essence a theological fiat and for centuries philosophers lived under the grandiose spell of the transcendent universe of imaginary ideas and values; from time to time the subterranean stream of Sophist thought came to the surface—enriched by the empirical strands of Aristotelianism which had escaped the scholastic reinterpretation—and then the philosophical stance of marginal thinkers was sceptical, agnostic, empirical, and pragmatic. These moments in history revived the Sophists' early ethical relativism; when the dominant philosophy was challenged the spotlight shone on the struggle for power, individual self-interest, the manipulation of justice; then, the man-made, constantly changing nature of customs and laws was recalled. Roger Bacon, Marsiglio of Padua, Ibn-Khaldun, and Machiavelli were to varying degrees reincarnations of the Sophist spirit—this other source of Western thought.

But it was the Enlightenment that offered the first serious challenge to idealist philosophy. The eighteenth century witnessed the dissolution of intellectual energies and initiated what Heidegger calls the "darkening of the world" which proceeds through various episodes: the hegira of the gods, the plundering of the earth, the standardization of men, the supremacy of the mediocre. These episodes are inevitable installments to be paid for another kind of development: the progress of the scientific-technological-industrial realm and may in time be resolved.

Importantly, however, the Enlightenment-inspired change in the intellectual attitude has wrought irrevocable alterations in the view of mind: modern philosophy and social science move toward a view that makes mind reflective of time and circumstance, a view that is suspicious of the sovereignty of mind, of the independence and finally of the existence and necessity of truth.

In summary, the exhaustion of the intellectual attitude is a process beginning with the Sophists of ancient Greece; it continues subterraneously as a thin strand connecting the thought of marginal philosophers and it breaks through to the surface as soon as the medieval spirit has been sufficiently emasculated to permit the eruption. This essay begins as the process widens during the age of Enlightenment and follows it into the twentieth century where the sociology of knowledge stands out as the perhaps most dramatic single expression of a new and total mistrust of the intellectual attitude as such. At this frontier the notion of truth stands unmasked as the obsolete remnant of a defunct theological tradition, and in the end values are discarded in favor of operational definitions and the mathematical interpretation of the universe.

These, then, are the dynamics embodied in the primary assumption of this essay. The secondary assumptions relate to it as verification relates to hypothesis; they are:

1. The loss of intellectual certainty is accelerated by increasing knowledge; mental entropy is a process which is also furthered by the activities of intellectual workers who battle it, because the process operates Hegelian fashion "behind their backs." The essay as a whole is intended to corroborate this assumption. Advanced scientific inquiry is subject to the process as well, since factors such as those conceived in the "Heisenberg principle" represent basic obstacles to the growth of knowledge in the direction of the absolute: this much is clear, if the most sophisticated act of observation destroys the phenomena intended by the observer.

2. The process of mental entropy can be traced back to certain "philosophical presuppositions" which are also cardinal prerequisites for the formation of the sociology of knowledge. Behind the current mistrust of the intellectual attitude—expressed in this sociology—lies, in short, a development of doubt in the potency of mind which includes the British Empiricists, Kant, Hegel, Dilthey, some Neo-Kantians, and Husserl. This is the first development; in it mind becomes epistemologically ever more dependent and "fragmented."

3. The process of mental entropy has been accelerated by a second

sequence in Western thought, introducing certain "conceptual presuppositions" such as *historism* and *ideology;* this sequence begins with Francis Bacon, runs through the French philosophers, Marx, Nietzsche, and Freud, and is concerned with showing that the mind is fettered by idols, dogmas, superstitions, self-interest, or by economic position, the lust for power, or by biological necessity.

4. The first development of philosophical presuppositions comes together with the second development of conceptual presuppositions to form the background of the sociology of knowledge.

5. These developments in the area of intellectual inquiry are accompanied by similar processes in the life of the general public. The special intellectual current coalesces with the general public current to form the modern mentality; this parallelism of forces affects all of us and warrants immediate attention.

The Varieties of Suspicion

The social and cultural conditions of life in the twentieth century have created a wide array of sceptical attitudes: doubt and suspicion are no longer menacing the probing and searching intellectuals alone who have known their disquieting murmur during the many lonely nights of human thinking and questioning that have passed into history. Ever since the dissolution of the medieval world, doubt and suspicion have spread to touch the daily lives of more and more people until the present distinction between a nontheoretical and theoretical level has become possible.[2]

On the *nontheoretical* level the attitudes of doubt and suspicion take the form of an overdetermined, mutual distrust between groups; they intensify the strains which complicate the international and domestic relations of contemporary societies and they deepen the split between political and cultural units. Men in the "less-developed areas" are suspicious of colonialism. Elsewhere, the fear of manipulation by the mass-media and powerful organizations increases individual insecurity and fosters the practice of *debunking.* Modern authors are often iconoclasts shattering idols that symbolized success. (Of all the elevated themes of contemporary literature none succeeds better than failure.) The promoters of "youth culture" have escalated idiocy into the ultimate of "artistic" expression, thereby completing a development which the "literary" henchmen of manufacturers and merchants initiated with the advent of radio and television.

[2] This distinction has also been made in my paper, *The Age of Suspicion: A History of the Sociology of Knowledge on Two Continents*, Read to the Fifty-Fifth Annual Meeting of the American Sociological Association, August 31, 1960, New York City.

Where the nontheoretical level reaches into the *popular* level, doubt and suspicion find their expression in cynicism and the practice of debunking; the climate of opinion takes on a sharply penetrating, urban, "breezy" atmosphere. The "unholy" insolence of the metropolitan cynic is rapidly diffused throughout society and the most articulate spokesmen of this mentality "arrive" as "cultural" heroes.

On the *upper reaches* of the nontheoretical level the cynicism is often the outgrowth of lacerating insight and despairing realism: Bertolt Brecht saw the world pass into the hands of the "Macky Messers" and remarked not without bitterness *"von Deinem Kopf lebt höchstens eine Laus."*

On the popular level the cynicism becomes often frivolous and "Mack the Knife" passes into the hands of the music hucksters. Kurt Tucholsky summed up the political qualities of the National Socialist Party by having one of his lower-middle-class characters say that they served soda pop with booze at their rally.[3] But, whereas Tucholsky committed suicide in his Swedish exile, the wisecracking greengrocer probably joined the murderous schnapps-dispensing Nazis.

In Europe the cultural diffusion of distrust proceeded from identifiable centers of intellectual and artistic gestation which often attained the pull of tourist attractions.

This theme connects the *Romanische Café* in the Republican Berlin of the 1920's with the Paris of the late 1930's, where Jean-Paul Sartre, at the *Café de Flore*, unwittingly initiated the fusion between the nauseating world of the entertainment industry and his nauseated philosophy of the world: a philosophy that is in itself a fusion of such disparate elements as Husserl's phenomenology, Hegel's and Heidegger's metaphysics, and Marx's social theory into a system of disgust, where nothingness lies coiled in the heart of being, like a worm.[4]

The acrid quality which the European *Zeitgeist* assumed early during this century was the pertinent reflection of a definite set of cultural and social conditions: with mounting social conflict the warring groups developed values, attitudes, and thought-styles distinctly their own. Soon incompatible differences overshadowed whatever these factions had shared before. The emergence of separate thought-styles with their corresponding universes of discourse has two consequences: each of these universes develops a paranoidal response to all the others, since its exponents experience the existence of conflicting interpretations and views as a threat to the truth and rightness of their own universe of discourse.

[3] Cf. Kurt Tucholsky, *Gruss Nach Vorn* (edited by Erich Kästner), Stuttgart, Hamburg: Rowohlt Verlag, 1946, p. 123.
[4] Cf. Jean-Paul Sartre, *L'Etre et le néant: Essai d'ontologie phénoménologique,* 43rd edition, Paris: Gallimard, 1955, p. 57.

Second, the process of meaningful communication between these mutually distrustful universes comes to a virtual standstill. Eventually all objective and factually grounded inquiry into the content of out-group utterances is replaced by the suspicious query: What are the ulterior motives behind the outside point of view?

The functional analysts in modern sociology tell us that "just as a discourse needs to be coherent and consistent to be convincing, a social system needs to be integrated to be productive."[5] Undoubtedly, the fragmentation of modern discourse cannot be without serious consequences for the integration and productivity of modern social systems.

When communication stops in the distrustful context of group conflict, force provides the most commonly adopted alternative. European varieties of totalitarianism and American varieties of thought-control have one thing in common: they represent attempts on the part of specific groups to establish a monopoly for their own universe of discourse. The immediate result is, as Judge Learned Hand warned in 1952, the spreading of a ". . . spirit of general suspicion and distrust which accepts rumor and gossip in place of undismayed and unintimidated inquiry."[6] As a companion consequence human relations begin to deteriorate: ". . . how, in the cramped surroundings of a loyalty hearing, with fear pressing in on all sides, do you speak warmly and naturally of your friends? Will not McCarthy jump up in the Senate and declare: 'See? I told you! That's not just friendship . . . They belong to the same gang!' "[7]

The spread of suspicion is also wasteful and, ultimately, detrimental to the political equilibrium of a democratic social system. The Oppenheimer case—by now resolved—". . . was an instance in which the American people fell into the unpardonable sin of accepting detraction against evidence, and if a long and honorable career is not accepted as in itself a refutation of slander, then the people's capacity to govern themselves comes into serious question."[8]

Suspicion engenders repressiveness and the two tendencies combine to threaten both the normality of intergroup relations and the psychic well-being of the individual. Close surveillance of his actions, ideas, and associations causes the individual not only anxiety but may impair his psychic functions. If censorship and interdiction wall off part of the object-world, ". . . if the impulse to adventure is checked by a restrictive culture, the free functioning of the ego is impaired. No less subject to

[5] Harold Fallding, "Functional Analysis in Sociology," *American Sociological Review*, Vol. 28, No. 1 (February, 1963), p. 12.

[6] Quoted in Harold Mehling, *The Great Time-Killer*, Cleveland and New York: The World Publishing Company, 1962, p. 104.

[7] Owen Lattimore, *Ordeal by Slander*, New York: Bantam Books, 1951, pp. 166–167.

[8] Gerald W. Johnson, "Robert Oppenheimer," *The New Republic* (April 20, 1963), p. 10.

injury is the super-ego . . . 'a mature super-ego can optimally develop only in a free and democratic society.' "[9]

The theme of *loneliness* in the modern world intimately connects with that of suspicion and distrust. Significantly, David Riesman and his co-authors entitled their analysis of the changing American character *The Lonely Crowd*. Premonitory rumblings of this research orientation echo through the works of Max Weber, and Ortega y Gasset; Alfred Weber actually raises the menacing question: *The Third or Fourth Man?*—indicating that also in Europe a human type is growing old and is in danger of being replaced by the humanly underdeveloped, technical functionary of overdeveloped social systems.

In Paris, Jeanne Hersch remarked in 1956 that European liberals exhaust an already almost empty tradition, that their excessive patience and their small improvements which are completely out of proportion with the giant size of the threats, sufferings, and expectations of this century depreciate the very values establishing their progressive position. "And they know of no cure for the modern drift into loneliness. Confronted with the social conditions their spirituality ruins finally, as that of the conservatives, not only their own existence, which would not be too bad, but also the very faith in the mind."[10] There are, indeed, similarities between the European and American climate of opinion.

On the *theoretical* level we doubt what we know and, at times, even whether we *can* know. Advanced theorists question, condemn, secularize, ridicule, and devalue thought and belief. From related presuppositions emanate the sociology of knowledge, psychoanalysis, behaviorism, ideological analysis, propaganda analysis, semanticism, neopositivism, quantum mechanics, and Heisenberg's uncertainty relations which—in quantum theory—put a ". . . definite limit on the accuracy with which positions and momenta, or time and energy, can be measured simultaneously."[11]

The critics of modern civilization evidence a similar problem-awareness. Thus, Sorokin complains: "Since everything is temporal and subject to incessant change, and since sensory perception differs in the case of different organisms, individuals, and groups, nothing absolute exists."[12]

[9] Lionel Trilling, *Freud and the Crisis of Our Culture*, Boston: Beacon Press, 1955, p. 43.

[10] Jeanne Hersch, *Die Ideologien und die Wirklichkeit: Versuch einer politischen Orientierung* (translated by Ernst von Schenck), München: R. Piper, 1957, pp. 116–117. The ramifications of the modern drift into scepticism and loneliness for the religious institution are already clearly visible. Cf. my article "Die Religion der einsamen Masse," *Kölner Zeitschrift für Soziologie und Sozialpsychologie*, Vol. 16, No. 4 (November, 1964), pp. 742–756.

[11] Werner Heisenberg, *Physics and Philosophy: The Revolution in Modern Science* (Introduction by F. S. C. Northrop), Harper Torchbooks, New York: Harper & Row, Publishers, 1962, p. 162.

[12] Pitirim A. Sorokin, *The Crisis of Our Age*, A Dutton Everyman Paperback, New York: E. P. Dutton, 1957, p. 97.

After 1903, when he turned his back on the conventional preoccupations of academic philosophy, John Dewey investigated and maintained the thesis that the character and derivation of logical and epistemological formulations is historically occasioned. The late C. Wright Mills remarked that "there have been and are diverse canons and criteria of validity and truth, and these criteria, upon which determinations of the truthfulness of propositions at any time depend, are themselves, in their persistence and change, legitimately open to social-historical relativization."[13] Turning in the direction of social-psychological analysis he observed eleven years later: "The personality market, the most decisive effect and symptom of the great salesroom, underlies the all-pervasive distrust and self-alienation so characteristic of metropolitan people."[14]

In Europe the break between individual and society was revealed by Marx and Freud and attained the rank of sociological principle in Max Weber's analyses of bureaucracy, Georg Simmel's delineation of the blasé attitude, Hans Freyer's studies of industrial societies, and Norbert Elias' theory of civilization which describes the dissolution of an older, naïve center of awareness into the conflicting notions of self-image and social image. Ultimately, society became—to paraphrase Ralf Dahrendorf—an "annoying fact," whereas the self developed into what Elias calls an "apparatus of self compulsion" (*Selbstzwangsapparatur*). At this point the possibilities of image manipulation become, as Hans Peter Dreitzel recently suggested, data for empirical investigation.[15]

On the theoretical level of doubt and suspicion the *sociology of knowledge* occupies a particularly prominent place: this specialized area of sociological inquiry contains a highly conscious and consistent theoretical formulation of these mental sets. Furthermore, the discipline itself is a product of an era dominated by suspicion. It is no accident that the main varieties of the sociology of knowledge developed in the distrustful climate of the Weimar Republic. Similarly, intellectual circles in the United States were receptive to the sociology of knowledge mainly ". . . because our society has come to have certain characteristics of those European societies in which the discipline was initially developed."[16]

---

[13] C. Wright Mills, "Methodological Consequences of the Sociology of Knowledge," *American Journal of Sociology*, Vol. XLVI, No. 3 (November, 1940), p. 318.

[14] C. Wright Mills, *White Collar: The American Middle Classes*, A Galaxy Book, New York: Oxford University Press, 1956, pp. 187–188.

[15] Cf. Hans Peter Dreitzel, "Selbstbild und Gesellschaftsbild: Wissenssoziologische Überlegungen zum Image-Begriff," *European Journal of Sociology*, Vol. III, No. 2 (Fall, 1962), pp. 181–228.

[16] Robert K. Merton, *Social Theory and Social Structure*, New York: The Free Press of Glencoe, 1957, p. 457.

CHAPTER 2

The Sociology of Knowledge in the French Tradition

I

N A GENERAL AND PARTIAL WAY, we may characterize the sociology of knowledge as a specialized area of modern sociological research which has made it possible for us to discern and describe the differences in human thought among different groups and at different times. Much like the historian of art who distinguishes different styles of art, the sociologist of knowledge distinguishes different styles of thought. In France, Émile Durkheim, Henri Lévy-Bruhl, and their followers established an important starting point for this type of sociological research when they revealed the system of logic peculiar to "primitive tribes."

The Durkheim School

Durkheim (1858–1917) went beyond the generalities of his predecessors who had taught that thought depends upon language, and language upon society; he took the next step when he tried to show in detail how both the forms of logical classification and the basic categories of cognition have been produced by society.

In collaboration with Marcel Mauss, Durkheim discussed the problem of classification and showed that the present concept of a "class" does not go back beyond Aristotle: our modern forms of logical classification such as class and subclass, species and genus are not innate but based upon ". . . a hierarchical order for which neither the sensory world nor our own minds offer us a model."[1] Durkheim and Mauss believed, however, that they had discovered the resemblance of such a model when their studies of the logical classifications of primitive men revealed that these classifications closely reflect the social organization of the tribe. Thus the hierarchical nature of logical classes was seen as the reflection of the hierarchical order of earlier (primitive) forms of social structure.

The Australian aborigines, for example, classify objects as belonging to different phratries: the moon may belong to one of two phratries, the sun to the other. Each of these primary tribal subdivisions may again

---

[1] Émile Durkheim and Marcel Mauss, "De quelques formes primitives de classification," L'Année sociologique, Vol. VI (1901–1902), p. 6.

be subdivided into two matrimonial classes; they in turn will serve as class categories for things. The first "classes," then, were classes of men and the importance of these "social" classes was carried over to the non-social objects in the corresponding logical classes: all the objects and animals in the environment were classified as belonging to a certain tribal subdivision or kinship group. In this manner Durkheim and Mauss explain the social origin of logical relations: the tribe is the logical ancestor of the genus, the phratry the ancestor of the species. The association of certain objects with members of certain social groups originated the classification of these objects with these human beings—the hierarchy of tribe, phratry, and clan led to the hierarchy of genus, species, and class and from the unity of society we came to imagine the unity of the universe of things, the supreme logical whole.[2]

Furthermore, this primitive classification is not primarily conceptual, but has its basis in the emotional values inherent in all psychical, associative processes which involve elements of social life. Scientific classification emerges when social sensibility and sentiment diminish in importance and when conceptions having such emotional values are subjected to free and rigorous examination. But—concludes Durkheim in his arbitrary manner—contemporary scientific classification has its source in these emotional, mythological classifications based on collective representations: the mental habits which help us organize facts in groups (themselves hierarchically related) bear the indelible mark of a social genesis.[3]

This general argument is repeated with only minor modifications in Durkheim's daringly speculative work *Les Formes Elémentaires de la Vie Religieuse* which introduces a sociologistic explanation of the categories of the understanding. By the analysis of the simplest religion known (the totemic practices of Australian tribes) Durkheim wants, first, to determine what are the elementary forms of religious thought and practice and, second, to demonstrate how the categories of the understanding have a religious (religion is itself the product of social causes) and, therefore, a social, origin.

La Vie Religieuse contains—mainly in the introduction—the rudiments of a sociological theory of knowledge which Durkheim develops with the hope of settling the dispute between empiricistic and *a priori* epistemology. He recalls that our judgments rest upon certain basic ideas which determine the nature and form of our intellectual activities. These

---

[2] Cf. *Ibid.*, pp. 9–13.

[3] Cf. *Ibid.*, pp. 66–72. Durkheim's attempt to make the logical powers of classification posterior to and dependent on the classificatory powers derived from the structure of the group is open to various forms of criticism—above all we may ask whether, if primitive men did not already possess at least a general power of classification, they could recognize human beings as constituting a class distinct from the animals or could arrive at such conceptions as phratry, clan, or family.

are the general concepts which philosophers since Aristotle have called the categories of the understanding such as time, space, class, number, cause, substance, totality, etc. The categories correspond to the most universal properties of things and provide the framework which makes the normal working of the intellect possible. Human thought cannot divorce itself from them ". . . without destroying itself, for it seems that we cannot think of objects that are not in time and space, which have no number, etc."[4]

The religious and consequently social origin of the categories may be observed, for example, in the category of time which was derived from social rhythms based on the concentration and dispersion of the social group; the divisions into days, weeks, months, and years correspond to the periodic recurrence of religious ceremonies and social activities— a calendar expresses the rhythm of collective life and simultaneously assures its regularity. The determination of these different moments and sequences of time is an entirely extra-individual affair, free from the whims and arbitrary decisions of any particular person. Individual man, to maintain his temporal relations with others, is forced to conform to this collective system of ideas and measurements.

Similarly the category of space was derived from the territory occupied by the society and the number of the fundamental regions of space varied historically with the variation in the fundamental number of clans. Next Durkheim explains the category of force as the logical formulation of the "mana" of primitive man's practical cosmology, as an objectified collective force (social constraint) projected into things, as an efficient force upon which the category of causality depends. The all-inclusive category of totality is the logical expression of the totality most familiar to primitive man: the whole social group. Finally, Durkheim suspects that even the idea of contradiction is a function of given social conditions since the power of this principle has varied from one historical epoch and one society to the next. Durkheim concludes that all the variations undergone by the rules determining contemporary logic prove that ". . . far from being engraven through all eternity upon the mental constitution of men, they depend, at least in part, upon factors that are historical and consequently social."[5]

In this manner Durkheim believes to have accomplished his objective; the negative aspects of the empiricistic and apriorist theory of the origin of the categories are eliminated while their viable elements are fused

[4] Émile Durkheim, *The Elementary Forms of the Religious Life* (translated from the French by Joseph Ward Swain), Third Impression, London: George Allen & Unwin, 1954, p. 9. Durkheim explains that he calls time and space categories because he does not see any difference between the role which these ideas play in the intellectual life and the role which falls to the ideas of class or cause.

[5] *Ibid.*, p. 13.

into his "social origin" hypothesis: the categories are collective representations imposed upon the individual; they impress man as universal and necessary. Consensus about these basic modes of thought is of signal importance for cooperation and thus for the very existence of the group and this explains the uniformity of the categories *within a given group*. In the interest of survival each group must enforce this measure of logical conformity and impose the categories upon its members with ". . . a special sort of moral necessity which is to the intellectual life what moral obligation is to the will."[6] The impression of necessity which the categories give is due to the fact that they are social representations with all the prestige bestowed by such an origin: the categories are therefore, for the individual mind, *a priori*, whereas their origin outside the individual mind satisfies the empiricist's positive desire to remain anchored in the objective universe of observable phenomena.

The categories are of religious origin, yet they remain at the foundation of man's intelligence; they appear now as "priceless instruments of thought" which men created over many centuries and where they have accumulated their most valuable intellectual assets.[7]

Durkheim held, then, that religion furnished the early (primitive) intellectual and attitudinal framework wherein the categories were first elaborated. The religious attitudinal matrix he derived, however, from a wider complex of experience that incorporates the totality of social existence which consists of religious and secular elements. Durkheim found the real basis determining both the forms and practices of religious life and the forms and practices of intellectual life in the various factors constituting the structure of society: the stratification of groups, power relations, ecological and economic conditions, the division of labor, familial and kinship relationships, socially sanctioned moral imperatives, and so forth. When Durkheim revealed these social factors he also identified the objective patterns which make up the substructure molding the forms of knowledge during their inception. The forms of knowledge, however, cannot be derived directly from the social substructure; what must now come into play is a meaningful subjective element that is to inform and express the responses of human agents to the objective social conditions of their existence. This subjective element Durkheim found in the primitive attitudinal matrix wherein the universe appears as a plenum of supernatural forces. The ideas of religion, therefore, furnished the attitudinal structure which coalesced with the natural and social aspects of primitive life to determine both the emergence and early expression of the categories. Durkheim views the attitudinal structure—existing within the minds of individuals—as the product of collective

---

[6] *Ibid.*, p. 18.
[7] *Ibid.*, p. 19.

experience. This structure is reflected by "collective representations" which combine the experiences of many persons; it is the process of social interaction that makes these representations binding on all group members.[8]

Durkheim contributed to the sociology of knowledge—which is essentially the doctrine of the determination of cognition and knowledge by social reality—by describing the interaction between the structure of nonliterate societies, the complex of their religious attitudes, and the genesis of the categories of the understanding. Durkheim did more than most of the German sociologists of knowledge, who only posited the interrelationship between social structure and thought, because of his willingness to analyze ". . . the problem in terms of concrete historical material derived from the best empirical sources in the field of anthropology which were available to him at the time of his research."[9]

Durkheim and his school were not preoccupied with political conflict and class struggles and the absence of any particular commitment enabled them to focus their attention upon social interaction in its entirety; therefore, these French sociologists emphasized from the onset the all-pervasiveness of social influences in the intellectual life of men in society.

The Work of Granet

This emphasis is prominent in the approach of the sinologist Marcel Granet (1884–1940), who employs Durkheim's methodology in his works on Chinese language and culture. Granet recalls that all thinking is clothed in words; words are social formations, stemming from social interaction and, therefore, all thinking is rooted in and colored by concrete social life.

[8] Cf. Gerard L. DeGré, *Society and Ideology: An Inquiry into the Sociology of Knowledge* (Ph.D. Thesis), New York: Columbia University Bookstore, 1943, pp. 74–75.

[9] *Ibid.*, p. 75. Kant had already tried to protect himself against attacks upon his universal, *a priori* view of the role played by the categories in the cognitive process when he rejected the psychological approach to epistemology. In our century it was especially Ernst Cassirer who fought most resolutely against all attempts to undermine the Kantian position by way of psychologistic, sociologistic, or historicistic reinterpretations. From a position that strives to retain the purity of Kant's basic question the categories appear as pure, formal concepts without any concrete content. As pure forms they have no relation whatsoever with an historically accumulated collective *experience*, or its counterpart. Those who claim an historical changeability of these pure forms simply confuse pure formal concepts with materially determined general concepts. Cf. Ernst Cassirer, "Der Kritische Idealismus und die Philosophie des 'gesunden Menschenverstandes,'" *Philosophische Arbeiten* (edited by Hermann Cohen and Paul Natorp), Vol. I, No. 1, 1906. Also see, Ernst Cassirer, *Das Erkenntnisproblem in der Philosophie und Wissenschaft der neueren Zeit*, 3 Vols., Berlin: B. Cassirer, 1922–23.

This observation led Granet to an attempt at the application of Durkheim's sociological theory of the categories. He published the results in 1934 in his book on ancient Chinese thought, *La Pensée Chinoise*.[10] The work endeavors to reveal the rules and symbols governing Chinese mentality and opens logically with an analysis of Chinese language: although a written language has been extant in China since about 1800 B.C. it remained monosyllabic, restricted in phonetic scope, and dependent on word order for clarity and pitch for diversity when spoken. The grammatical apparatus of accidence and syntax is missing. Consequently, Chinese language is a poor vehicle for the communication of abstract and analytical forms of thought. This tongue is, however, rich in highly concrete images (emblems) conveying values and stimulating action. Chinese language is a powerful medium for the expression of sentimental, emotional attitudes and the suggestion of forms of conduct. As a moral, social, and ritualistic control device it expresses emotion, judges conduct as proper or improper, and assigns whatever is symbolized by the word to a definite place in the social order.[11]

Since this language opposes itself to all attempts at the economization of mental effort and the development of analytical and abstract thought, we are not surprised to find that the ideas which are directive of the operations of the Chinese mind are different from the categories determining the intellectual life of the Occident. Being basic, these "directive ideas" (*idées directrices*) still possess the value of categories—but they are synthetic and concrete, instead of analytic and abstract.[12]

Undoubtedly, Granet suggests a social genesis of the categories. The Chinese conception of time, he argues, was deeply emblematical and reflective of the dynastic and feudal structure of ancient China. There, no thinker conceived of time as a monotonous duration constituted by repetition; time derived its meaning from a definite order of eras, seasons, and epochs; time was intimately associated with the notions of the calendar and of dynastic succession. Chinese time was not an abstract addition of quantitatively equal and qualitatively indistinguishable units. Each period of time was inseparable from a certain circumstance and occasion. Moreover, considerations of time were never separated from those of space which appeared as a complex of singular domains and climates extending into different directions. Chinese space was not abstract like Kant's pure and homogeneous medium; but, like time, it was highly heterogeneous and hierarchical.

---

[10] This book is devoted to Chinese thought. It is, however, complimentary to *La Civilization Chinoise* (1929), where Granet portrays the social and political system of the ancient Chinese. Cf. Marcel Granet, *Chinese Civilization* (translated by K. E. Innes and M. R. Brailsford), New York: Alfred A. Knopf, 1930.

[11] Cf. Marcel Granet, *La Pensée Chinoise*, Paris: La Renaissance du Livre, 1934, p. 37.

[12] *Ibid.*, p. 83.

For the Chinese, space was not extension as such; it was square and faded into four vague regions (The Four Seas) in or near which lived the animal-like barbarians—only the Chinese were human and lived in civilized space. At the center, space was densest and purest: here the group fully realized its diversity, hierarchy, and order. The site for this sacred, central square must be near the celestial palace; it must be a site where the convergence of rivers and of climates marked the genuine center of the world. To connect time and space and to ensure, thereby, celestial and social harmony, the chief must reside in various sections of the empire and he must reach each portion at a certain season to receive in audience the vassal from this sector. Traveling with the sun from the east, it took the sovereign five years to complete his tour of the empire.

This conception was the creation of a feudal society and since this society remained feudal, space ". . . never ceased to be imagined as a hierarchical federation of heterogeneous extensions."[13] Together, the concrete ideas of space and time furnished an organon for the art of mastering, by ritual and symbol, the world and the society of civilized men at its center: they provided a framework for the mature art of ruling.

The Chinese combined an extreme respect for numerical symbols with an extreme indifference for all quantitative conceptions. Mere ordinal succession and quantity played almost no role in their thinking, apart from worldly trade and technology. For the Chinese philosophers numbers were manifestations of the structure of reality, means of arranging objects, actions, and people in hierarchies of essential value: these hierarchies were ultimately founded on the ranks of the feudal system and the power vested in the sovereign; they were, therefore, determined by social considerations. Numbers were important because of their polyvalence, as this made them remarkably suitable for efficacious manipulation. Numbers revealed the form or value of objects, because numbers symbolized the composition and power of social groups in relation to these objects which were associated with them. Therefore, the Chinese thinkers were able to ". . . represent with the help of numbers the protocol order that governs the universal life."[14]

Numbers had a logical function which was classificatory. This function resided in the distributing of all things within the categories *Yin* and *Yang*. The classificatory usage of numbers, odd and even, connected with the other function of numbers: the protocol function. With the aid of numbers the sages were able to represent the protocol order which governed the life of the universe. Numbers established the etiquettes for the different groups they classified.

[13] *Ibid.,* p. 95 (my translation).
[14] *Ibid.,* p. 297 (my translation).

Yin and *Yang* are specifically Chinese categories which have a directive function and instill everything with a "rhythm." Granet assumes that they originated in the semiannual ceremonies and the occupational divisions and cycles of the social structure which are determined by the principle of sex. Essentially, all that is masculine in nature may be classified under *Yang* and all that is of feminine nature under *Yin*. Like so many other Chinese "emblems," however, *Yin* and *Yang* are not principles of classification in an abstract sense—they emphasize and reveal concrete qualification and differentiation. What they emphasize are mainly alternating and contrasting social arrangements and segments such as the social division of labor and the occupational cycles of men and women which coincide with the changes in season.

The spring and autumn assemblies which play an important part in Granet's explanation of the genesis of these categories are sexual rites (*fêtes sexuelles*) which bring these social facts into focus: the male members of the group appear on one side of a river-bound valley, where they are revealed by the rising sun to the women who stand in the shadows, facing the men. These positions evoke essential attributes of *Yang*, such as the north of a river, the south of a hill, the sun, penis, and other attributes belonging to *Yin*, such as shady, the south of a river, cold, mysterious, vagina.

Between the men and the women has been divided the work during the year. The oncoming orgy will now bring into focus their complementary character in ritual form: men and women will fuse in sexual union and the emblems *Yin* and *Yang* will be evoked in all their rich meaning. *Yang* evokes the image of an open door, of generation, and of spring, when the men go out into the sunlit fields to produce the food that maintains life. *Yin* evokes the image of a closed door, of the hibernation of the time of winter when the women weave and do their share of the common labor. But now *Yin* and *Yang* are one, harmonizing as they are called back and forth, the cosmos of man and nature. Now time and space blend perfectly, because the site and the occasion are perfect: there is order and harmony and there exists a unity between man and that universe of which he is a solid part.[15]

The two sexes have obeyed the command of an antithetical discipline; as rival groups they have communicated with emblem and deed: they have become parts of something larger than and embracive of all of life and time and space. Their close union under the domination of *Yin* and *Yang* has made men and women into a total and harmoniously related

---

[15] Cf. *ibid.*, pp. 139–148. Cf. also O. Z. Fang, *Complete Chinese-English Dictionary*, quoted in H. G. Creel, *Sinism: A Study of the Evolution of the Chinese World-View*, Chicago: Open Court Publishing Company, 1929, p. 28.

society focalized in a rite and this is projected mythically: *Yin* and *Yang* are *Tao*.[16]

"All *Yin* and all *Yang*, this is *Tao*." *Tao*, the All-Encompassing, embraces all the other symbols; it is a total made up of two aspects which are totals themselves, because they are mutually substitutable. *Tao* is, however, not their sum, but the regulator of their alternance. Literally *Tao* means way or road, but its deeper meanings, contained in the classics, are always those of social and cosmic order, totality, responsibility, and efficacy. *Tao* is supreme. *Tao* is total efficacy, a center of responsibility, and finds its expression above all in the sovereign ruler who manages the world and animates it. *Tao* is the unique principle of all success and it is geared to the total art of ruling. According to Granet, *Tao* begins by evoking the image of the chief's journey which signifies the power of regulation and orderly efficacy vested in him.

The sovereign lord makes his tour of the empire, imitating the march of the sun and is considered by the Heavens as a Son. This unique man maintains the communication between the sovereign heaven and earth and, thereby, their felicitous harmony. This virtuous chieftain is the pivot of a great axis. Once more, Granet tries to reveal the essentially social character of a Chinese symbol: *Tao* is the concretion of notions evolving around the sovereign, his domain, the feudal hierarchy, the harmony of society and nature. *Tao* is the supreme emblem of social monism and the final assertion of man's oneness with the cosmos. Man's social arrangements, his ritual and etiquette, give expression to the all-pervading *Tao* in exactly the same way as do natural phenomena. He who knows the *Tao* of anything, knows the *Tao* of everything. The great of this world rule by the power of their "saintly" wisdom: *"ce Savoir agissant, c'est le Tao."*[17]

From Lévy-Bruhl to Halbwachs

Granet gives rise not only to the thought that the categories are socially determined but also to the suspicion that there exists a radical cleavage of categorial systems, that there are no common and universally valid denominators of conception and thought. A similar argument resides in Lévy-Bruhl's concept of the "prelogicality" of the primitive mind. Prelogical thinking is said to follow "affective categories" which are expressive of impulses and emotions. This primitive thinking is determined by

[16] Cf. Granet, *La Pensée Chinoise*, p. 120.
[17] *Ibid.*, p. 326. Cf. also C. Wright Mills, "The Language and Ideas of Ancient China," in C. W. Mills, *Power, Politics and People* (edited and with an introduction by Louis Horowitz), New York: Ballantine Books, 1963, pp. 469–520.

the social group, and its connection with the world is largely a matter of "mystic participations" and "exclusions." The primitive is alleged to have no clear idea of substance and attribute, cause and effect, identity and contradiction—his outlook is dominated by confused superstition. With Lévy-Bruhl (1857–1939) the continuity leading from "primitive" to "civilized" thoughtways becomes ruptured.[18]

Contemporary anthropologists have rejected the assumption that primitive mentality is basically different from modern, "rational" mentality and argue to the contrary that the thoughtways which Lévy-Bruhl alleged to be typically primitive occur also among the members of developed societies. No matter how civilized and rational we may pride ourselves to be, we, as well, see the elementary threats—illness, death, insanity—through a vague emotional fog which becomes ". . . denser and more impenetrable as the fateful forms approach. It is indeed astonishing that 'savages' can achieve such a sober, dispassionate outlook in these matters as they actually do."[19]

Not only do civilized men exhibit traits of the primitive's mentality but "primitives" also exhibit traits of civilized mentality and that to a significant degree. Bronislaw Malinowski claims that his observations among the Melanesian and Papuo-Melanesian tribes of Eastern New Guinea and the surrounding archipelagoes ("the classical land of magic") prove that there is knowledge of the rational and empirical variety ". . . among savages living in the age of polished stone."[20]

The primitive does not only have one (prelogical, superstitious) domain of reality, but two. He has his everyday world of practical activities and this is directed by rational knowledge and experience. Besides this domain he has his region of belief and cult; primitive men use magic whenever they have to cope with mysterious and hostile forces, or with the ". . . great unearned increment of fortunate coincidence."[21]

Malinowski is certain that his data prove that there are no irreconcilable differences between primitive and civilized mentality when *comparable* domains of thought and activity are considered. If we accept Malinowski's position we come to suspect that Granet is subject to a fallacy which is not unlike that of Lévy-Bruhl. Is it correct to compare—as Granet does—factual, technical-scientific concepts with conceptions that are not factual but traditional, not technical-scientific, but notions born of magic and ritual? Probably not and ". . . in a wide range of actual

[18] Cf. Lucien Lévy-Bruhl, *How Natives Think* (translated by Lilian A. Clare), London: George Allen & Unwin, 1926, and *Primitive Mentality* (translated by Lilian A. Clare), London: George Allen & Unwin, 1923.

[19] Bronislaw Malinowski, *Magic, Science, and Religion and Other Essays*, A Doubleday Anchor Book, Garden City, N. Y.: Doubleday & Company, 1954, p. 32.

[20] *Ibid.*, p. 27.

[21] *Ibid.*, p. 29.

practices, the Chinese did not *act* on the assumption that 'time is round' and 'space, square.'" Granet, therefore, only ". . . demonstrated qualitative differences of concepts in *certain contexts,* but not within such comparable contexts as, say, that of technical practice."[22]

A modification of Durkheim's position—especially by way of a psychological approach—was brought about by Celestin Bouglé and Maurice Halbwachs. Significant portions of their work are reminscent of sociology of knowledge in the Durkheimian tradition—but in contrast to him they also proceed along the lines of primarily speculative social psychology.[23]

This injection of psychology, however, seems to have helped the acculturation of a sociology of knowledge derived from Durkheim in the United States. The germs of a peculiarly American sociology of knowledge are contained in the social behaviorism of G. H. Mead, which is a similar attempt to show the operation of those psychic mechanisms through which objective social constraints acting upon the individual become internalized within the private attitudinal complex of the person.[24] Soon American social psychologists developed experimental techniques that made it possible to empirically study the influence of group situations upon the individual's perception and judgment.[25]

The social psychology of G. H. Mead gives direction to the work of Florian Znaniecki, who wants to restrict the sociology of knowledge to the study of the carriers of knowledge—to the analysis of a certain complex of human interaction.[26] Znaniecki wants to demonstrate how men of knowledge orient themselves to special segments of society which have special criteria of validity determining what is "important" knowledge. These segments of society which influence men of knowledge in their work, he calls "the social circle." The emphasis on the brain worker's "audience" explains why this typically American variant of sociology of knowledge was destined to fade into the field of communications, public opinion, and propaganda analysis. It is symptomatic that Znaniecki's narrow approach to the sociology of knowledge was greeted by Robert K. Merton, who has worked along similar lines in the area of public com-

[22] Robert K. Merton, "The Sociology of Knowledge," in Georges Gurvitch and Wilbert E. Moore (editors), *Twentieth Century Sociology,* New York: Philosophical Library, 1945, p. 388 (emphasis in original).

[23] Cf. Celestin Bouglé, *The Evolution of Values* (translated by Helen S. Sellars), New York: Holt, Rinehart & Winston, 1926, and Maurice Halbwachs, *Les cadres sociaux de la mémoire,* Paris: F. Alcan, 1925, and *La mémoire collective,* Paris: Presses Universitaires de France, 1950.

[24] Cf. G. H. Mead, *Mind, Self and Society,* Chicago: The University of Chicago Press, 1943.

[25] Cf., for example, Kurt Lewin, *The Conceptual Representation and the Measurement of Psychological Forces,* Durham, N. C.: Duke University Press, 1938.

[26] Cf. Florian Znaniecki, *The Social Role of the Man of Knowledge,* New York: Columbia University Press, 1940.

munications, as ". . . a procedure which promises to take research in the sociology of knowledge from the plane of general imputation to testable empirical inquiry."[27]

[27] Merton, *op. cit.*, p. 398. Cf. also Paul F. Lazarsfeld and R. K. Merton, "Studies in Radio and Film Propaganda," *Transactions of the New York Academy of Sciences*, 6:58–79, 1943. Cf. also Dorwin Cartwright, "Some Principles of Mass Persuasion: Selected Findings of Research on the Sale of United States War Bonds," *Human Relations*, 1949, 2, 253–267, Gordon W. Allport and Leo J. Postman, "The Basic Psychology of Rumor," *Transactions of the New York Academy of Sciences*, Series II, 1945, viii, pp. 61–81. For an analysis of the social conditions which influence the production, distribution, and consumption of various kinds and quantities of "knowledge" and a statistical description of such "knowledge-industries" as communication media, information machines and services, education, research and development, etc., see Fritz Machlup, *The Production and Distribution of Knowledge in the United States*, Princeton, N. J.: Princeton University Press, 1962.

CHAPTER 3

Marxist Sociology of Knowledge

THE SOCIOLOGY OF KNOWLEDGE does not only aim at the discovery, analysis, and description of different thought styles. The discipline is more than that; it is also a theory of the relation of ideas and reality asserting the primacy of reality and the determination of ideas by reality.[1] Karl Marx developed a theory asserting the primacy of economic reality and the determination of ideas, or rather of the ideological superstructure, by this economic reality. It is more than a poetic gesture to call Marxism the "storm center of the sociology of knowledge" because much of this sociology is a development of Marx's hypothesis and a struggle with the problems unleashed by his analysis of the order of things.

The heritage left by Marx was so problematic that even his followers found it impossible to agree on a singular Marxist sociology of knowledge. Instead, there are several ranging from Max Adler's Kantian version to Emil Lederer's sociology of culture. In a manner of speaking we may, however, make a major distinction between a "positivist" and "historicist" branch of Marxist sociology of knowledge.

The historicists are informed by the earlier writings of Marx which intimately connect with Hegel's thinking. The positivists, on the other hand, stress the later scientistic Marx-Engels tradition; consequently they arrive at a narrow, empiricist attitude and deny the existence of everything but matter which exhibits its stubborn factness in the social world by economic relationships.

The Positivist School

Bogdanov's writings are permeated by this emphasis on empiricist attitudes and the methods of physical science and he clearly belongs in the camp of the positivists or—as the historicists were fond of saying— "vulgar" Marxists. The Russian physician, philosopher, and sociologist Alexander A. Bogdanov was inspired by Ernst Mach's positivist-pragmatist system, Ostwald's energetic philosophy, and Avenarius' empirical criticism, and followed through with his own attempt to reduce history to an epiphenomenon of technological change. Bogdanov's sociology of knowledge is contained in the three volumes of his *General Theory of Organization: Tectology* (1925–1929). The outlines of his position can,

[1] For a detailed definition and discussion of the "range of the subject matter" see Kurt H. Wolff, "The Sociology of Knowledge: Emphasis on an Empirical Attitude," *Philosophy of Science*, Vol. 10 (April, 1943), pp. 107–109.

however, already be detected in his earlier works on sociology, *Psychology of Society* (1904) and *The Science of Social Consciousness* (1914). Here he maintains that social adaption and biological adaption are essentially the same. Variations in the social forms are due to changes in the natural environment. The few new social forms that manage to survive in the struggle for existence are adaptions. There are two main types of social adaption: technical and ideological, the latter being dependent upon the technical adaptions. All the ideological forms are "organizing adaptions" of the technical forms.[2]

Transforming Marx's position into a naive and unsystematic dogmatism, Paul Szende argued that sense experience as such is reliable: only its interpretation is socially determined. These socially determined interpretations combine into an ideology which conceals reality in the interest of the ruling class.[3]

Otto Bauer made the attempt to develop an empirical interpretation of the genesis of worldviews. The reality factor determining the worldview of a given class can be found in man's work experience: the members of the capitalist class are rooted in a working experience which consists essentially of the planning of work carried out by others. Therefore, they develop a worldview in which the notion of an overall plan is paramount, i.e., idealism. The members of the working class, on the other hand, are determined in their thinking by a work experience which brings them into direct, physical contact with the forces of nature and the properties of matter—they arrive at a worldview evolving around the same principles of force and matter: materialism.[4]

The Historicism of Georg Lukács

An historicist version of Marxist sociology of knowledge was developed by the Hungarian Georg Lukács and, to some extent, by his Polish-born follower Stanislaw Warynski (Leo Kofler).[5] In as much as Lukács is an orthodox left-wing Marxist, who came to accept the Leninist interpretation of Marxism, this deviation into "relativism" indicates that a measure of cerebral self-torture is not absent from the workings of the more subtle and creative minds in the totalitarian intellectual universe which is usually dominated by the naive and narrow thought-ways of lower-middle-class mental types. (Here Communists, Fascists, and American apostles

[2] Cf. Alexander A. Bogdanov, *Die Entwicklungsformen der Gesellschaft und die Wissenschaft* (translated by I. Dursky), Berlin: Nike Verlag, 1924.

[3] Cf. Paul Szende, *Verhüllung und Enthüllung*, Leipzig: Cl. Hirschfeld, 1922.

[4] Cf. Otto Bauer, "Das Weltbild des Kapitalismus," in O. Jenssen (editor), *Der Lebendige Marxismus: Kautsky Festschrift*, Jena: Thüringer Verlagsanstalt und Druckerei, 1924. See also A. Fogarasi, "Die Soziologie der Intelligenz und die Intelligenz der Soziologie," *Unter dem Banner des Marxismus*, Vol. IV, No. 3 (1930).

[5] Cf. Stanislaw Warynski, *Die Wissenschaft von der Gesellschaft: Umriss einer Methodenlehre der dialektischen Soziologie* (translated by Kazimierz Malecki), Bern: A. Francke, 1944.

of thought-control share, by the way, common ground.) This biographical datum also explains why the historicist element in Lukács' earlier writings is not something that meets the eye, but rather a subterranean current detectable only by intimate comparison of his thoughts with those of Marx. There are, of course, these more obvious facts: Lukács' book contributing to the sociology of knowledge and the sociological analysis of the ideology problem met with the disapproval of the Communist Party and he, in turn, abandoned eventually his objectivistic philosophy of history to regain the blessings of official doctrine.

Lukács' controversial book *History and Class-Consciousness* implicitly rejects all positivist and Neo-Kantian attempts to construe Marxism as either positive or idealist historical and social science. In contrast to the vulgar Marxists, Lukács (1885–   ) returns to the specifically Hegelian ingredients in Marx's thinking and comes to use historical materialism as a *method* leading to a universal understanding of historical reality and the dialectic totality of the elements constituting this reality.

Lukács is convinced that the Hegelian conception of the dialectic guarantees the scientific value of Marxism. He proceeds to oppose both the limitation of the dialectic to the conceptual realm and its materialistic reconstruction. He arrives at a realistic version of the dialectic which is equally far removed from the idealist dialectic of the Neo-Kantian Marxists, on the one side, and the dialectical materialism of the positivist Marxists, on the other. Turning directly against dialectical materialism, Lukács restricts his conception of the dialectic to the movement of historical reality; it is applicable to the social world only and serves no useful purpose in the interpretation of the physical universe. (Similarly, Karl Mannheim excludes the thought products of the physical sciences from his doctrine of the existential determination of knowledge.) For Lukács the dialectical movement of the historical process is *ens realissimum*, and in a typically Hegelian and historicist assertion he denies the existence of all suprahistorical factors. Inevitably, there germinates in his thinking the notion that, as a method, historical materialism has to be applied upon itself, thereby becoming subject to historical and social relativization.[6]

[6] Cf. Georg Lukács, *Geschichte und Klassenbewusstsein: Studien über marxistische Dialektik*, Berlin: Malik-Verlag, 1923. In 1953, Lukács' account of irrationalist philosophy, *Die Zerstörung der Vernunft*, appeared in East Berlin. Certainly Lukács had lost all appetite for even the slightest trace of relativism. Mannheim's sociology of knowledge figures in Lukács' reckoning with irrationalism as a "relativist caricature" which denies that cognition can have any objectivity. (Cf. Georg Lukács, *Die Zerstörung der Vernunft, Georg Lukács Werke*, Vol. 9, Neuwied am Rhein, Berlin-Spandau: Hermann Luchterhand Verlag, 1962, pp. 549–550.) A lessening of Lukács' doctrinaire attitude and a greater receptiveness for some of the concepts of his earlier work are apparent, however, in his more recent book, *Wider den missverstandenen Realismus*, Hamburg: Claassen Verlag, 1958. It is possible that the change was occasioned by the problems and conflicts which Lukács experienced when he participated in the government of Nagy.

Marx had never wavered in his conviction that all societies—ancient and modern alike—are under the mind-determining influence of the economic sphere; that, in other words, all societies have to be explained with the hermeneutic principle provided by historical materialism. In contrast, Lukács thinks that the economic conception of history is fully applicable only to the interpretation of modern capitalistic society and brings about the subtle, historical relativization of a principle that Marx had meant to be universally and eternally valid. It was correct, argues Lukács, to apply historical materialism unconditionally to the history of the nineteenth century. In the precapitalistic societies, however, the intensity of economic life which has been reached in capitalistic society did not yet prevail. Therefore, historical materialism cannot be applied to the precapitalistic social structures in the same way as to those forming part of capitalistic development. Here we need much finer analyses to reveal, on the one hand, what role the purely economic forces have played among the forces propelling society, provided such forces existed then in such "pureness," and on the other hand we need them to demonstrate how these economic forces acted here upon the other structural elements of society. The vulgar Marxists completely ignored this difference. Their application of historical materialism fell into the same error which Marx saw in vulgar economics; merely historical categories—in the first case categories of capitalistic society—were mistaken for eternal categories.[7]

His interpretation of historical materialism shows that Lukács was open to the suggestion that thought is existentially determined; he, obviously, realized that historical materialism had to be applied upon itself: in this view historical materialism stood revealed as the function, the expression of a determinate complex of social conditions. Yet at this exciting junction in the development of Marxist thought Lukács cautioned that this application upon itself neither leads to a complete relativism nor to the abdication of historical materialism as the right method. Following the dynamics of his initial reasoning Lukács concludes his observations, however, by saying that the truths contained in historical materialism resemble the truths which Marx saw in classical economics, in as much as they are truths within a given order of social life and production—only as such are they unconditionally valid. Societies may develop, however, wherein ". . . because of the nature of their social structure, validity will belong to other categories, to other contexts of truth."[8]

In the historicist mood of his youth, Lukács did not only display impatience with "eternal categories"—there grew in him the suspicion that the so-called "hard facts," i.e. the data furnished by experience, are, if seen in isolation, nothing but dead "fetishes." For the young Lukács the problem of truth appears in an entirely new light and in his Hegelian

---

[7] Cf. Lukács, *Geschichte und Klassenbewusstsein*, pp. 244–245.
[8] *Ibid.*, pp. 234–235 (my translation).

terminology he asserts that he sees "becoming as the truth of being, process as the truth of things." This leads to the historicist assumption that historical development is ontologically more real than the "facts" of experience.[9] What Lukács wants to destroy is the methodological priority of facts. This he deems necessary to reveal the true nature of all phenomena which are essentially processes. For Lukács, all so-called facts are likewise constituted of processes. Facts are nothing but ". . . artificially isolated and frozen *moments* of the total process."[10]

Lukács contends, then, that facts are killed if they are isolated from the movement to which they belong in life. With this contention he also establishes the connection with a concept that is central to his thinking: *reification*. With this concept Lukács tirelessly attacks men's eagerness to abandon the flowing totality for the static system, their inability to see human relationships other than in the shape of relations between things, their tendency to transform the historical and the relative into the eternal and absolute. The disposition of men toward reification not only endangers the vitality of individual facts—this disposition threatens movement as such by destroying its meaning and, thereby, ruling out truthful statements about it. Like Marx, Lukács views the problem of commodities as the most typical manifestation of the phenomenon of reification (*Verdinglichung*). Relations among people take on the character of a thing (*Dinghaftigkeit*); they receive a "ghostly objectivity" which makes them look like strictly closed systems operating on natural law principles. In this way there remains no trace of their true nature, namely that they were relations between human beings.[11]

As a historicist, Lukács claimed that the historical process is reality itself, as a relativist he announced that our loss of the sense for the historical movement as a whole prevents the apprehension of the truth of the world which we experience, and as a sociologist he saw the collapse of our cognitive apparatus determined by a social situation. As a Marxist, however, he identified this social situation in the bourgeois conception of the world and in the capitalistic mode of production.

In Lukács' view it is the capitalistic mode of production which leads to the substitution of things or fetishes for human relationships, to the functioning division between head and hand, between theory and action, and thus to the bourgeois conception of the world that postulates stability where it should discern movement. Reification is central to bourgeois thinking; the members of this class are divorced from reality. The bourgeois always tend to reify relations or conditions among persons—they are the true victims of the intellectual impasse created by the separation of subject and object, theory and practice and they are doomed to remain

[9] Cf. *Ibid.*, p. 198.
[10] *Ibid.*, p. 202 (emphasis in original; my translation).
[11] *Ibid.*, p. 94.

the prisoners of a social and intellectual situation which is of their own making. For the bourgeois—scholars and scientists are no exception— the essential quality of life is masked and what is warm and changeable freezes into cold, rigid forms: "a mentality which can take in neither the human character of the social world nor yet its historical quality is manifestly condemned to miss the true meaning of reality and is in fact a mentality 'every cognition of which is necessarily wrong.' "[12]

The Marxists coined the term "false consciousness" to convey the idea that there is a totally distorted mind that falsifies everything it touches upon.[13] Lukács uses this concept to penetrate the entire realm of mental activity. "Bourgeois philosophy," for example, is the degeneration of philosophical speculation into an exercise in shadowboxing. The phantasmagoric, mythological, and metaphysical varieties of this philosophy stem from its false premise that true theory must be separated from practice, that only a contemplative attitude will produce valid philosophical ideas. Inevitably, the "bourgeois philosopher" creates out of his deluded imagination the unrealistic division of thinking and being. Similarly, "bourgeois historians" create out of their false consciousness a perversion of history; they distort history—the clearest expression of movement— into a frozen landscape, robbed of all depth, mutilated beyond recognition.[14]

For the bourgeoisie the cognitive catastrophe is total and there is no room for hope: this class is forever sunk in error, its conception of the world is of necessity unrealistic. The individual members of this class are inevitably deluded by false consciousness and, therefore, incapable of penetrating to an understanding of the real interconnection of things with totality. The bourgeois is barred from the view of truth by his particular position inside the process of production; this is a collective fate: because of their class position the members of the bourgeoisie are actually unconscious of their own position in the historical and social process. This limitation transforms bourgeois class-consciousness immediately into false consciousness; it is not an incidental, psychological limitation, but one that arises as the objective consequence of the economic structure of capitalistic society.[15]

Moreover, Lukács is convinced that truth is revealed in action, that reality can only be known by those who function inside it, who participate in the true historical reality which is the "totality of the historical

[12] Werner Stark, *The Sociology of Knowledge: An Essay in Aid of a Deeper Understanding of the History of Ideas*, New York: The Free Press of Glencoe, 1958, p. 308.
[13] Cf. Franz Mehring, *Geschichte der deutschen Sozialdemokratie*, Vol. I, fourth edition, Stuttgart: J. H. W. Dietz, 1909, p. 386.
[14] Cf. Lukács, *Geschichte und Klassenbewusstsein*, pp. 58–59 and 172–173.
[15] Cf. *Ibid.*, pp. 63–65.

process." Only those who have been called and who have the will to usher in the future, ". . . can see the concrete truth of the present."[16]

The historical process which is reality becomes conscious of itself in the proletariat: the subject *and* object of history. The workers represent the first class in history which can have an adequate social consciousness.[17] The social consciousness of the working class is adequate because it is in harmony with the facts and movement of reality, but it is also determined by a social situation: the proletariat is capable of grasping the essence of capitalism and of the historical process leading to its destruction since—as a class—it occupies a social position in capitalistic society, where the naked and inhuman reality of this doomed order is directly experienced. The proletariat, Lukács maintains, holds in Hegelian fashion the key that will unlock the mystery of history: proletarian class-consciousness is the mentality which is ideally suited to the objective position of this class in society and history. The proletarian who is conscious of his class position understands life with its continuing, important struggles; he never loses his sense of the total historical process; he comprehends the truth of the future which he creates and which will be fully revealed to him at the moment of revolution when proletarian science and proletarian class-consciousness must achieve its full logical adequacy, since it will be in this instant of decision that consciousness is dialectically transformed into action, and theory into practice.

The proletariat, in recognizing itself, simultaneously achieves the objective recognition of society as a whole.[18] Only with the appearance of the proletariat does the understanding of social reality reach their completion: this class must fully understand its position in society in order to exist and to act; its class position becomes understandable only through the understanding of society in its entirety. This dialectical situation explains the unity of theory and praxis; because in the perspective of the proletarian self-recognition and recognition of the totality of history and society coincide: "the proletariat is both subject and object of its own understanding."[19]

Knowledge of truth spells ideological ruin as far as the bourgeoisie is concerned; for the working class, on the other hand, this knowledge is a weapon that must be wielded relentlessly to bring victory.[20] Class struggle is not an exclusively economic fight; class struggle is also a battle about the official interpretation of reality: bourgeoisie and proletariat compete for the "consciousness of society." The victor in this competition

---

[16] *Ibid.*, p. 223 (my translation).
[17] Cf. *Ibid.*, p. 217.
[18] Cf. *Ibid.*, p. 165.
[19] *Ibid.*, p. 34 (my translation).
[20] Cf. *Ibid.*, p. 80.

will not only emerge as the ideological ruler; his superiority will also offer him the chance to lead society.[21]

As soon as the bourgeoisie begins to realize that the ascending proletariat reveals truth, its false consciousness becomes "a falseness of consciousness."[22] Falseness moves from the noological to the psychological level: unintentional, unconscious object-inadequacy becomes intentional, deliberate concealment of a basically correct insight into reality; ideology changes into the lie and what started as a theoretical problem ends as a moral issue. Lukács believes that ever since the beginning of the nineteenth century the ideology of the bourgeoisie reflects its desperate fight not only against the understanding of a social system of its own making, but also against an awareness of its situation as a class.[23]

With a typically Leninist turn Lukács concludes that it is the task of the Communist Party—that "sublime" expression and culmination of true proletarian consciousness—to educate the workers so that they will become in reality what they are ideally already: the true, empirical proletariat. It is the educative mission of this elitist party to induce the personal consciousness of individual proletarians to reach the level of the ideal, collective consciousness possessed by the proletariat as a class; this mission is consummated in the Revolution. In this process the party plays the star role; it embodies and safeguards the class-consciousness of the proletariat; the party preserves the conscience of the workers' historical mission.[24]

Lukács the historicist, relativist, and sociologist was thus overcome by Lukács the Marxist-Leninist, who claims for the proletariat that it owns the future and is, therefore, able to see ". . . the concrete truth of the present."[25] His attempt to guarantee absolute truth to one social class and especially to the Communist Party indicates that Lukács never battled the problem of relativism seriously. He raised the problem, but proceeded to limit the consequences by holding to account only the thoughtways of the bourgeoisie. Exempting the proletariat and the party elite from the charge of relativism, Lukács took a way that leads out of the impasse but not toward reason; instead it leads to the misty regions of myth and religion. Lukács refused to think through the challenge of relativism; he failed, in the end, to turn the critical probe inward, upon his own position and that of the working class; instead, he used the lever

---

[21] *Ibid.*, p. 234.

[22] Cf. *Ibid.*, pp. 77–78.

[23] Cf. *Ibid.*, pp. 78–79.

[24] Cf. *Ibid.*, p. 53. For Lukács, *history* is the genesis of *class-consciousness*, of that mentality that reaches its perfection and annihilation in the same flash of historical significance: the proletariat annihilates itself together with its opponent at the moment of revolution and at that same moment class-consciousness becomes totally real to immediately leave the stage of history, forever. (Cf., *Ibid.*, pp. 62, 86, 89.)

[25] *Ibid.*, p. 223.

of faith to raise one privileged intellectual and social position out of the darkness of relativism: by a bold decree he declared it to be the absolute.

Of course, Lukács' attempt to settle the matter of relativism by escaping from the arena of reasoned and empirically anchored discourse is not remarkable as such; others, too, have sought refuge in those regions, where the scientific method of proof is overruled by the fiat of faith. While the Communist Lukács found comfort believing in the messianistic role of the proletariat and the priestly aloofness of the party, the Catholic Scheler found his distant safety-zone in the imaginary world of Platonic essences.

CHAPTER 4

MAX SCHELER
Quest for a Catholic
Sociology of Knowledge

$\overbrace{\qquad\qquad}$

Max Scheler is remarkable for his attempt to integrate the sociology of knowledge into the structure of a philosophical worldview and to reconcile the new perspective which this sociology opens up with the metaphysics, ontology, and epistemology underlying the worldview. "This accounts for the fact that he more or less ignored the internal conflicts inhering in this new intellectual orientation and the dynamic implications and new problems arising out of it."[1] This statement from the pen of Karl Mannheim shows that he considered Scheler's approach to the sociology of knowledge as being essentially in the nature of an opposition. The argument between Mannheim and Scheler does, indeed, represent one of the most challenging debates in the further development of the field.

Scheler's importance, however, transcends the function of forcing Mannheim to clarify and declare his own position. Apart from the scholarly sophistication and philosophical depth of his work, Scheler was the first writer who gave form and conceptual self-sufficiency to the discipline. Actually, it was Scheler (1874–1928) who first used the term "sociology of knowledge."[2]

Scheler's School

Furthermore, Scheler and his followers (Paul Honigsheim, Wilhelm Jerusalem, Helmut Plessner, Justus Hashagen, et al.) systematically

[1] Karl Mannheim, *Ideology and Utopia: An Introduction to the Sociology of Knowledge* (translated by Louis Wirth and Edward Shils), seventh impression, London: Routledge & Kegan Paul, 1954, p. 279.

[2] Scheler used the term *Soziologie des Wissens* in 1924; cf. Max Scheler (editor), *Versuche zu einer Soziologie des Wissens*, München: Duncker and Humblot, 1924. In 1909, however, the term "sociology of cognition" was used already by the Austrian, Wilhelm Jerusalem. Cf. Wilhelm Jerusalem, "Soziologie des Erkennens," *Die Zukunft*, 1909. For a discussion of the term *"Wissenssoziologie"* see Irving Louis Horowitz, *Philosophy, Science, and the Sociology of Knowledge* (with a Foreword by Robert S. Cohen), Springfield, Illinois: Charles C Thomas, Publisher, 1961, p. 140. For a detailed comparison of Scheler and Mannheim see Hans-Joachim Lieber, *Wissen und Gesellschaft: Die Probleme der Wissenssoziologie*, Tübingen: Max Niemeyer Verlag, 1952.

analyzed the social processes, groups, and structures that are bound up with different types of knowledge-acquisition, knowledge-conservation, and knowledge-distribution. These attempts led to the establishment of a particular form of quasi-empirical research in the sociology of knowledge which may be roughly characterized as the social and social psychological investigation of knowledge-production, knowledge-distribution, and knowledge-consumption. (The team emphasized academies, universities, philosophical and literary schools and circles, religious groups, etc.)[3]

Scheler also raised the question concerning the social determination of knowledge and thus contributed to this second and major form of research in the sociology of knowledge. In view of his earlier research interest it is not surprising that his answer to this crucial question implied that social factors influence merely the selection of ideas, in as much as they instigate or impede their dissemination; in view of his religious and metaphysical inclinations it is not surprising either that Scheler stressed the contention that social factors do not determine the content or validity of ideas.

Scheler and Mannheim

Both Scheler and Mannheim were influenced by Husserl's phenomenology. But, whereas Scheler regarded the cognitive act as insight into eternal essences, as a contemplative participation in these eternal truths, Mannheim viewed the cognitive act as bound up with the models to which it aspires, both in its existential and meaningful quality, as an ". . . instrument for dealing with life-situations at the disposal of a certain kind of vital being under certain conditions of life."[4] Whereas Scheler found the secret of historical knowledge in values transcending the flux and flow of the empirical world—values that only an immediate and convincing flash of emotional insight can reveal to us—Mannheim claimed that the ideal of truth which we construct from the products of thought is conditioned by three factors which influence the results of our mental activities: 1.) The thinker's response to reality. 2.) The thinker's constitution as a biological and historico-social being. 3.) The peculiar conditions under which the thinker responds to reality.[5]

In the phenomenological camp, Scheler was the foremost defender of the objectivist, absolutist theory of values which claims that truths of timeless validity (concrete, material values) can be grasped in "essential

[3] Cf. Scheler, *Versuche zu einer Soziologie des Wissens*. For a similar orientation see also Alfred von Martin, *Soziologie der Renaissance*, Stuttgart: Ferdinand Enke, 1932, and *Geist und Gesellschaft*, Frankfurt am Main: J. Knecht, 1948.

[4] Mannheim, *Ideology and Utopia*, p. 268.

[5] Cf. *Ibid.*, p. 268.

intuition" (*Wesensschau*):[6] Mannheim opposed this contention. What he shared with Scheler was the phenomenologists' rejection of positivism—that "philosophy of no-philosophy"—which so grossly neglected the phenomenological difference between the physical and the historic-social universe.[7] Still Mannheim was mainly and passionately concerned with the possibility of thinking "through" the phenomenological surface of ontic differences to reach the substantial core of social and historical reality. Much like Lukács, he believed that this intellectual advance could only be carried out by the active, genuinely committed personality.[8]

The intellectual careers of Mannheim and Scheler reflect powerful, dialectical reversals. Both men were influenced by the philosophy of the phenomenological school—Scheler leaned more strongly toward these ideas than Mannheim; both were fascinated by the tremors of historicism —Mannheim gave himself more fully to this wave of ideas than his opponent, but retreated as he grew older. Scheler began as a devout Catholic and ended on a note of rebellion bordering on atheism—Mannheim at first showed a cold and hostile indifference toward religion and was later drawn to the ". . . wealth of religious experience."[9]

Scheler's inability to remain aloof to the challenge of historicism becomes understandable if we recall the direction of his work and the stucture of his personality: in his work he found himself irresistibly driven to the new field of sociology, for which he meant to create a systematic basis in keeping with his metaphysical and philosophical convictions. Yet, once inside the arena of early twentieth-century German sociology he had to face the winds of historicism. Then, Scheler was the kind of man who felt close to the reality of his day; his strong personality did not permit him to shirk the responsibility of coping with novel intellectual developments. In this respect he was already different from the other scholars in his circle who peacefully continued to interpret the world through the optic of their Catholic tradition. In contrast to them, Scheler was a restless and sensitive philosopher, who tolerated neither boundaries nor hard formalism. Scheler declined to live forever with a

[6] Cf. Max Scheler, *Der Formalismus in der Ethik und die materiale Wertethik: Neuer Versuch der Grundlegung eines ethischen Personalismus*, third edition, Halle: M. Niemeyer, 1927.

[7] In a similar way, Scheler argued that Comte's and Spencer's positivism was no philosophy at all—it was merely a specific type of West European ideology reflecting the social reality created by late occidental industrialism. Cf. Max Scheler, *Die Wissensformen und die Gesellschaft. Gesammelte Werke*, Vol. 8 (edited with commentaries by Maria Scheler), Bern and München: Francke Verlag, 1960, pp. 66–68.

[8] For Mannheim's stand on positivism see his essay, "The Problem of a Sociology of Knowledge," in Karl Mannheim, *Essays on the Sociology of Knowledge* (edited by Paul Kecskemeti), New York: Oxford University Press, 1952, pp. 150–152.

[9] Cf. Karl Mannheim, *Diagnosis of Our Time*, London: Routledge & Kegan Paul, 1943, p. 118.

wall separating eternity and temporality; he wanted to explain ". . . the new cultural factors emerging in the world."[10]

However, the structure of an argument will be subject to perilous tensions if a conservative mode of thought and experience has to accommodate so strong a feeling of affinity to the present. Caught between the immediate claim of historicism and the remote but powerful lure of phenomenology, committed to the theory of supertemporal values, and drawn to the movement of the world of reality, Scheler was forced into a daring synthesis: he had to work out the position of historicism and sociologism within the confines of a philosophy of timelessness.

Scheler acknowledged his affinity to the empirical world with the statement that the thinkers of the nineteenth and twentieth centuries produced their greatest insight when they grasped ". . . that knowledge is determined by society."[11] To avoid the sociologistic implication that this social determination of knowledge also conditions its validity, he fell back upon the phenomenological contention that "factual" knowledge is entirely different from "essential" knowledge. This division between two fundamentally different forms of knowledge reflects the phenomenologists' separation between Being and Meaning, and Scheler proceeded from these premises when he bolstered his argument with the construction of a dualistic metaphysics, claiming there are two separate realms of being, a realm of ideal value-essences and a realm of concrete existential facts.[12]

Scheler finds the link connecting his metaphysics with his sociology in his philosophical anthropology which clearly separates two realms of being: mind and life; it is man who acts as mediator between these two independent spheres, for man is both, mind and life.[13] One of the major functions of sociology is equally dualistic: the researcher in this field investigates the social determination of human actions that are above all determined by the mind sphere—actions which aim at mental or "ideal" goals; but, he also does the same with actions that are mainly determined by basic drives, such as the sex, hunger, and power drive. In the case of mainly drive-determined actions, men strive to accomplish "real" alterations in the structure of the empirical world. (Every concrete human action is, of course, a mixture of both elements.)

His dualistic philosophical anthropology enables Scheler to distinguish two major forms of sociology which provide the poles of a continuum making possible the typological characterization of all sociological phe-

---

[10] Mannheim, *Essays on the Sociology of Knowledge,* p. 155.

[11] Scheler, *Die Wissensformen und die Gesellschaft,* p. 52n (my translation).

[12] *Ibid.,* pp. 359–360.

[13] Cf. Max Scheler, *Die Stellung des Menschen im Kosmos,* Darmstadt: Verlag Otto Reichl, 1928.

nomena: he sets the "sociology of the superstructure" (*Kultursoziologie;* the sociology of knowledge is part of it) apart from the "sociology of the substructure" (*Realsoziologie*). This Marxist-inspired distinction draws upon differences in human intentions which direct actions either toward "ideal" entities or—as in the instance of *Realsoziologie*—toward empirical reality: "At one time activity terminates in the ideal world, at another in the real world."[14]

Scheler's Major Task

It was Scheler's major task to decide upon the exact nature of the social determination of all culture content. To accomplish this task Scheler introduced a further, though related, distinction: he claimed that there is "objective spirit" with its subjective human correlate, the "mental structure" which give us the "ideal factors" (*Idealfaktoren*).[15] Then there

---

[14] Scheler, *Die Wissensformen und die Gesellschaft,* p. 19 (my translation). In contrast to Marx, Scheler developed a detailed differentiation of the superstructure, based on his theory of "cultural change." First of all, there are the "relatively natural world views" (*relativ natürliche Weltanschauungen*) constituting "organic growths" (*organische Gewächse*) which develop only in very large timespans and contain everything that the members of a group accept without question as "naturally" given. In any fundamental sense they can be changed only through race mixture and the eventual mixture of language and culture. The great blocks of these world-views support various types of knowledge belonging to the "relatively artificial forms of worldview" (*"Bildungs" weltanschauungsformen*). These are ordered in seven classes, according to their degree of artificiality. Beginning with the forms of knowledge that are least artificial, Scheler establishes a classification ranging from myth and legend through philosophical-metaphysical knowledge to technological knowledge. The rate of change increases with degree of artificiality and, while myth and legend or religious knowledge change very slowly, positive science and technology change from hour to hour. (Cf. *Ibid.*, pp. 61–64.) Scheler's theory of relatively natural worldviews implies his rejection of Kant, whose table of categories is "only the table of categories of European thinking." Scheler assumed that the nature of relatively natural worldviews changed from group to group and, within one group, from one stage of development to another. With Lévy-Bruhl and other students of primitive mentality he claimed that these differences reached into the very structure of cognition. (Cf. Scheler, "Weltanschauungslehre, Soziologie und Weltanschauungs-setzung" in *Schriften zur Soziologie und Weltanschauungslehre, Gesammelte Werke,* Vol. 6, second edition (edited by Maria Scheler), Bern and München: Francke Verlag, 1963. See also Scheler, "Die geistige Einheit Europas" in Scheler, *Der Genius des Krieges und der Deutsche Krieg,* Leipzig: Verlag der Weissen Bücher, 1915.)

[15] Much like Hans Freyer, Scheler differentiates various manifestations of objective spirit. He explains that "objective spirit" can be found wherever and whenever we encounter human society: objective spirit is meaningful content embodied in matter or reproducible psychophysical activities (tools, works of art, language, institutions, customs, rites, ceremonies, etc.). Objective spirit has its subjective correlate in the changing structure of the group's "spirit" which the individual experiences as having binding significance and power. (Cf. Scheler, *Die Wissensformen und die Gesellschaft,* p. 24 and Hans Freyer, *Theorie des objektiven Geistes,* third edition, Leipzig and Berlin: B. G. Teubner, 1934.)

are "real life relations" (*Reale Lebensverhältnisse*) with their subjective human correlate, the "structure of human drives" which combine into "real factors" (*Realfaktoren*).

Scheler's decision is contained in his "law of the order of effectiveness of the ideal factors and real factors" (*Gesetz der Ordnung der Wirksamkeit der Idealfaktoren und Realfaktoren*) which implies that mind is a "factor of determination" but not a "factor of realization." Mind, finding its expression in the ideal factors, determines what works and thoughts *can* be created by a culture. The particular combination of the real factors prevailing at the time will, however, determine what actually *gets* created. Thus, the social conditions or real factors do not determine knowledge; they merely have the function of making a selection among the possibilities made available by mind. Because of their selective function the real factors control the ideal factors: only those potential works and thoughts actually occur that are permitted into empirical existence by the real factors.

The substructural forces, i.e., the particular combination of the real factors in the interplay of power relations, economic factors, quantitative and qualitative demographic factors, geographical and geopolitical factors, perform the function of "negative factors of realization." In a Nietzschean turn, Scheler finds his "positive factor of realization" in the "free action" and "free will" of the leaders, models and pioneers—those few who are imitated by the masses, thereby making possible the diffusion of culture. To pass from potentiality to actuality a possible cultural achievement, therefore, depends upon the "negatively selective power" of *real factors and* the "free volitional causality" of the *élite* whose mentally creative and aggressive members help to push open the "sluice gates" for the mental stream by preparing the masses for new ideas.[16]

Scheler's rebuttal of relativism depends on the thought that the real factors do *not* determine the positive content of meaning of mental productions. "Real history" only hinders or facilitates, retards or accelerates, the *realization* of this content of meaning: real history "opens and closes in a certain manner and order the sluice gates of the mental streams" so that ideas and works may pass from possibility to actuality. (Major real factors are: "blood, power, the economy." The real history of any given supranational culture, i.e. *Hochkultur,* can be summed up in a "law of three phases." This "*Gesetz der drei Phasen je vorwiegender Primärkausalität der Realfaktoren*" implies that in the first phase, blood-relationships with their regulative kinship institutions form the independent variable of the sociohistoric process; during the second phase the primary effectiveness, i.e. *Wirkprimat,* is embodied in political power; during the third

---

[16] Scheler, *Die Wissensformen und die Gesellschaft,* pp. 21–22.

phase economic factors primarily determine the processes of real history by controlling the sluice gates for the mental stream.)[17]

Scheler's synthesis which permitted him to work out the position of historicism and sociologism within the confines of a philosophy of timelessness rests, of course, upon his dualistic metaphysics. On this basis he found it possible to reconcile the view that the genesis of ideas and works does not affect their content and validity with the assumption that it is important to trace their genesis. In other words, Scheler held that the *content* of knowledge belongs to the realm of timeless essences, whereas the *forms* of intellectual *activity* belong to the realm of existence; they are, therefore, socially determined. This line of reasoning leads Scheler at the same time to the establishment of his sociology of knowledge: he states that all knowledge including the forms of thinking, intuition, and cognition are undoubtedly of sociological character. This sociological determination does not affect the content or validity of knowledge. We must realize, however, that the dominant, interest-bound social perspective determines the selection of the things we want to study. There is no question—the *forms* of thought ". . . are always and *necessarily sociological,* i.e. *co*-determined by the structure of society."[18]

Scheler, in this fashion, limited the influence which society exerts upon knowledge to the function of selection; he thereby succeeded in establishing a moderate version of the sociology of knowledge—he failed, however, in his attempt to overcome relativism. His solution is reminiscent of Benedetto Croce: all ideas and works appearing in real history are partial and relative, since they are released by existentially determined interests—only the one "eternal, objective Logos" incarnates ulti-

---

[17] Cf. *Ibid.*, p. 40. For the "law of three phases" see *Ibid.*, p. 47. In suggesting a *variation* of effective existential factors, Scheler turned upon the three naturalistic theories which rely exclusively either on race (Gumplowicz, Gobineau), politics (Ranke's school), or economic factors (Marx) and which hold that real factors *unequivocally* determine the *content* of the cultural works and thoughts. Equally wrong are, in his opinion, all ideological, spiritualistic, and personalistic views of history which maintain that real events and social phenomena can be understood as a unilinear sequence to the history of mind. (Cf. *Ibid.*, pp. 40 and 42.) Scheler believes that his position, as expressed in the law of three phases, is supported by the evidence produced on various fronts; he points in particular to the findings of ethnologists concerning the importance of blood-ties among nonliterate peoples and to the historical analyses of Werner Sombart demonstrating the limitations of the economic interpretation of history. (Cf. *Ibid.*, pp. 42–44.) Scheler also deduces the "law" from his theory of the structure of human drives (sex, power, hunger) and from the "laws of vital-psychic aging" which claim that the three phases of the lifespan are dominated by different drives: in youth the sexual-procreative drive is predominant, during maturity the desire to have power over men and nature is paramount, and with the onset of old age, men fall under the spell of economic motivations. These changes, related to aging in the individual, correspond to a kind of "aging" of human societies where the sequence in the drives undergoes similar changes. Thus Western culture becomes now increasingly dominated by the economic interests in production and property. (Cf. *Ibid.*, pp. 49–51.)

[18] *Ibid.*, p. 58 (emphasis in original; my translation).

mate, objective truth. This solution may represent sound metaphysics, but it certainly does nothing to help us decide how true any given "truth" actually is. "In this 'escape' from relativism, as in so many others, the ultimate conclusion that we are forced to reach is that relativism is a fact stronger than much metaphysical theory: in the end it will break its way through any tissue of speculation which once affords it tenancy."[19]

Karl Mannheim, protagonist of the radical sociology of knowledge, was perturbed in particular by Scheler's attempt to establish a mental realm with an immanent logic of meaning in relation to which the empirical realm with its real factors plays merely a selective role. Mannheim critically confronted Scheler's "static conception" with his own "dynamic position." He saw the relationship within the "possible" and "actual" differently: "For us, too," Mannheim argued in the vein of Husserl,

> there is at each moment that which is actual, surrounded by a horizon of possibilities; this horizon, however, is not the abstractly "possible as such," but contains merely that which is possible in a given situation as a result of a certain constellation of factors. This "horizon," in turn, is merely the starting point of a new process leading to new actualities; this always involves the completely new, creative role of the moment and of the unique situation. For our conception of the world, then, it is not the abstractly possible that is higher; the value accent rests upon the emerging and the actual. The real is not, as in Scheler's system, an always inadequate selection from a transcendent treasure of forms, but a creative concretization flowing from historically unique constellations.[20]

[19] From *The Problem of Historical Knowledge,* by Maurice Mandelbaum. By permission of Liveright, Publishers, New York. Copyright © renewed, 1966, by Maurice Mandelbaum, p. 155. Both Scheler and his literate interpreters realized this problem. Scheler meant to overcome it by postulating—not unlike Mannheim—a collective "mission" of *all* epochs and civilizations which would lead to the historical "synthesis" of all the essences that had been partially intuitioned by different individuals and groups in the course of history. For the implications and shortcomings of this germ of a "solution" see Werner Stark, *The Sociology of Knowledge: An Essay in Aid of a Deeper Understanding of the History of Ideas,* New York: The Free Press of Glencoe, 1958, pp. 341–344 and Mannheim, *Essays on the Sociology of Knowledge,* pp. 166–179. See also Scheler, *Die Wissensformen und die Gesellschaft,* pp. 26–27.
[20] Mannheim, *Essays on the Sociology of Knowledge,* p. 165.

CHAPTER 5

The Radical Sociology of Knowledge and Beyond

D EVOID OF THE METAPHYSICAL DEVICES of his predecessors, it was
Mannheim who had to experience the full impact of relativism. The
radical branch of the sociology of knowledge—emphasizing that *all*
aspects of culture are determined by society—contains two subdivisions.
One approach establishes a *causal* determination of culture, the other
proclaims a *functional* state of dependency. While Marx is customarily
associated with the idea of causal determination, Mannheim's radical
sociology of knowledge belongs to the functional variety of absolute cultural sociology. (Mannheim continues Max Weber's functional analysis.)

Mannheim (1893–1947) distinguishes between two different interpretations of mental products in establishing the sociology of knowledge as
the central science. He declares the sociology of knowledge to be an
extrinsic interpretation and sets it apart from the *immanent* interpretation of thought products.[1] The immanent interpretation is based upon an
understanding of the intellectual *content*; it is thereby limited to the
theoretical content of knowledge. The extrinsic interpretation is based
upon the understanding of *manifestations*; it sees culture content as the
manifestation of an absolute stratum (*Absolutschicht*).

This differentiation between two types of interpretation enables Mannheim to designate a logical place for the sociology of knowledge within
the scientific system. Along with other disciplines such as psychoanalysis,
the sociology of knowledge stands opposite the traditional human sciences, which seek the immanent meaning of mental products through
the understanding of the mind (*Geistverstehen*). Thus, cultural sociology
interprets culture and the sociology of knowledge interprets knowledge
through the understanding of manifestation as an emanation of *ens
realissimum*: social reality. In other words, the sociology of knowledge
as an extrinsic interpretation functionally relates intellectual statements
and judgments to social reality as the absolute stratum.

Mannheim claims in support of the sociology of knowledge that its
fundamental thesis was not established arbitrarily. Rather, the sociology
of knowledge must be understood as the conceptual expression of con-

[1] Cf. Karl Mannheim, "Ideologische und soziologische Interpretation der geistigen
Gebilde," *Jahrbuch für Soziologie*, Vol. II (edited by G. Salomon), Karlsruhe: G.
Braun, 1926, pp. 424–440.

temporary historical experience which has *social reality* at its vital center and which conceives of all manifestations of life as dependent upon the socio-economic orders and their transformations.[2]

The Method of Wissenssoziologie

The idea of an "existential determination of knowledge" forms the central theme of Mannheim's sociology of knowledge. By equating reality to social reality he establishes the actual relevance (*Geltungsrelevanz*) of societal life for all intellectual utterances. According to Mannheim, the method of sociology of knowledge becomes effective only where content and form of judgement are dependent on a specific constellation of social life. Thus, the concept of "socio-existential determination of knowledge" expresses the theory that the absolute stratum, i.e., societal life centered around socio-economic orders, not only has importance for the realization of judgements *hic et nunc,* that it not only possesses factual relevance (*Faktizitätsrelevanz*) but also that it influences the *content, form,* and *structure* of intellectual utterances.[3]

This peculiar influence of the absolute stratum upon the products of thinking is not direct; rather, it is *mediated* by the carrier of knowledge, by the space- and time-bound and always historical subject of cognition. This perceiving subject is always fitted into the historical-social process of life in a specific way: he always has a particular "standpoint" in the all-embracing totality of life. Therefore, an object of cognition never totally discloses itself to man. Rather, every agent of cognition sees only a partial aspect and that only from his own cognitive standpoint (*Denkstandort*).

Presumably this perspective extends into the product of thinking. Now, the term perspective context (*Aspektstruktur*) is introduced to point out how a perceiving individual sees an object, which of its elements he grasps, and how he constructs a context in the process of thinking. Apart from thought products of the type $s = \frac{g}{2} t^2$ or $2 \times 2 = 4$, the results in the human sciences which rest on metaempirical worldview presuppositions can only be formulated in perspective contexts. The existentially determined *standpoint of thinking* thus *extends* via perspective context into the content of a judgement, leaving its imprint on the *entire* utterance since it exerts a decisive influence even upon the *categorical apparatus.*[4]

[2] Cf. Karl Mannheim, "Das Problem einer Soziologie des Wissens," *Archiv für Sozialwissenschaft und Sozialpolitik,* Vol. 53, No. 3 (September, 1925), pp. 632–633.

[3] *Ibid.,* p. 635.

[4] Cf. Karl Mannheim, *Ideology and Utopia: An Introduction to the Sociology of Knowledge* (translated by Louis Wirth and Edward Shils), second edition, New York: Harcourt, Brace & World, 1940, pp. 26, 243–244, 263–264.

The first period of Mannheim's work ends with his article *Wissensso-ziologie* (sociology of knowledge), published in 1931.[5] In it Mannheim still attempts to clarify epistemological and ontological issues concerning a sociology of knowledge that follows the main stream of cultural sociology and tends towards a problem awareness resting on the larger question of a sociology of the mind.

Mannheim's theorizing in this first period must be understood against the background of the Weimar Republic. Political and social life of this period resembled a kaleidoscopic display, with the observer witnessing constant changes of the most varied philosophical, political, social, and cultural tenets.

Because of these and other experiences and influences, including Marxist economic determinism and the various methods of unmasking ideologies that were advanced by Nietzsche, Freud, and Marx, Mannheim in time came to a basic doubt regarding man's intellectual behavior. The impact on him of Life-Philosophy (*Lebensphilosophie*) and historism increased and accentuated his doubts and distrust until he eventually arrived at the question of the basic meaning of mind and culture.[6]

Sociology of Knowledge and the Modern Mentality

The following discussion deals with the "antecedents of the sociology of knowledge" or, to word it differently, with the growth of doubt and suspicion. The sociology of knowledge—the probably most specific expression of sceptical relativism—is seen as the erstwhile end product of a long chain of developments in intellectual and social history.

These developments have not only led to the formulation of this particular area of specialized sociological inquiry. They have also signally affected the intellectual attitudes and research orientations that are generally manifest in modern schemes of scientific and philosophical analysis. Moreover, the slow but rather steady accumulation of suspicious and distrustful mental attitudes has an immediate bearing upon the unmistakable penetration of doubt and suspicion into the nontheoretical level of everyday living. It is probably here that these mind-sets create the greater turmoil and confusion. Whereas theoretical men have lived with these problems for centuries, as the subsequent analysis will show, their counterparts have not, and only the twentieth century has forced the insecurity born of gliding standpoints and shifting realities upon the bewildered mass of literate humanity.

[5] Cf. Karl Mannheim, "Wissenssoziologie," in Alfred Vierkandt (editor), *Hand-wörterbuch der Soziologie*, Stuttgart: F. Enke, 1931, pp. 659–680.

[6] Cf. my article, "Karl Mannheim: Revision of an Intellectual Portrait," *Social Forces*, Vol. 40, No. 1 (October, 1961), pp. 23–30. In this article I have also traced the changes in Mannheim's thinking that became noticeable after his emigration to England in 1933.

Accustomed to the static, ontologically and epistemologically conservative frame of reference provided by the "conventional wisdom"—to use Galbraith's term—modern men of "practical" orientation are especially helpless in the agitated sea of modern relativism and cling all the more stubbornly to the archaic signposts of an intellectually and socio-politically defunct past. The fatal split of the world into an aggregate of isolated, noncommunicating, disparate universes of discourse can only be brought closer to healing after Nietzsche's dictum has been widened into the statement that not only science but the world at large is a "graveyard of discarded hypotheses." We all must learn to live with the insight— already part of the scientist's and intellectual's workday world—that the insistence upon "truth" may be noble (often it is manipulative or puerile) but that an orientation toward relative operational stages may be more functionally related to the needs of the human animal. "True" is after all only an adjective ". . . applied to propositions that satisfy the forms of an accepted model of verification"; and in our time there does not exist a ". . . common form of validation to which all will submit their assertions."[7]

Because of these wider ramifications of our problem the following essay will be mainly concerned with those antecedents of the sociology of knowledge that have more than technical significance and form actually part of the mainstream of Western intellectual history.

We will be concerned, first of all, with the phenomenon of *doubt*. Our initial question is: When and how did doubt emerge, that is, doubt in the potentialities of the human mind as an instrument of cognition and a vehicle for the acquisition of knowledge? This sociologically-grounded investigation into the problems of epistemology begins with Immanuel Kant, who closed the significant chapter of the Enlightenment and, thereby, ushered in the critical spirit of modern times.

Kant's thinking was propelled by a fundamental doubt in the efficacy of all philosophy as he knew it, by a doubt in the possibilities of an unlimited progress of human knowledge into the secrets of reality. With Kant, the invasion of the epistemological and ontological frontier by the forces of scepticism resulted in a disturbing contraction of man's cognitive potential.

With Hegel's ontological reduction in the spirit of *historical consciousness*, man experienced a shocking diminution of the world of his present, which shrank to a mere link in the oceanic process of continual historical transformation. With Dilthey, the movement had gathered enough momentum to annihilate Kant's *consciousness as such* and to oust his universal *a priori*, which was replaced by the relativistic life philosopher's

---

[7] C. Wright Mills, "Methodological Consequences of the Sociology of Knowledge," *American Journal of Sociology*, Vol. XLVI, No. 3 (November, 1940), pp. 325 and 326.

historicized worldview a priori that limited the cognitive agent to his specific historical and social position. Finally, Husserl's phenomenological attitude initiated the fragmentation of the physical universe into a series of *perspective variations,* the reduction of the objective world to something that does neither exist, nor not exist, but that *we believe* to exist.

This development of specific "philosophical presuppositions" constitutes to a considerable extent the *sine qua non* of the evolution of certain "conceptual presuppositions" which in their entirety represent the clinical history of both the modern mentality and the radical sociology of knowledge. Two concepts are especially prominent: *historicism* and *ideology;* they directed the labors of numerous thinkers.

The historicists introduced the notion that human behavior must be understood as something that is relative to a specific historical situation. They taught us to view every historical (cultural) phenomenon, every human experience, social system, and belief as something that is temporal, historically conditioned, relative, and limited.

The spread of such intellectual and moral relativism accelerated the growth of the *suspicion of ideology* which began to invade the serene world of classical idealism when Francis Bacon declared that human reason was not a clear light and set out to develop a fairly comprehensive list of disturbing influences with his enumeration of the *idols* of the mind. Less direct but not less significant for the development of ideology was the reversal of classical idealism that occurred when the modern idealist philosophers placed "ideal reality" in the *consciousness of man.* Since Locke's epistemological inquiry, Berkeley's and Hume's empiricist attitude, and Kant's critique, "reality" and "truth" were reduced to a dependency on the human mind which became problematic as soon as this mind became questionable.

The thinking of Locke and Bacon provided a source of inspiration for those who were to take this fateful step: the philosophers of the Enlightenment in France. The *philosophes*—especially Helvétius and Holbach —declared man to be subject to errors and deception which distort his relationship with the objects that constitute his world. Now the suspicion of ideology finds its first formulation on a *psychological* level: man is able to conceive a true reality but he rejects it because truth conflicts with his interests. An important variant of this interest theory no longer credits the falsifier of truth with good faith; it indicts him as a deliberate *liar.*

With Karl Marx the suspicion of ideology becomes *total:* now the *entire* mind is seen to be ideological—not just certain ideas; now the social situation does not merely condition the psychological manifestation of concepts but penetrates to the *noological* meanings, to the very core of thought products. Marx turns this total suspicion of ideology against the thought of his adversaries; the suspicion of ideology becomes the most important weapon of the proletariat in the class struggle. Marx declares the bourgeois thinkers to be incapable of grasping the movement of "true" reality.

Also on other fronts the traditional concepts of reason and truth are under attack. Friedrich Nietzsche—the great "sham-smasher" as Mencken calls him—channels much of his dark brooding to the development of an *irrational* theory of ideology. At the dawn of our century Freud's *biological reduction* of reason is already complete and the devaluation of ideas is making rapid strides: terms such as rationalization, illusion, verbal facade, myth, vital lies, derivation, and ideology become part of everyday language.

Thus ends the story of the antecedents of the sociology of knowledge: that field of inquiry where not only error or illusion but also the *discovery of truth are seen as socially and historically conditioned,* where not merely the ideas of our enemies but those of all groups—including our own—are recognized as socially determined; therefore, temporal, relative, limited.

Neither Mannheim nor his predecessors could bring themselves to fully accept this final conclusion and much of their thinking was equivalent to the intellectual self-torture of a fight against relativism. In our discussion of the antecedents of the sociology of knowledge we will, time and time again, encounter the often heroic attempt to firmly anchor knowledge, to guarantee *truth.* Much in the earlier writers strove toward prophecy and the promise of a more satisfactory world—intellectually as well as morally. But the spectre of relativism would not fade and even the most hopefully conceived idea system would ultimately, and often against the intentions of its originator, contribute to the further growth of doubt and suspicion, the advance of relativism. Even the radical Mannheim preferred to speak of "relationism" and arrived after various other attempts to overcome the problem of relativism at the dubious construction of a so-called *socially unattached intelligentsia* that is allegedly able to rise above the unavoidable chaos of diverse standpoints, to engage— because it has no special axe to grind—in adjusting and synthesizing activities which would initiate a process that leads *in infinitum* toward truth.

Current Sociology of Knowledge

More recently, practitioners of the sociology of knowledge have exhibited considerable fascination for an organicist, a-historical construct derived mainly from social psychology, cybernetics, and semantics: *the image.* In 1955, this concept was introduced by Gardner and Levy within the general framework of motivational research. A year later Boulding defined an image as the structured totality of ". . . messages filtered through a changeable value system."[8]

The fascination for the concept of the image displayed by contemporary sociologists of knowledge is understandable; they have so far failed to discover a satisfactory or logically tenable correspondence between thought and reality. The theory of the image, however, contains a fiat which is of signal importance for the dismantlement of this dilemma: "We can never examine the correspondence of the image with reality, whether in the field of value or in the field of fact."[9]

According to *eiconics* (the theory of the image) there are, to begin with, no facts—rather individuals and organizations receive sensory and symbolic messages from their environment; they filter these messages selectively through the screen of their variable scales of valuation and develop a subjective knowledge structure, an interpretative conception of reality: the image.

It is not reality, but this image and its value system that determine the current behavior of all organisms and organizations—our responses to reality are always mediated by the image. Individuals and groups, for example, that adhere to a distrustful and hostile image of the world will soon find their suspicions confirmed: their behavior will create the enemies which are necessary for the self-justification of their image.

Images are both private and public: the personal elements result from an individual's projections of his personality into the world and express weak or strong feelings of pleasure and fear. In varying degrees, also images contain social elements, represented by expressions of the normative expectations which each group maintains with regard to the behavior of its members.

Images become social phenomena and objects of sociological interest as soon as they exist as symbols and representations of reality directing

---

[8] Burleigh B. Gardner and Sidney J. Levy, "The Product and the Brand," *Harvard Business Review,* Vol. 33, No. 2 (March–April, 1955), pp. 33–39. Kenneth E. Boulding, *The Image: Knowledge in Life and Society,* Ann Arbor: The University of Michigan Press, 1956, p. 14. Cf. also Ralf Dahrendorf, "European Sociology and the American Self-Image," *European Journal of Sociology,* Vol. II, No. 2 (Fall, 1961), pp. 324–366, and Hans Peter Dreitzel, "Selbstbild und Gesellschaftsbild," *European Journal of Sociology,* Vol. III, No. 2 (Fall, 1962), pp. 181–228.

[9] Boulding, *op. cit.,* pp. 174–175. Mannheim's immediate followers showed little concern for the lack of a satisfactory correspondence between thought and reality. Their work shows that in their time the sociology of knowledge was still dominated by the historical dimension. Cf. Hans H. Gerth, *Die sozialgeschichtliche Lage der bürgerlichen Intelligenz um die Wende des 18. Jahrhunderts: Ein Beitrag zur Soziologie des deutschen Frühliberalismus,* Berlin: V.D.I.-Verlag, 1935. Ernst Kohn-Bramstedt, *Aristocracy and the Middle-Classes in Germany: Social Types in German Literature 1830–1900,* London: P. S. King & Son, 1937. Hans Weil, *Die Entstehung des deutschen Bildungsprinzips,* Bonn: F. Cohen, 1930.

the behavior of not only one person or a few individuals, but the actions of large groups and entire societies.

The stability and durability of an image depends on the intensity, the strength of group norms and group discipline. Most of the images maintained by members of pluralistic, relatively open societies are, therefore, less stable and less enduring than the images that direct the behavior of individuals in relatively closed and authoritarian social systems. Boulding asserts, however, that neither democratic nor authoritarian organizations are in this respect inherently stable; it is actually an oscillation between the two forms of organization that constitutes the general political dynamic.

Images are representations of reality which consist of accumulated informations about reality. New informations, in turn, may modify or annihilate existing images; they may also replace them with novel images. The value scales of individuals or groups mainly determine the effect of the information they receive on their image of the world. Men exhibit an intense and constant need for new information—a need that does not only reveal the importance of up-to-date information for the mastery of novel situations but also a strong desire to find support for their current image of reality.

At this point a responsible analysis and description of modern consciousness must turn its spotlight on a process which is, as an undercurrent, of ancient origin but which was endowed with the force of an intellectual movement by the philosophers of the Enlightenment and brought to maturity by modern technology and industry. This process—the unfolding of the scientific-technological-industrial worldview—was from the start inspired by the secular-scientific attitude and logically concludes by giving science the monopoly over all questions concerning physical and social reality.

The scientific-technological-industrial process depended for its development on an immense proliferation of information and, in turn, unleashed an excess of information—an inflation of messages—which seriously threatens the formation and survival of images of the world and society, because it robs everything that is not narrowly scientific and technical of all certainty and normative relevance.

World and society, therefore, confront contemporary men as objective, barely comprehensible forces; modern men react by keeping their distance from these annoying, unsettling aggregates of short-lived, relative, abstract data. Modern life recoils upon itself, upon the small world of privacy; it tends—as Dreitzel correctly observes—toward personal isolation and lonely individualism. This tendency finds its most bizarre expression in the improbabilities of the electronic nightmare which the average television viewer has accepted so that he may send the world and society to hell.

So far it seems the sociology of knowledge has not gained more from its association with the theory of the image than a different rock upon which to shatter: in its classical stance this sociology sank into the sea of relativism—now it totters at the abyss of commercialized nihilism.

We should, however, not overlook what may well turn out to be the central weakness of the image concept in its present formulation: the retention of value conceptions. We have seen how images that are structured around value systems are weakened and eventually destroyed by an unavoidable inflation of messages since their value systems cannot assimilate all of the new, often contradictory information that bombards them incessantly. It may well be that images can only survive as forces capable of directing human behavior if their normative structure can be changed into an entity that conforms to science and thrives on the heavy traffic of messages. In other words, if modern man cannot live with value-oriented images, he must live with images that have a different normative structure. This different normative structure, it seems, science offers itself: *quantitative conceptions.* Similarly, Krysmanski demands that value conceptions must be transformed into "metric conceptions."[10]

Because of its essentially transcendent origin and inflexible nature a value system does not offer a durable structure for the consciousness of modern man, condemned as he is to the inflation of messages. A system of quantitative or metric conceptions, on the other hand, can follow all the expansions and changes that modern consciousness must undergo, because such a system is as incomplete and evolving as its source: scientific quantification. A value system is rigid, rooted in socio-economic and political interests and incapable of compromise; a quantitative system, conversely, convinces because of its provisional, flexible, negotiable characteristics. It is no accident that in popular thinking, too, quantitative communication has been widely accepted to neutralize differences in experience and outlook: contemporary men speak of $30,000 statues, 300-feet high monuments and the day may not be far when the relevance of ideas will be measured by the bushels of wheat they were capable of directing to the hungry multitudes of the world.

This new approach to the image has its methodological basis in the development of symbolic logic which fused mathematics and logic, thereby terminating the century-old tension that had kept the humanistic and mathematical traditions of the West apart. The reconstruction of the image found its preparation in the work of Freyer and Geiger and rests now on the assumption that modern society is no longer a value-oriented social system, but rather a consumption-oriented, semi-scientific

[10] Cf. Hans-Jürgen Krysmanski, "Metrische Vorstellungen: Zur wissenssoziologischen Beschreibung modernen Bewusstseins," *Soziale Welt,* Vol. 14, No. 3/4 (November, 1963), pp. 297–310.

system that is at present precariously balanced on the remnants of value systems which stand unmasked as ideologies.[11]

Modern consciousness, however, needs to be structured around guiding principles that are reality-adequate and such principles are momentarily represented only by quantitative conceptions and numerical relations.

Prophecy is both an amusing and foolish game, as J. W. Allen remarked in 1928, and so the most recent thought-style in the sociology of knowledge does not wish to announce that tomorrow computers will be kings or kings will become computers.[12] The consciousness of men is principally open and the emphasis on mathematical-quantitative systems is seen as a necessary but transitory phase in the—hopefully—long-lived drama of human development.

[11] Cf. Bertrand Russell, *Principles of Mathematics*, New York: W. W. Norton, 1903, pp. 3–10. Hans Freyer, *Das soziale Ganze und die Freiheit der Einzelnen unter den Bedingungen des industriellen Zeitalters*, Göttingen: Musterschmidt, 1957. Hans Freyer, *Über das Dominantwerden technischer Kategorien in der Lebenswelt der industriellen Gesellschaft*, Wiesbaden: F. Steiner, 1960. Theodor Geiger, *Arbeiten zur Soziologie*, Neuwied am Rhein: Hermann Luchterhand Verlag, 1962.

[12] Cf. J. W. Allen, *A History of Political Thought in the Sixteenth Century*, revised edition, London: Methuen, 1957, p. 516.

PART TWO

PHILOSOPHICAL
PRESUPPOSITIONS

CHAPTER 6

IMMANUEL KANT

The Limitations of Reason

T<small>HE CONTRIBUTIONS</small> of the German philosopher Immanuel Kant (1724–1804) to the advancement of human thought are manifold. Within the confines of the present analysis, it will be sufficient to delineate merely those ideas for which Kant is probably most widely known, i.e., the essentials of his epistemology.

We should recall that the question concerning the possibility and origin of cognition has been an early concern of thinking man. In the terminology of the philosopher, this question gives rise to the opposing doctrines of rationalism and empiricism. According to the latter position, all knowledge is derived from experience. The dogma of rationalism, on the other hand, claims that scientific knowledge can never originate in the senses: the criteria of this type of knowledge are generality and necessity; therefore, scientific knowledge is a product of reason. The rationalist argues that truth may be obtained by reasoning from "self-evident" premises; the empiricist typically rejects such premises.

The Rationalist Origin of Philosophy

When we turn the spotlight of the historian upon the scene of this old feud between the two varieties of epistemology we realize that the rationalist theory began to form as soon as philosophy departed from the common conception of the universe. After his separation from the common sense explanation of things, the philosopher claimed a different origin for his ideas. Common knowledge might well be based upon sensory experience, he argued, but scientific knowledge or philosophy does not at all stem from such experience; it originates in thinking or reason.

This is one element that the first systems of Greek philosophy had in common: truth does not stem from sensory experience. Thus, Heraclitus (*ca.* 535–475 B.C.), asserted that the senses are unreliable witnesses that teach only those who know how to interpret their evidence critically. Harsher still was the verdict of the Eleatic school: sense perceptions and change are illusory; truth resides only in reason. Zeno of Elea (*ca.* 490–

ca. 430 B.C.) employed thinking to demonstrate the impossibility and unreality of the empirical world. On this point, even Democritus (*ca.* 460–370 B.C.) and Plato (427?–347? B.C.) agreed: only reason leads to truth, not sense perception.

The first systems of modern philosophy were also predominantly rationalistic in their epistemology, a fact which is rather obvious to anyone who views the theories of Descartes, Hobbes, Spinoza, and Leibniz in this light. With mathematics for their vantage point, ultimately aiming at a mathematical theory of the universe, these early modern philosophers had as little use for perception as anyone who was mainly interested in pure mathematics. Furthermore, some of the new philosophers were intent on proving the existence of God and the immortality of the soul, another enterprise where experience was rather useless.

Thus, rationalism was the first form in which epistemology appeared. Empiricism was of later origin, taking shape as a criticism of metaphysical systems and their epistemology.[1] Among the various types of rationalism, the mathematical rationalism of the seventeenth century is of special interest to the analyst of Kant's position. The adherents of mathematical rationalism proclaimed that all science had to take the shape of mathematics, i.e., the form of a demonstrative system derived from basic principles: Descartes and Hobbes met on these premises. Spinoza tried to execute this idea formally in his *Ethica Ordine Geometrico Demonstrata;* Leibniz meant to preserve the notion within certain limits that sprang into focus after his encounter with the unfolding empiricist criticism.

The philosophy of René Descartes (1596–1650) aimed, first of all, at demonstrating the possibility of purely mathematical physics. In his attempt to apply mathematical methods to philosophy, Descartes took universal doubt for his fundamental premise. One thing, although, could not be doubted: doubt itself. What, then, leads out of this dilemma into truth? Only the rational faculties of the human mind. According to Descartes, truth is whatever I understand clearly and precisely. Every concept that is clear and distinct in itself possesses in this, its thinkability or possibility, the guarantee of its validity. From absolute doubt, Descartes proceeded to the absolute certainty of his famous *cogito ergo sum*—I think, therefore, I am. In the third of the *meditationes de prima philosophia,* Descartes developed his central formula into a statement that obviously originated in mathematical thinking: *quidquid clare ac distincte percipio, verum est.*[2]

---

[1] Early attempts at empiricism must, of course, be acknowledged (to some extent Aristotle, more so, Epicurus, Roger Bacon, Francis Bacon). Such empiricist strands are, however, overshadowed by a dominant rationalism.

[2] René Descartes, "Meditationes de prima philosophia," in R. Descartes, *Opera philosophica,* Amsterdam: Typographia Blaviana, 1685, p. 15.

Philosophy in the Empiricist Mood

Mathematical rationalism found its critic and opponent in the second great sequence of modern philosophy, viz., British empiricism. The main representatives of this camp were John Locke and David Hume. Empiricism differentiated two types of science which were set apart by their very nature and method. The one type was conceptual, as mathematics; the other, empirical, as physics and psychology. According to empiricist philosophers, the rationalists erred when they hypostatized the one type, mathematics, attempting to mold all other sciences after the mathematical image: this the empiricists claimed was an impossible enterprise; the factual sciences, specifically the physical sciences, and the moral sciences were entirely different from mathematics in content and method.

The empiricists argued that the mathematician does not make assertions about the existence and the dynamics of the empirical world, but that he makes inferences from concepts and definitions. The empirical sciences, on the other hand, present an entirely different picture. The physicist and psychologist intend to demonstrate the reactions of phenomena that exist independently from our concepts. How can we acquire knowledge in this case? The empiricists asserted: only through experience.

John Locke (1632–1704) initiated these reflections. He meant to prove that all our concepts were derived from experience. In his famous essay, he maintained that the mind is a blank at birth, that it is a *tabula rasa,* upon which human experience inscribes all knowledge.[3]

David Hume (1711–1776) pressed the analyses of Locke into a determined, thorough-going scepticism. He turned his battery of guns mainly upon the concept of cause and effect, trying to blast one of the major strategic points of rationalism.[4] Hume believed that relations of ideas were discoverable by the mere operation of thought, but matters of fact, which were the second kind of objects of human reason, were not ascertained in the same way. This crucial distinction, he maintained, escaped the rationalists, whereby they arrived at their faulty concept of cause and effect, assuming that the knowledge of this relation was discoverable by reasoning *a priori.* According to Hume, the knowledge of the cause-and-effect relation arose entirely from experience, when we found that two sensations were customarily joined.

[3] John Locke, *An Essay Concerning Human Understanding,* 40th edition, London: W. Tegg, 1877.
[4] Cf. David Hume, *An Inquiry Concerning Human Understanding* (edited with an introduction by Charles W. Hendel), New York: Liberal Arts Press, 1957.

The Kantian Synthesis

This, in brief, was the philosophical heritage that Kant found upon his arrival in the arena of thought. It was mainly a heritage of disunity and confusion. The importance of Kant's contribution to the advancement of human thought can only be appreciated through the revelation of this dilemma which remained after practically two thousand years of philosophical inquiry. How did the German thinker, then, enter into the debate? What solution did he have to offer?

From the foregoing, it should be apparent that the controversy between rationalism and empiricism culminated in the central question: Is knowledge based upon *a priori* cognition of objects, upon pure reason, or is knowledge attained by way of sensory experience? The rationalists voted for the first proposition: pure reasoning gives us the absolute knowledge of phenomena which we could never acquire through the senses. The empiricists decided in favor of the second proposal: "we only have knowledge of objects through perception, through sensory experience," whereby they implied that we do not possess absolute knowledge.

In the light of modern knowledge, Kant's solution seems amazingly simple. He cut the Gordian knot by salvaging from each one of the doomed theories the segment that he considered to be true and by putting them together again. This synthesis gave birth to a new theory. Now, human knowledge was declared to be a product of both pure reason and sensory experience. Against Hume's empiricism, Kant restored the old dogma of rationalism: knowledge of objects *a priori* is extant; yet, simultaneously, he hastened to repudiate the rationalism of the Leibniz-Wolffian system by adding: but only knowledge of things as they appear in our experience (*phenomena*), not knowledge of things-in-themselves (*noumena*), which the intellect cannot actually fathom. The main characteristic of Kant's epistemology is this fusion of phenomenalism or idealism with rationalism. Hitherto, rationalism had always been realistic, while empiricism has assumed idealistic features with Berkeley and Hume.

The Critique of Reason

The dynamics of his thinking practically forced Kant to take upon him the involved task of formulating the critique of reason—pure, practical, and synthetic. Three monumental works were the result: *The Critique of Pure Reason* (1781), *The Critique of Practical Reason* (1788), and *The Critique of Judgement* (1790).

The first part of the *Critique of Pure Reason*, viz., "Transcendental Analytic," aimed at the construction of a new epistemological system. The latter half of Part II, called "Transcendental Dialectic," clarified how the new philosophy compared to the old metaphysics. Here, Kant demonstrated the impossibility of a purely rational psychology, cosmology, and theology. Reworded: the first half of the book asserted the possibility of a phenomenalistic rationalism, while the second part demonstrated the impossibility of a realistic rationalism.

Technically, Kant had first of all to overcome Hume's scepticism which maintained that we could not arrive at general and necessary laws about empirical facts. But no science could be built upon mere associations, the only basic element that Hume admitted. Hume drove his scepticism *ad absurdum* when he went beyond physics and metaphysics and touched upon mathematics. The factual existence of mathematics revealed the insufficiency of the principles of empiricism. Therefore, Kant had actually only to show how these sciences were possible. He had to ask: How is pure mathematics, how is pure physical science, how is metaphysics possible? Or, to use his technical formulation: How can we explain the possibility of "*a priori* synthetic judgements?"[5] Since this question had no psychological intent, but a strictly epistemological connotation, it ultimately asked: How can statements derived neither from experience (i.e., judgements *a priori*) nor from logical inference (analytic judgements) attain the status of objective knowledge (synthetic judgements)?

This was the important question that Kant had to argue. His answer was that such statements could only attain objective validity as long as reason itself created the objects about which the statements were made. Reason knew objects *a priori*, as long as reason created the objects. Reason did just that much in mathematics. The geometrician could state space properties and relations of figures and their elements in space in the form of synthetic judgements *a priori*, because he created these objects himself. Basically, the same held true as far as physics was concerned. The objects of the physicist were natural phenomena; in a fashion such phenomena were products of the observer to whom they appeared, and as such, they depended in their general form upon the constitution and activity of the observing subject. But there could be no *a priori* knowledge of nature, if nature was conceived as absolute reality, existing without any relation to the cognitive subject. Reason could not help us to gain *a priori* knowledge of things as they were in themselves, viz., independent from the subject. Furthermore, reason could neither help us to gain *a posteriori* knowledge of things-in-themselves; as they would have to enter into our perception, would have to become phenomena in order to become knowledgeable. Therefore, metaphysics was not possible, if the term was to denote, as customary, knowledge of things-in-themselves. Metaphysics, according to Kant, was only possible if the term did not imply anything more than "pure physical science," i.e., a general phenomenology of nature.

[5] Immanuel Kant, *Critique of Pure Reason* (translated by Norman Kemp Smith), London: Macmillan, 1956, p. 55.

Obviously, Kant was primarily interested in the formal or technical aspects of knowledge. He tried to establish how and what we can know. Thus, he had to reveal the formative elements which he assumed to be identical in every cognitive act. He arrived at the conclusion that there were two types of form elements: the forms of the intuition and the forms of the understanding. Furthermore, there were two forms of the intuition, viz., space and time. With the help of formal logic and its classification of judgements, Kant arrived at twelve forms of the understanding which he called categories, such as quantity, quality, relation, and modality. It is important to realize that time and space were not conceived as existent realities outside the subject of cognition, but only as synthesizing functions peculiar to the human mind. Kant believed that these functions of synthesis on the side of the subject established order and unity in the tremendously varied and, otherwise chaotic, content of the intuition.

According to Kant, this, then, was the nature of the principles of rational knowledge: they were given as synthetic functions which the human intellect practices always and everywhere in identical fashion. Mathematical and physical axioms were formulas expressing these functions and, consequently, principles of cognition *a priori*. We were not born with these functions. They developed, as all other functions, in the course of life. But they did not enter from the outside; our sensory impressions and experiences were only accidental causes of their development. This was Kant's position above the extremes of empiricism and rationalism. The empiricists maintained, *nihil est in intellectu, quod non antea fuerit in sensu*, and they were right. But something was missing and Kant added the necessary element: *nisi intellectus ipse;* everything is derived from experience, except the faculty to make experiences.

Kant compared the decisive turn that he had given to epistemology with the Copernican revolution of the *worldview in astronomy*.[6] Prior to it, the phenomena in the sky had been explained by reference to the revolution of the celestial bodies around the earth. Copernicus assumed more simply that the observer himself was turning around them. In similar fashion empiricism had explained cognition by assuming that the external order of nature affected the mind. Kant proposed to establish a new center of knowledge. This new center was to be the mind itself. Kant saw the failure of his predecessors in their attempt to make knowledge center in the object, while they expected that the mind should reflect, either by perception or reason, the nature of an outward and independently existing phenomenon. Kant construed cognition on the basis of his expectation that the objects conformed to the mind: human thought *formally* created its objects (not in an ontological sense, of course). Nature was now seen as the original creation of the mind.

[6] Cf. *Ibid.*, p. 25.

Nature owes all of its arrangements and connections, even its very distribution in space and time, to the constitution of the knower. The mind imposes its conditions on the object, and thus gets out of nature what it has already put into it. Therefore, reason can know the objects in so far in *a priori* fashion, and, furthermore, formulates knowledge in general and necessary statements. The axioms of geometry and the law of causality are necessary and generally valid for all objects of our cognition. But rational knowledge ends where this determination of the objects by reason cannot take place. The "things-in-themselves" are not subject to the synthesizing function of human intelligence, and, therefore, rational knowledge of absolute reality, metaphysics in the traditional sense, is impossible.

A summary of the preceding discussion reveals the following major traits: Kant was instrumental in ending the philosophical deadlock resulting from the extremism of pure empiricism and pure rationalism. These two currents had hypostatized either one or the other of the two important sources of human knowledge, sense perception or reason. For the empiricists the senses were everything, while reason reigned supreme in the rationalist camp. Absolute empiricism or sensationalism seemed to have reached the end of the road in Hume, while rationalism deteriorated into empty formalism and semantics in Wolff. Kant's *Critique of Pure Reason* aimed to remedy these extreme conceptions by allowing for both sense-perception and reason. The German philosopher proclaimed that perception without conception is blind, while conception without perception is empty. He fired his first volley at the overemphasis on sense-perception. He argued that the mere sequence of sense-impressions can never yield the connections, necessities, unities, and laws, which are the prerequisites for science. The intellect must furnish these itself. They constitute what Kant called "categories," the tools which the human mind must use when it operates in that specific way which is referred to as knowing. Kant then turned his battery of high-powered guns on the other target—extreme rationalism. Kant was convinced that the process of how we come to know is the main problem of philosophy and that a critical method must be developed which would distinguish between the area of certain knowledge and that of hypothetical speculation. Therefore, Kant could not stop at the demolition of the empiricist hegemony. Kant realized that these above-mentioned instruments of the mind are not by themselves sufficient for knowledge. They cannot themselves be known in the ordinary way as they are what one knows with. Since they are instruments, they need some material to work upon; they cannot spin knowledge out of thin air. Therefore, it follows that the data supplied by sense-perception are the other necessary elements of cognition. Hence, to know is to synthesize, by the forms native to the mind, the content conveyed by the senses. Thereby, Kant delimited the area of human knowledge by demonstrating that the only certain and rational type of knowledge is phenomenal knowledge, the knowledge about the universe which we receive through the senses. Our knowledge of this outer world is not an exact reflection of it, for the unity which we see in this world is something given it by the instrumentalities of the mind, first by the *a priori* forms of the intuition—space and time—and then by the schemata and the categories of the understanding. Thus, the human mind lends form to the world surrounding it and, ultimately, makes it intelligible to itself. We are, therefore, forever barred from knowing absolute reality, the world of "things-in-themselves," which Kant fathomed beyond the forms of time and space. Ideas such as God, immortality, and freedom, the main objects of traditional metaphysics, can never be proven or disproven by way of scientific inquiry. They must be left to the other great sphere of human existence: belief.

Kant and the Modern Mentality

Kant's impact upon the further development of human thinking transcends the limits of epistemology. Modern theories with a systematic emphasis on doubt and suspicion have one of their important roots in Kant's critical philosophy. Undoubtedly, Kant's own thinking was propelled by a fundamental doubt in the efficacy of all philosophy before and during his time. Equally obvious is the suspicion characterizing his approach to reason, his doubt in the possibilities of an unlimited advance of human knowledge into the deepest secrets of reality. Compared to his rationalistic predecessors, he himself was one of the first great systematizers of doubt and suspicion.

Such rather general designation, though, does not help us to arrive at a more complete account of his importance for the subsequent formation of theories that have doubt for their central motive. These ramifications of Kant's thinking can only be detected through a somewhat more detail-conscious analysis of some of his major concepts and premises.

Kant's line of inquiry inevitably led to a revision of the concept of reality; thereby, the door was opened to those frontiers of knowledge which constitute the main concern of our analysis. In the refutation of his one-sided predecessors, Kant demonstrated how nonsensical it was to imagine reality as independent from human cognition. The significance of Kant's contribution in this instance can only be fully appreciated if we examine the situation before his revision of the concept of reality, if we visualize the implications of the earlier naive realism that largely dominated epistemology up to the appearance of Kantian criticism.

The sharpest realization of Kant's contribution, though—and we are going to take it up first—emerges when we contrast it with the "common sense" epistemology of everyday life. For the uncritical mind reality does not exist: the phenomena are simply there or they are not there. At this precritical stage the human mind is unaware of the fact that the phenomena are there—the universe surrounds man with immediate and thoughtless reality. In this context the question whether the world is real or illusionary cannot yet arise. How could I assert the reality of the things that I perceive, if I have not even pondered the question whether or not they are? On this level of critically uninterested day-by-day living, we have not yet confronted ourselves with our cognition; we find ourselves right in it and not even in it *qua* cognition but as the world pulsating around us. On this level where experience is merely "lived," reality is not known yet, since this living has not yet been consciously confronted with its content. In this stage, thinking about the things does not yet confront the things. Only when deception has aroused man does he start to think about his experience, only then does the thing as "illusion" or "only in the mind" oppose the thing "in reality." The unity of the world view only falls apart in the sharp light of critical thinking. Experience divides itself into truth and appearance, splits into possibility, reality, necessity, and its opposite, only after the mind has commenced to reflect upon the immediacy of experience. Reality of experience originates when man's subjectivity enters experience. Experience becomes more than mere mind content as soon as it is immediately related to man's subjectivity as the unifying center. Reality, instead of being the opposite pole to the subjectivity of our consciousness, is actually its corollary. Things as such are not real; they are only real in relation to a center of judgement that they correspond to.[7]

It is our assertion that the characteristic approaches of ideological analysis and sociology of knowledge alike would not have been possible without the criticistic elevation of thinking. In the succeeding stages of this analysis it will become clear that this genetic relationship is especially important in the case of the radical branch of the sociology of knowledge. But apart from these finer distinctions, Kant's ideas were germinal to the entire current of systematic doubt, which constitutes our larger category.

All these theories rest on certain premises which would be unthinkable without the "Copernican revolution" that Kant unleashed in epistemology, and, as might be added already, also unthinkable without the subsequent work of the exponents of philosophical criticism. As its object of cognition a sociology of knowledge establishes the dependence of knowledge on social reality. This premise would be meaningless if it were derived from a crude realism that has the subject of perception confronted with an autonomous object which has merely to be registered in photographic

---

[7] Cf. Max Adler, *Das Soziologische in Kants Erkenntniskritik: Ein Beitrag zur Auseinandersetzung zwischen Naturalismus und Kritizismus,* Wien: Verlag der Wiener Volksbuchhandlung, 1924.

fashion. In the case of naive realism, perceiving man could never exert any influence upon the object of cognition. Such influence is only conceivable if we assume that the object of cognition is constituted by a creative act of the perceiving individual.[8]

Thus, the particular question posed by the sociology of knowledge presupposes the object-constituting function of cognition, as such function was affirmed by the Copernican turn of Kant. Also in the human sciences (*Geisteswissenschaften*) all preobjective material—which is immediately accessible to the subject—is only transformed into an object of cognition in the method-conscious process of perception.

An example of Kant's far-reaching influence and importance can be furnished by the following passage taken from the most resolutely developed sociology of knowledge:

> The world is known through many different orientations because there are many simultaneous and mutually contradictory trends of thought . . . struggling against one another with their different interpretations of "common" experience. The clue to this conflict, therefore, is not to be found in the "object in itself" (if it were, it would be impossible to understand why the object should appear in so many different refractions), but in the very different expectations, purposes, and impulses arising out of experience.[9]

Apart from certain later modifications and delimitations of Kant's epistemology, the basic content of his thinking proved viable—especially the emphasis upon the importance of the subjective factor in experience which equated reality with the lawful order of human consciousness. Kant significantly believed that the life of men has as many realities as there live different kinds of consciousness in men. Reality is man's own activity—not the material quality of an alien entity confronting him; therefore it is as real as man is real. The lawful workings of consciousness are equally important in the determination of the various types of evaluation that men engage in: only, while the relation to our "I" necessarily recedes where the activity of our consciousness confronts us with the reality of nature, it will, on the other hand, necessarily assume central importance where other forms of activity create the realities of aesthetic, moral, and religious values.[10]

---

[8] Cf. Kant, *op. cit.*, p. 22.

[9] Karl Mannheim, *Ideology and Utopia: An Introduction to the Sociology of Knowledge* (translated by Louis Wirth and Edward Shils), seventh impression, London: Routledge & Kegan Paul, 1954, p. 241.

[10] The critical reader will recognize that even such specific concepts as Mannheim's "cognitive standpoint" (*Denkstandort*) have already been formally suggested by Kant. In the latter case see, especially, Kant's "Refutation of Idealism," where the critical analysis of the concept "I" suggests the relation of thinking to a center of consciousness viz. the quality of consciousness. The world is only my conception of it, does not mean, it is only mine, but the world is, necessarily, someone's conception seen from someone's standpoint, i.e. in the language of every I, "my" conception. (Cf. Kant, *op. cit.*, pp. 244–246.)

CHAPTER 7

GEORG WILHELM
FRIEDRICH HEGEL
God in Prussia

THE STORY OF GERMAN PHILOSOPHY after Kant is largely an account of the development of the various stages of idealism—roughly the narrative about a current leading from Fichte's subjective to Hegel's objective idealism. Strangely, the main disturbance that Kant left after his thunderous appearance was not so much caused by the technical aspects of his epistemology which aroused the spirits of a later generation; Kant's more immediate followers were, above all, excited by the problem concerning the relation of experience to reality. Again, the voices expressing concern about ultimate reality became forceful. The reappearance of questions concerning the thing-in-itself constituted a reaction against the limitations that Kant had imposed upon knowledge.

The German idealists reached a finality of philosophical conviction in their basic assumption: the secret of the universe is reason. With the proceeding clarification of this idea the assumption actually came to mean that, if God is a spirit and thinks, if God created the universe on thought, then all is reducible to thought, and *l o g i c* is the name of the whole.

In Quest of the Absolute

The initial thrust in this direction was launched by the subjective idealism of Johann Gottlieb Fichte (1762–1814).[1] But Fichte's emphasis upon the creativity and unity in the inner life terminated his interpretation of the universe at a relatively early stage, a stage where the ego was wrapped up in self-reflection. In the diverse thought systems of Friedrich Wilhelm Joseph Schelling (1775–1854), reason loomed large

[1] This account of post-Kantian philosophy is selective only because of the properties of our frame of reference, wherein certain dynamics of intellectual development are more relevant than others. Therefore, our emphasis is upon the idealistic current of the post-Kantian era—to the expense of those resisting a sceptical outlook in the vein of phenomenalism. Thereby, we also must neglect the advocates of feeling, like Georg Hamann, G. von Herder, Romanticism, and F. Schiller's attempts at a reconciliation between freedom and necessity.

in the origin of all phenomena, but reason was still something dark, something not yet conceivable, it was the "night of the absolute." For Schelling ultimate reality transcended all finite distinctions, the absolute was not yet defined. Then, Georg Wilhelm Friedrich Hegel (1770–1831) brought his objective idealism to bear upon the problem, intending to grasp the absolute, to fully conceive ultimate reality. He believed that the absolute was represented by spirit and to him spirit was the central principle of the universe. Hegel taught that it is the essence of spirit to become conscious of the contradiction that it embodies within itself. Therefore, spirit is essentially a process, a becoming, that proceeds from the in-itself of the unconscious to the for-itself of the conscious phase. Obviously, Hegel's thinking was dynamic. Consequently, traditional logic with its static character was no longer sufficient; the revolution in thinking called for a revolutionary method. The speculative, dynamic thinking of reason found this method in the dialectical process which makes it possible to grasp the unity of contradictory concepts. The reflection of difference into identity was now seen as the principle of truth, as the one concrete principle in the world.

Thus, Hegel tried to find a genuine synthesis, a unity in differences. For Kant the organic unity of experience was represented by the intelligent self. He believed that the necessary synthesis was embodied in his *transcendental apperception*.[2] For Hegel it was the dialectical activity of thought that sparked the progressive organization of differences into higher and higher unities. Since he regarded this dialectical process as inherent in all thinking, philosophy must depart from this logical premise.

Hegel took his dynamic logic based on the systematic principle of thesis-antithesis-synthesis for his vantage point, because he felt this dialectical triad to be more than just a logical method; he saw in it the operational manifestation of a profound and final principle: Hegel believed that he had found the key that would unlock the secret of the absolute, of ultimate reality. He conceived of the dialectical process as the secret of the universe, as the continuous progress and rhythm of all reality.

In Hegel's dialectic, one concept like Being (thesis) inevitably evokes its opposite like Non-Being (antithesis), and the two interact to form a new and more elevated concept like Becoming (synthesis) which in turn becomes a new thesis. Since the synthesis represents a new and qualitatively higher expression of the mind, which becomes the starting point for a new triad designed to overcome the limitations of the just-found level of understanding, the universe is seen as engaged in a dialectical process of perpetual self-creation: the Spirit (the essence of absolute reality) pursues his predetermined road leading from the germi-

---

[2] Cf. Immanuel Kant, *Critique of Pure Reason* (translated by Norman Kemp Smith), London: Macmillan, 1956, pp. 135–161.

nal, unconscious state of existence to his final and inherent goal of full consciousness and self-realization by positing a long chain of triads as his manifestation on the various stages of existence.

But Hegel was only concerned with logic because he saw in logic the starting point for a metaphysical system conceived of as a cosmic-philosophical triad. The Spirit contains both the beginning and the end, but this end can only be reached if the Spirit leaves his initial, unconscious state of dormant possibilities. This can only happen if the Spirit confronts himself with his own being by positing his opposite: the thesis (*Idea*) must be confronted with its antithesis (*Nature*). Idea and Nature are then raised to the higher level of their synthesis (*Spirit*) where the full insight into reality begins. The process nears its completion: through the different triads of subjective spirit, the higher level of objective spirit is reached, and these two dialectical opponents finally attain their synthesis—the highest synthesis of all—in Absolute Spirit: art, religion, and philosophy. In philosophy, spirit or mind has reached its inevitable destiny: self-knowledge or rational cognizance of itself. Now the spirit is in-and-for-itself.

However, it takes man's activity and thinking to foster the actualization and self-knowledge of the Spirit: for his unfolding, the Spirit needs many human generations, entire nations and, therefore, the progressing self-development of Spirit takes place in History, better, is History.

The Cunning of Reason

In Hegel's description the Spirit "uses" different nations, expresses himself in their temporal reality as carriers of the Spirit, and discards them with the impartial detachment of a higher, impersonal force once they no longer suffice to serve as adequate expressions of his nature. Then another nation is chosen by the Spirit because it can present him with a new platform whereupon the higher and more developed phase of self-knowledge can be more fully realized; similar is the role of the great historical personages. Also, the hero is "used" by the Spirit to bring about the necessary developments leading to greater self-knowledge. The hero *unconsciously* acts as the agent of the World Spirit in his course toward the absolute phase from one historically relative phase to the next. The thoughts and actions of the human agents are, in other words, not equal to the superior "cunning of reason" operating behind the backs of men.

At this point Hegel's philosophy acknowledges the existence of two disparate levels of consciousness: one is occupied by the Spirit and this is the level of true, reality-adequate consciousness; the other affords tenancy to men and this is the level of a false consciousness which is reality-inadequate. In this manner it is reason itself that renders human thought ideological. Hegel assumes that the world is a unity and is conceivable only with reference to a knowing subject—because of its own nature, this unity is caught up, however, in a process of continual historical transformation. For this dialectical process the world, which is the world of Spirit, needs the thoughts of men which of necessity become totally ideological as soon as the Spirit has accomplished a phase of historical transformation and makes ready to move onward so that the unity of the world may find the restoration of its equilibrium on still higher levels.

Hegel admitted currents of thought into the realm of philosophy which arose from social interaction and politico-economic conflicts; he arrived at a position from where the experiences of human life can no longer be accepted at face value, but must be analyzed in all their implications.

The Sociological Dimension

Hegel knew that the historian must apprehend his subject matter faithfully; he knew, moreover, that such general terms as "faithfully" and "apprehend" conceal an ambiguity: "Even the average and mediocre historian, who perhaps believes and pretends that he is merely receptive, merely surrendering himself to the data, is not passive in his thinking. He brings *his categories with him and sees the data through them.*"[3]

Thus Hegel added the historical and sociological dimension to the great transformation which Kant set in motion: he thereby completed the destruction of that century-old ontological dogmatism which pictured the "world" as existing independently of men in a fixed and final form.

The rise of thought from its century-old dogmatic slumber can surely not be contributed wholly to theoretical, philosophical currents. A tremendous driving force was generated by the developments in political and socio-economic reality. Thanks to the powerful handwriting of history it is sufficient to merely point to the flaming signal of the Great French Revolution. How much the thinkers who launched modern thought owe to the rejuvenating heat of this explosion in socio-politico reality can probably never be fully assessed. The ideas of the thinkers themselves, on the other hand, clearly reveal their influence on the subsequent acts in the drama of human thinking.

It would be difficult, indeed, to fathom the development of historical thinking without reference to Hegel's logic and his metaphysics of history. Of course, as in the case of practically all innovators, there are the forerunners who have greatly helped to set free man's historical awareness. In the case of Hegel, especially, we have to mention the influence

[3] G. W. F. Hegel, *Reason in History: A General Introduction to the Philosophy of History* (translated, with an introduction by Robert S. Hartman), New York: The Liberal Arts Press, 1954, p. 13 (my emphasis).

of Rousseau, Montesquieu, and Herder. Herder, above all, awakened Hegel's sensitivity for the steady flow of history. He, furthermore, set the stage for Hegel's dialectical conception of the universe when he sensed that life radiated through the manifold forces of the world, that the contradictory content of human experiences pointed to a meaningful whole which was ultimately accessible as the concrete idea.

On the other hand, without Hegel the historical schools in law, political economy, and other fields of human knowledge would hardly have made their important contributions. It would be difficult to account for the powerful current of historicism would there not have been Hegel's ontology. The meaning and role of history in Hegel's system and its relation to his dialectics must be understood before we can grasp the essentials of the great debate on historism that was waged mainly by these men: Dilthey, Windelband, Rickert, Simmel, Max Weber, Troeltsch, Sombart, Meinecke, Litt, Spranger, Rothacker, and Mannheim.

Despite the pioneering of Dilthey and Windelband[4] it has not been fully realized that the understanding of Hegel is not possible solely on the basis of his major works but only if his early writings are included in the overall assessment.

The Young Hegel

A survey of Hegel's early manuscripts[5] reveals that his intellectual development was mainly characterized by the following dominant theme: while Kant's question was based on the mathematical physics of Kepler, Galilei, and Newton, Hegel immediately concentrated on life and history and the alleviation of the contradistinctions of his era. His question was— how is life, how is history possible? Furthermore, where is the vantage point for resolving the manifest contradictions of existence? Thus, from the very beginning Hegel's philosophy is philosophy of life, philosophy of history, and social philosophy. The youthful Hegel is fascinated by two major contradictions: the contradiction between the positive, empty rationalism of the Churches and the genuine religiosity of the people and the clash between the petrified dead constitution of the State and the living community of men, based upon freedom. He decides that the frozen social structure must be revived. What he advocates is unity of

[4] Cf. Wilhelm Dilthey, *Die Jugendgeschichte Hegel's, Gesammelte Schriften,* Vol. IV, Leipzig: B. G. Teubner, 1921. Cf. also Wilhelm Windelband, *Die Erneuerung des Hegelianismus,* Heidelberg: C. Winter, 1910. More recent research results and analyses are available in the work of Friedrich Bülow. See, especially, Friedrich Bülow, *Die Entwicklung der Hegelschen Sozialphilosophie,* Leipzig: Felix Meiner, 1920, and *Hegel: Recht, Staat, Geschichte,* Stuttgart: Kroner, 1955.

[5] Such an overview has become possible since Nohl published Hegel's early manuscripts under an admittedly misleading title. Cf. Hegel, *Theologische Jugendschriften* (edited by Hermann Nohl), Tübingen: J. C. B. Mohr, 1907.

existence, living morality, humane religion, and mastery of life in a social entity that is as dynamic and complete as the Greek *polis* at its vital peak. His anthropology sees the whole of man and tries to embody all the manifold aspects of human existence in the social scheme. Politics and religion must allow *man* to live as fully as his nature demands: phantasy and reason, heart and sensuality, must be acknowledged equally.

For Hegel the word "life" represents a rather complex concept: life is not only unification of impressions, it is also contradiction. Hegel's concept of life is social, is the product of a thinking process that was inflamed by an era full of disharmony and contradiction. Here we find the origin of his dialectic which reflects a world fraught with social contradictions and absurdities. In the dawn of the social question, dialectic is the logic that makes it possible to grasp the social process, as well as a world that lacks stability because of the historical struggle involving men and institutions.

Already in Hegel's early writings it becomes apparent that, for him, there is only one reason and one truth, viz., historical reason and historical truth. There is no *a priori* reason, there are only individual people expressing an absolute principle at different stages of development. Now history manifests itself as the fate of the spirit. The ontological property of reality is movement. The processes and conflicts in the economy, in law, in ethics, and in the State are now seen neither as chance happenings nor as immutable eternal truths, but as manifestations of life. This life is realized in history and, therefore, subject to metamorphoses which must be understood in the light of reason.

The Worship of Success

The secret of Hegel's metaphysical supertheory must reveal itself in the equation that seems to underlie his titanic brooding. This equation should also prepare the final understanding of the ramifications and consequences of his thinking. The equation reads: *History is life and life is history.* What, then, are the ultimate characteristics of historical life? The basic phenomenon of historical life is first of all the continuous change of nations and individuals, the constant rhythm of birth and death, growth and decay, building and destruction. Nothing lasts in the sphere of human activity and suffering, neither crimes nor heroic deeds have any permanency. Gigantic efforts crumble into nothingness and petty events have great historical consequences. Eras of energetic freedom and golden wealth decline into times of cowardly subservience and miserable poverty. If this drama of human passions and sufferings, of stupidity and brutality, is viewed objectively, world history reveals neither an idea nor a reasonable goal. In this perspective, world history is a heap of rubble, a graveyard of scandalized ideas, and a slaughterhouse where the happiness of nations and individuals is senselessly sacrificed. This immediate view of history stimulated Hegel to raise the question: What is the meaning, the ultimate purpose, of all these happenings? Hegel believed that he could provide the answer as a Christian philosopher. His solution was the secularized version of Christian belief in divine Providence. He turned the Christian story of salvation into a worldly theodicy, where the divine spirit pervades the world, where the State is a terrene god, and where history is of divine nature.

Hegel assigns the task of discovering the principle inherent in all changes to the philosophy of history, which is equipped with the "eye of the concept." The philosophy of history sees the world in the perspective of reason and, therefore, discovers the meaningful content of world history—continuous progress in the consciousness of freedom.[6] "God governs the world. The actual working of His government, the carrying out of His plan, is the history of the world . . . Philosophy wishes to recognize the content, the reality of the divine Idea, and to justify the spurned actuality, for Reason is the comprehension of the divine work."[7]

Compared to the empirical, immediate view of history, Hegel's construction is extravagant, indeed.

How could this intellectual *tour de force* become popular? The answer is contained in the very core of Hegel's own philosophy which can easily be stripped of its Christian-theological cloak. Hegel designed his superstructure by measuring the pace of history in temporal progress. He started with the last step, assuming that the preceding ones necessarily led up to this last step. This emphasis upon a temporal sequence implies that only consequential events count in world history, that all happenings must be evaluated according to their success. Success is the highest criterion in Hegel's construction—whatever is successful has proven its higher right over whatever is unsuccessful:

> The nation to which is ascribed a moment of the Idea in the form of a natural principle is entrusted with giving complete effect to it in the advance of the self-developing self-consciousness of the world mind. This nation is dominant in world history during this one epoch . . . In contrast with this its absolute right of being the vehicle of this present stage in the world mind's development, the minds of the other nations are without rights, and they, along with those whose hour has struck already, count no longer in world history.[8]

This center piece of Hegel's speculation could become popular because of its vicinity to the widespread belief that only the most success-

[6] Cf. G. W. F. Hegel, *Philosophy of Right*, (translated with notes by T. M. Knox), London: Oxford University Press, 1953, par. 342, p. 216.

[7] Hegel, *Reason in History*, pp. 47–48.

[8] Hegel, *Philosophy of Right*, par. 347, pp. 217–218.

ful is also the most legitimate. In the nineteenth century this belief was
further strengthened by Darwin's "law of natural selection" whereby
the higher species develop as a consequence of the struggle for existence
which permits the fittest to survive the ones that are less fit. Much as
Darwin, Hegel infers from the fact of success that the winner's emergence
was necessary and justified:

> It is the absolute right of the Idea to step into existence in clear-cut laws
> and objective institutions . . . whether this right be actualized in the form
> of divine legislation and favour, or in the form of force and wrong. This right
> is the right of heroes to found states.
>
> The same consideration justifies civilized nations in regarding and treat-
> ing as barbarians those who lag behind them in institutions which are the
> essential moments of the state.[9]

But success in itself is a relative variable, and any philosophy that ultimately leads to the worship of success throws the doors to cynicism and
relativism wide open: often success was bestowed upon the vile and
stupid, the vicious and mad personages of history. Was there ever an
historical power that came into existence without brutality, legal viola-
tions, and crimes? No metaphysics of history can evade this question,
however elaborate and abstract it may be.

The great iconoclasts were quick in realizing these implications of the
Hegelian supertheory. Thus, Nietzsche felt that this philosophical historicism had dangerous effects upon German culture and education,
leading to the *idolatry of factual reality*. He knew that man could only
prostrate himself before success if every victory was seen as the manifestation of reasonable necessity, as the triumph of the idea.

Eventually, Hegel's metaphysical historicism replaced the waning es-
chatology of the Christian religion. Historicism—the belief in the meaning of history—became the religion of the educated man, whose scepticism was too weak to do without any kind of faith. Hegel's students
transformed his metaphysics of the history of spirit into an absolute historicism. They retained merely the element of historicity from the historical unfolding of the absolute. They established the temporal process
as the supreme power ruling over philosophy and the spirit alike. History
would reveal the truth of an era by establishing its success.

As far as religion itself was concerned, Hegel proceeded to "elevate"
religion by taking it out of the form of feeling and intuition and putting
it into the form of the concept. This elevation was never free from ambiguity as Hegel thereby intended both to justify and to criticize religion.
This ambiguity inflamed all of the post-Hegelian criticism of religion.
The religious orthodoxy banned his interpretation as unchristian, and
his more radical students complained that Hegel still retained dogmatic

[9] *Ibid.*, p. 219.

Christianity in the form of the concept. The historical result of Hegel's conceptual elevation of religion was a determined destruction of Christian philosophy and religion. Hegel wanted to transpose religion from the sphere of emotion and mere intuition to the highest realm of his philosophical system. He meant to give it the dignity and conceptual clarity of philosophical existence. The final result was a powerful upsurge of a consistent and systematic antireligious current.

The consequences in terms of basic suspicion and doubt actually transcended the religious field as the dynamics of thought, once set free, even corroded the substitute that the post-Hegelian foes of religion had established in its place by worshipping the image of man. In the thinking of Hegel's radical followers, man became autonomous in opposition to Christian religion. Originally, the concepts of man and of humanity were intimately related to Christian thought. This connection was severed, and the first step was actually to replace Christianity with humanitarian ideals. In the thinking of Feuerbach, Ruge, and Marx, the concepts of man and humanity figured prominently as the beginning and end of all philosophy. But eventually even the ideal of humanity became suspect, the dehumanization of man began and the stage of philosophy darkened with the arrival of Stirner, Kierkegaard, and Nietzsche.

CHAPTER 8

WILHELM DILTHEY
The Fragmentary Nature of Life

W ILHELM DILTHEY's philosophical career unfolded to a large extent
in the powerful intellectual field of German idealism that Kant and Hegel
had established. Kant provided the inspiration and the conceptual tools
for Dilthey's endeavor to create the critical epistemological foundation
for knowledge in the historically oriented human sciences. Later in his
career, Dilthey allied himself to an extent with Hegel, who had widened
the critical framework by including a number of "human studies" such
as ethics, law, art, religion, and philosophy within it. Furthermore,
Hegel's concept of a dynamic reason pervading man's creations in history
was akin to Dilthey's approach to the study of history, which was to
result in the philosophical interpretation of the history of ideas in their
total socio-cultural setting. Dilthey's writings lack the architectural unity
of Kant's work and the systematic and logical consistency of Hegel's
idealistic superstructure. But despite the often fragmentary nature of his
expositions, his main contributions to the growth of modern philosophy
can be summarized by pointing out that he discovered the integrity of
meaning in a complex historical situation, thereby rejuvenating more
than the thoughts and personalities of individual thinkers by actually
bringing back to life the spirit of their entire historical era. Thus, Dilthey
was able to give us real biography and real history, transcending the
merely external or abstract special accounts of past historians.

In the course of his thinking, Dilthey abolished all eternal criteria of
truth—Kant's transcendental apperception and timeless *a priori* as well
as Hegel's personal guarantee of supertemporal knowledge.[1] Dilthey had
no use for metaphysics as he was determined to establish that experience
was the basis of all knowledge. His central argument was that *life* gave
rise to philosophy. Since life transcends all artificial limitations, all

---

[1] Cf. Immanuel Kant, *Critique of Pure Reason* (translated by Norman Kemp
Smith), London: Macmillan, 1956, p. 136. Hegel feels himself allied with the spirit
of the world. This spirit reaches his ultimate destiny and goal when he reaches full
self-consciousness and self-knowledge in the realm of philosophy, i.e., in Hegel's
philosophy. Despite all the manifold fluctuations and contradictions of this process,
Hegel presents this personal guarantee of truth as he assumes the status of the philosopher of the spirit of the world.

attempts to force it into a static metaphysical frame must be futile. Dilthey was deeply convinced of the fragmentary nature of life; he, consequently, upheld the idea that life manifests itself differently in each moment in the course of historical evolution. In the light of his thinking: "Each world-view is historically determined, therefore, limited, relative."[2] This is the point where Dilthey (1833–1911) manifests tendencies that are important for the particular purposes of our analysis. Before we embark upon this line of study, it seems appropriate, though, to introduce a more complete characterization of Dilthey's position within the intellectual field of his time.

History or Science?

Dilthey's thinking was shaped mainly by two sets of factors. On the one hand, he engaged in the battle between historicism and positivism waged by European intellectuals during the 1860's, and, on the other hand, he began to assimilate the ideas of the German idealists, largely as a result of his investigations of Schleiermacher's and Hegel's philosophy and the personal influence exerted by his mentor and teacher, Adolf Trendelenburg.[3]

Dilthey came under the influence of historicism mainly through personal contacts with its second generation of exponents at the University of Berlin—men of the historical school like August Böckh, Leopold von Ranke, and Karl Ritter who challenged the philosophers of the Enlightenment with their belief in a natural law of causation which they alleged to have universal validity. While the philosophers of the Enlightenment proclaimed that this natural law was accessible to empirical study, the historicists of the second generation maintained that human activities were not understandable within this static frame of analysis. On the contrary, such understanding could only develop by reference to the dynamic and everchanging element of historical variability.

The influence of the earlier historicist movement also planted the germ of Dilthey's life-long concern with the critical foundation of the human studies. According to the earlier historicists, the methods of the physical sciences were not appropriate as conceptual tools for the analysis of human culture and society. Dilthey initially accepted this challenge and

---

[2] Wilhelm Dilthey, *Weltanschauungslehre: Abhandlungen zur Philosophie der Philosophie, Gesammelte Schriften,* Vol. VIII, Leipzig and Berlin: B. G. Teubner, 1931, p. 224 (my translation).

[3] For an account of these different influences see Wilhelm Dilthey, *Die Geistige Welt: Einleitung in die Philosophie des Lebens, Gesammelte Schriften,* Vol. V, Leipzig and Berlin: B. G. Teubner, 1924, pp. 3–7.

joined in the search for the necessary methods of understanding adequate to the qualitatively different subject matter of the human sciences.[4]

The historical school proudly proclaimed that it had discovered the true meaning of history, and this assertion invited the attack of those who had raised the banner of a different philosophy during the late 1850's and the 1860's. This positivistic countermovement was spearheaded by Auguste Comte in France and John Stuart Mill and Henry Thomas Buckle in England. The positivists reversed the trend that the historicists had advocated with regard to the epistemological, methodological, and interpretative bases of philosophy and history. The discussion was now carried out within the dynamic tension generated by polar conceptions. While the members of the historical school clamored for a different nonphysical scientific method in the human studies, Comte based his *philosophie positive* on the methodological presuppositions of mathematics and the biological sciences, and Mill hoped to advance the human sciences with the help of the methodological apparatus of the physical sciences.[5] Where Leopold von Ranke had visualized the State as something more than a mere subdivision of general categories, as "a living thing, an individual, a unique self,"[6] Comte saw only general laws of evolution and social organization, just a uniform pattern of causal sequences.[7] A look at Ranke's characterization of Pope Pius V reveals the emphasis that the historical school placed upon the reconstruction of individuals and their motivations from the investigation of documents relevant to an historical setting. A glance at Comte's positivistic assertions shows how history appears here as a result of natural laws operating through society as a collective aggregate rather than through particular individuals.[8] The exponents of the historical school were keen on the accurate investigation of individual data in their unique historical setting —the positivists disdained the mere accumulation of isolated facts, aim-

---

[4] Cf. Wilhelm Dilthey, *Einleitung in die Geisteswissenschaften: Versuch einer Grundlegung für das Studium der Gesellschaft und der Geschichte, Gesammelte Schriften*, Vol. I, Stuttgart: B. G. Teubner, 1923, p. XVIII, and Wilhelm Dilthey, *Der Aufbau der geschichtlichen Welt in den Geisteswissenschaften, Gesammelte Schriften*, Vol. VII, Leipzig and Berlin: B. G. Teubner, 1927: "Thus I have designated a critique of historical reason as the basic task of all reflections about the human sciences. We have to solve for historical reason the problem which was not yet fully grasped by Kant's critique of reason . . . We have to step out of the pure and delicate atmosphere of Kant's critique of reason to grasp the wholly different nature of historical phenomena" (p. 278, my translation).

[5] Cf. John Stuart Mill, *A System of Logic: Ratiocinative and Inductive*, 8th edition, New York: Harper, 1893, p. 521.

[6] Cf. Leopold von Ranke, *Politisches Gespräch* (edited by H. Ritter von Srbik), Leipzig: Insel-Verlag, 1943, p. 45.

[7] Cf. Auguste Comte, *Cours de philosophie positive*, 6 vols., Paris: Bachelier, 1830–42, IV, 17, 145, 287.

[8] Cf. Leopold von Ranke, *History of the Popes, Their Church and State* (translated by E. Fowler with introduction by W. Clark), Vol. I, New York: The Colonial Press, 1901. Cf. Also, Comte, *op. cit.*, I, 16; V, 14.

ing at generalizations about causal and natural laws of development. The earlier historicists advocated the free will of the individual—the positivist Buckle left nothing to chance in the human realm but stressed that every event was occasioned by the rigid determinism of the natural order.[9] The German philosophers and historians meant to explain human deeds by reference to the unique national heritage and the specific historical situation, but Comte and Mill were of the opinion that the human sciences had to be based on investigations of large collectives whose actions could be reduced by statistical analysis to natural laws. This view was strengthened by Buckle's efforts to illustrate the assumed uniformity and necessity in human affairs not so much from history as from statistics.[10]

The positivistic philosophers presented a collectivistic and mechanistic concept of man and of socio-historical reality. Dilthey joined the historicist opposition that held the polar conception with its individualistic and voluntaristic views of these phenomena.

The subsequent analysis of three principal factors will show why Dilthey helped to accelerate the growth of the modern mentality that views the importance, quality, and functional meaning of ideas with systematic suspicion.

In the case of historicism, the development is characterized by an interesting dialectical current. Dilthey was opposed to positivism, but he could not prevent his own contribution to the concepts and ideas of the historical school from aiding the rise of a new and different type of historicism which assimilated and practiced almost everything that positivism stood for. The earlier historicists had organically related the diverse manifestations of history to a transcendent unity, thereby finding reason and meaning in the plurality of absolutes. The later historicists experienced the same pluralism as a meaningless coexistence of manifold phenomena, as a mere chaos of worldviews. The procession into philosophical relativism and pessimism began.

Dilthey and Kant

Let us now consider the second factor explaining Dilthey's contribution to the development of modern systematic doubt with regard to intellectual manifestations. As already pointed out, Dilthey employed the basic conceptual and epistemological tools of Kant's critical philosophy in

[9] Cf. Henry Thomas Buckle, *Introduction to the History of Civilization in England* (with annotations and introduction by John M. Robertson), New York: E. P. Dutton, 1904, pp. 5–21.

[10] Cf. Wilhelm Dilthey, *Studien zur Geschichte des deutschen Geistes, Gesammelte Schriften,* Vol. III, Leipzig: B. G. Teubner, 1927, p. 145. Cf. also Mill, *op. cit.,* p. 529, Buckle, *op. cit.,* p. 164.

order to establish a firm foundation for knowledge in the historically oriented human sciences. In 1867, Dilthey publicly announced his allegiance and further intention ". . . to follow Kant's critical path, to establish an empirical science of the human mind in collaboration with researchers in other disciplines . . . to conceive the laws that dominate social, intellectual, and moral phenomena."[11] Thus, Dilthey went along with Kant in asking the basic epistemological question concerning the process transforming experience into knowledge in the mind; like Kant he also rejected all metaphysical conceptions of the universe and reality as obsolete foundations for philosophy. The importance of this second factor in our analytical frame, however, does not rest with these points of agreement, but rather with Dilthey's further development and modification of Kantian and Neo-Kantian philosophy.

The most basic criterion of science is the attempt to transcend the individual case and to arrive at generalizations about the uniform forces that operate behind the in-itself meaningless variety of empirical manifestations. In this sense, Kant had tried to show how mathematics and physics were possible by revealing the universal elements behind the physical scientific approach. His establishment of the physical sciences rests upon the assertion that the forms of knowledge come from the mind while the material of thought is given from without.

Dilthey was determined to achieve the same for the historically oriented human sciences, and, consequently, he had to reveal the basic universal factors that make history as a science possible. His question, therefore, was: Is there anything behind the great variety of historical manifestations that would make the universal stream of historical continuity accessible to the human mind? Initially, Dilthey had asserted that an interaction similiar to the one maintained by Kant existed in as far as the stream of historical continuity arose out of the life-situation in which the "inner" world of the mind interacted with the "outer" world of the physical and cultural environment. But the elements of universality and necessity were still missing, and Dilthey had to discover these factors if he wanted to establish the scientific basis for the investigation of the historical process. Dilthey believed that this elevation of the historical human sciences to the level of an exact science was possible through the application of the conceptual tool that Kant had forged with the principle of the categories of the mind. Therefore, Dilthey based his critique of historical reason upon the idea that these categories dominate the universal historical stream, that they lend necessity and universality to the manner in which the human mind operates in history, and that they establish the fundament for an accurate analysis of culture. Thus, Dilthey

---

[11] Dilthey, Vol. V, *op. cit.*, p. 27 (my translation).

viewed the categories, the forms of thought, as the motivating power behind all human thought and all human activity; he saw them as immanent teleological forces determining the general development of man's action and thought in history.

In the endeavor to arrive at generalizations and to discover uniformities the social sciences have been greatly helped by the construction of types which make it possible to conceive society as a whole. If history was to be advanced, the unique hero of historical biography had to be replaced by the type. Dilthey significantly contributed to this development when he turned from his analysis of human thoughts and actions in history to the study of man's psychological reactions and attitudes to the world, thereby arriving at the construction of types of worldviews —basic ways in which men perceive the external world.

Dilthey's attempt to develop a truly integral historical interpretation of man in his world culminated in his famous thesis that the history of ideas is coextensive with the history of three fundamental types of philosophical worldviews; each of these he conceived as a system of values and a system of knowledge complete in itself. He believed that scientific certainty would result from an understanding of these worldview types. Furthermore, he asserted that all human thought could be subsumed under one of these major types of thinking, thanks to the universal nature of the categories of the mind.

Dilthey's worldview typology is based on distinctions made by his teacher Trendelenburg and asserts the possibility of three attitudes toward the world. Dilthey describes the first type of worldview as (materialistic, positivistic) *naturalism*—in this instance the human mind functions like a mirror, passively reflecting the natural world. The second view is called *idealism of freedom*—taking this attitude man completely impresses the forms of his mind upon the understanding of the empirical world. Third, Dilthey explains that the worldview of the pantheistic life-philosophers represents *objective idealism*—in this case man's intelligence interacts with the surrounding world, partially reflecting it and partially molding it to the understanding.[12]

This typology enables Dilthey to trace a continuity which joins different intellectual representatives and systems in a unitary type. The first type embraces—in spite of the great diversity of the systems—Democritus, Lucretius, Epicurus, Hobbes, the Encyclopedists, the modern materialists, Comte, and Avenarius. Idealism of freedom affords tenancy to Plato, the Hellenistic-Roman philosophy of life (Cicero), Christian thought, Kant, Fichte, Maine de Biran, and Carlyle. The developmental stages of objective idealism are represented by Heraclitus, strict Stoicism,

[12] Cf. Dilthey, Vol. VIII, *op. cit.*, pp. 97–118.

Spinoza, Leibniz, Shaftesbury, Goethe, Schelling, Schleiermacher, and Hegel.[13]

Dilthey arrived at his universal knowledge of the past by assuming, first, that the historical process was identical with the evolution of ideas ". . . out of a life-situation and the progression of action from those ideas, (2) that ideas arose in history within certain necessary and universal types of worldviews, and (3) that the investigator's mind could understand those ideas because his mind functioned in similar patterns . . ."[14]

Dilthey meant this method to be universal in its application to the historical studies and felt he had achieved in this realm what Kant had achieved for the physical sciences in his *Critique of Pure Reason*—he had created the fundament for a scientific analysis of the historical world.

Thanks to the widening of critical epistemology by Wilhelm Dilthey and other representatives of life-philosophy as well as of historicism, Kant's insights—thus far limited to nature—could now at last be applied to the sphere of intellect (*geistige Welt*). The critical method which the Neo-Kantians had limited to the physical sciences had been extended to the human sciences and the field of history. Only the process of understanding (*Verstehen*) transforms the pre-objective material into the essence of an objective world. Kant's statement concerning the lawful order of the objects of the physical sciences is valid also in the world of ideas which constitutes the object of the human studies: the meaningful order of the world does not originate in the objects, but rather in the structure of the perceiving mind.

It was in this sense that Dilthey discussed the *establishment of the historical world in the human sciences.*[15] The object of the human sciences, too, takes shape in the process of cognition and is dependent on, or at least codetermined by, specific object-constituting formative factors which are located on the side of the perceiving subject. In analogy to Kant, these formative factors are called "categories of understanding."

The Transformation of Critical Philosophy

Dilthey searched—in particular—for the subjective conditions making possible the existence of "objective spirit"—understood as the fixed manifestation of mental structures. He meant to reduce the configurations of objective spirit (not to be confused with Hegel's objective spirit) to the subjective-mental life-structure. This line of thought resulted in significant modifications of the concepts of critical philosophy. Of special

[13] Cf. Wilhelm Dilthey, *The Essence of Philosophy* (translated by Stephen A. Emery and William T. Emery), Chapel Hill: The University of North Carolina Press, 1954, p. 63.

[14] William Kluback, *Wilhelm Dilthey's Philosophy of History*, New York: Columbia University Press, 1956, p. 69.

[15] Cf. Dilthey, Vol. VII, *op. cit.*, pp. 79–188.

importance was the injection of historical awareness into critical epistemology: Dilthey and his followers *historicized the a priori*. Without this
transformation of Kant's central concept such analytical schemes as the
one represented by the sociology of knowledge would not have been
possible.

How did this *historicization of the a priori* come about?

Kant had grounded the object-constituting principles of general and
a priori validity, i.e., the categories of thought in the *transcendental
apperception*, in a *consciousness as such*, pure, original, and unchangeable.[16] Dilthey transferred this epistemological orientation to the world
of ideas (*geistige Welt*), trying to reveal the "categories of understanding" which were understood as transcendental elements constituting the
ordered structure of the world. What happened to the pure concepts
of the understanding after this act of transference? They emerged as
modes of evaluation reflecting the particular worldviews of different
thinkers and were no longer universally grounded in a *consciousness as
such*. A different conception emerged: the evaluating subject of cognition
approaches the empirical, pre-objective material in the human studies
with the *a priori* of his worldview and makes a selection among these
mere data in correspondence with his worldview *a priori*. But this
worldview *a priori* is no longer the old universal *a priori* of Kant's epistemology. On the contrary, the *a priori* of Wilhelm Dilthey and his followers is a particular one that corresponds to the specific *historical and
social position* of the thinkers.

In this way Dilthey came to accept the unity of science and life; he
saw the world of ideas, i.e., the subject matter of the human sciences
engulfed by the all-embracing totality of life. Each human being experiences and evaluates his specific historical and social position within this
totality of life and, consequently, arrives at specific forms of world interpretation and worldview. These forms determine the shaping of the ideal
world which takes place within the cognitive process of the human
sciences. Furthermore, man makes his own social and historical position
part of the cognitive goal. Consequently, the objective intention upon
the cultural, historical subject matter is accompanied by the subjective
intention upon the thinker's specific social and historical position.[17]

All these assumptions led Dilthey to proclaim the identity of living,
evaluating, and perceiving man—the epistemological hallmark of the
human and social sciences.

[16] Cf. Kant, *Critique of Pure Reason*, pp. 135–136.

[17] Cf. Dilthey, Vol. VII, *op. cit.* Dilthey argues: "The individual in his self-
contained personal being is an historical creature. He is determined by his location
upon the time-continuum, by his position in space, his status in the cooperation of
culture systems and communities. Therefore, the historian must understand all of
the individual's life as manifest at a particular time and a particular place" (p. 135,
my translation).

Dilthey and Hegel

Finally, we will have to consider a third factor to fully understand Dilthey's contribution to the development of the modern mentality that approaches all claims of absoluteness and finality with suspicion and distrust. In this case we must investigate how he adopted and modified Hegel's ideas.

In November, 1905, Dilthey read his *Jugendgeschichte Hegel's* to the members of the Berlin Academy of Sciences[18] and joined the group of scholars that initiated the Hegelian Renaissance. Dilthey's analysis followed the lead that Karl Rosenkranz and Rudolf Haym had given, and he largely completed the work of these men by contributing an account of the evolution of Hegel's philosophy.

Thus the year 1905 marks the point where Dilthey turned toward the philosophy of Hegel and, as will become evident, he also began to follow ideas advanced by Husserl. Hegel's concept of "historical consciousness" exerted a particularly profound influence upon Dilthey; but he did not adopt Hegel's thoughts uncritically. On the contrary, he started with the assumption that Hegel's philosophy contained elements that would remain valid for future thinkers and elements that had only temporary significance, elements that were already defunct. It was the very concept of historical consciousness that provided Dilthey with a criterion appropriate for carrying out the crucial distinction between the lasting and the passing in Hegel's system. Taking an overall view, Dilthey pointed out that Hegel's philosophy suffered from a central contradiction: on the one hand, Hegel employed the notion of historical consciousness to show the limited, relative validity of historical data and ideas, but, on the other hand, he claimed for his philosophy universal, eternal validity.

Consequently, Dilthey rejected Hegel's logic and his philosophy of nature and, along with his religious philosophy, the idea that the Christian religion has any claim of absoluteness. The important, lasting part of Hegel's metaphysics can be found in the dynamic historical intentions contained therein—in the great and fruitful idea of evolution, in the postulate to understand the meaning of each manifestation of life historically.[19]

The spirit of the world, Hegel's absolute, is dead—long live the absolute: now Dilthey transforms the absolute into history. *The new absolute is history because history makes everything relative and temporal.* In Dilthey's philosophy, Hegel's inspirited universe becomes "socio-historical reality" and the latter is neither rational nor irrational

---

[18] This interpretation of the young Hegel and his early works was subsequently published. Cf. Wilhelm Dilthey, *Die Jugendgeschichte Hegel's, Abhandlungen der Königlich-Preussischen Akademie der Wissenschaften,* Berlin: B. Behrs, 1905.

[19] Cf. Dilthey, Vol. V, *op. cit.,* p. 406.

as such. This reality is only "meaningful" in a vague sense. Even this element of meaning does no longer originate in the world itself, but must be understood as a product of man's attitudes toward and interpretations of the world. The world does not give meaning to life. On the contrary, meaning and significance originate in man and his history. Theology and metaphysics must be replaced by the objective forces of human history, by the units of Hegel's objective spirit—largely social configurations, such as family, society, and State: only then will man be able to understand his life out of life itself without the crutches of dogmatic theology and metaphysics.[20]

In this manner Dilthey adopted the seed of historicism from Hegel's idea system and brought it to its fullest realization. Dilthey was enthusiastic in his acceptance of historical awareness, and he knew that scepticism and doubt inevitably follow in its wake:

"Yet beyond the depth and much of the skeptical conclusions from the contradictoriness of human opinions there extend certain doubts which have grown out of the continuous unfolding of the historical awareness of man."[21] History reflects the anarchy of all philosophical systems and ". . . the coming of an historical awareness, more so than the sweeping survey of the conflict of systems, destroys forever the belief in the absolute validity of any one philosophy which might have undertaken to interpret the world compellingly by an interrelation of concepts."[22]

The Supremacy of Life

To sum up the preceding discussion: the principle that explains the world is no longer inherent in the world. With Dilthey the world must be understood from a different vantage point: *life*. Similar to Husserl, Dilthey intends to establish philosophy in the image of exact science, and, for this purpose, he needs something more tangible than metaphysical belief: the objective manifestations of life constitute the subject matter of the human sciences. Philosophy is now philosophy of "objective spirit." Objective spirit is understood as the sum of the objective manifestations of a spiritual-mental entity. But these manifestations no longer reflect the spirit of the world; they are creations of subjective spirit; they result from the behavior of human individuals. Dilthey claims that the conditions which determine the existence of objective spirit must be

[20] Cf. Karl Löwith, *Von Hegel zu Nietzsche,* Stuttgart: W. Kohlhammer Verlag, 1953, pp. 130–140. See also Dilthey, Vol. VII, *op. cit.,* p. 278.

[21] Wilhelm Dilthey, *Dilthey's Philosophy of Existence: Introduction to Weltanschauungslehre* (translation of an essay with introduction by W. Kluback and M. Weinbaum), New York: Bookman Associates, 1957, p. 19.

[22] *Ibid.,* p. 20.

found in the cognitive subject—in man. Hegel's objective spirit still "floated" above the human individuals—this notion is now rejected by Dilthey. He reduces the manifestations of objective spirit, such as art, religion, and philosophy (notice the contrast to Hegel) to their point of origin: the subjective-mental structure of life. Dilthey proclaims: thought cannot go behind life ("*hinter das Leben kann das Denken nicht zurück-gehen*"). *Life is ultimate reality.*[23] Thus, the term objective spirit takes on a new meaning for Dilthey. Objective spirit now shows that a manifestation has taken its place in the intellectual sphere, that it has found its way from the inner world of the subject into the objective outside of historical reality. Dilthey implies that the manifestation can be better grasped on the outside than on the inside.

His formula for this grasping of manifestations reads: *Erleben—Ausdruck—Verstehen.* (Experience—Expression—Understanding.)[24] This, according to Dilthey, represents the method appropriate to the human sciences, while the objective manifestations of life represent their subject matter. This is Dilthey's establishment of the human sciences, his *Aufbau der Geisteswissenschaften*—scientific disciplines ". . . in which the chief aim is to understand some portion of mental life through the interpretation of its outward expressions in individual or social histories, in economic, political, or religious processes and institutions, or in the creative activities and products of the fine arts."[25]

Technically, Dilthey's *philosophy of philosophy* is to provide the different specialities within the human sciences with a common theoretical and methodological basis. Furthermore, Dilthey demands that we start with objective manifestations and go back to the nature of the expressing entity or, in other words, that we should understand the world around us by reducing each expression to the underlying human experience. This means that the mental world is a human world, an historical and social world. It also means that a meaningfully ordered historical world does not exist as such, but only comes about because of the activity of the historian who creates such meaning. From the vantage point of his present, the historian tries to grasp the past with the help of the category of meaning. He does so to give direction to the future. Thus, Dilthey evaluates the past under the aspect of its importance for the future. This was also Hegel's approach to history, but with him the future had practically ended and the question concerning historical importance was raised with regard to the *spirit of the world*. Dilthey, on the other hand, is open to the limitless possibilities of the future, and he brings up the

---

[23] Cf. Dilthey, Vol. V, *op. cit.*, pp. 4–5.
[24] Cf. Dilthey, Vol. VII, *op. cit.*, p. 191.
[25] Stephen A. Emery and William T. Emery, Translators' Preface to W. Dilthey, *The Essence of Philosophy*, p. x.

question concerning the importance of past events and ideas with regard to *man*.

With Dilthey, man's intellectual development has reached an important state—important especially as far as the growth of doubt and suspicion are concerned. *Dilthey brings functional analysis and extrinsic interpretation into being:* he creates the new mode of questioning which replaces the traditional one of earlier thinkers who practiced the traditional, immanent interpretation that inquired into the content of beliefs and ideas simply to prove or disprove them. Dilthey, however, wants to know how ideas and objective situations come into existence. *Now thought becomes functionalized—is interpreted as a function of life.*[26]

To some extent, the context of distrust and doubt—typical for functional analysis—was already extant in the case of Dilthey.[27] *Man became the center of philosophy*, or, rather life as lived, expressed, and understood by man. Dilthey boldly asserted that the only constant element in man was his changeability.[28] Furthermore, he maintained that the atheoretical manifestations of life were more relevant to our understanding of reality than thought. Ultimately, the world views were atheoretical units—not products of thinking. They did not result from the mere will to perceive, but from man's cravings and appetites.

This new emphasis upon the atheoretical elements, this attempt to approach thought from life must be understood as an important preparation of the idea that *thoughts are existentially determined*. Later, Marx will add the thesis that modern life reveals itself most genuinely in *social existence* and the basis for a sociology of knowledge emerges.[29]

[26] Cf. Dilthey, Vol. I, *op. cit.*: All intellectual work ". . . is determined by the relationship of a perceiving subject within his historical horizon to a certain body of data the scope of which is also determined by a certain horizon. For each the object presents itself only from a certain point of view. Each is, therefore, a particular, relative mode of seeing and perceiving its object. He who enters into these labors faces them as a chaos of relativities. *Subjectivity of the modern research intention*" (p. 413, my translation; emphasis in original). Cf. also Dilthey, Vol. VIII, *op. cit.*, p. 98.

[27] Cf. Dilthey, Vol. VII, *op. cit.* Dilthey says: ". . . we recognize not only intentions upon cultural values as active forces but also the will to power and the inclination to subjugate others." (p. 166, my translation.)

[28] Cf. *Ibid.*, pp. 290–291: "The historical consciousness of the finitude of every historical phenomenon, every human or social condition, of the relativity of every sort of belief, is the last step towards the liberation of man. . . . Life is liberated from perception through concepts; the mind becomes sovereign over all the cobwebs of dogmatic thinking. . . . We do not carry any meaning from the universe into life . . . meaning and significance only originate in man and his history." (My translation.)

[29] Dilthey was already very susceptible to "materialistic" interpretations of history and human life. See *Ibid.*, p. 260: ". . . the French's mentality is characterized by a clear insight into personal motives, money, social position, and they cannot understand the Germans' . . . sense of duty and their consequent *naiveté* in regard to personal purposes." (My translation.)

Moreover, Dilthey prepares the way for modern thought because of the elements of scepticism and relativism that are so conspicuous in his writings. He argues that man cannot grasp all of life and uses in the fashion of Husserl the concept of perspective variations: we can only see the pure light of truth in different, broken rays; we can only perceive life in its perspective variations. But the number of these different approaches to life is not limitless. They converge into types of worldviews; each of these reflects the life experiences and interpretations of historically determined men. Since these worldviews are determined by historical situations, their values are relative to these situations.[30]

Dilthey ends up with a polytheism of metaphysical positions, each claiming absolute validity for its assertion. This conflict of systems can only be solved by way of an arbitrary, purely subjective decision—the door to the modern theory of the existential determination of thought has been thrown wide open.[31]

[30] Cf. Dilthey, Vol. VIII, *op. cit.*, p. 224.

[31] Cf. *Ibid.*, p. 99: ". . . every metaphysical thinker . . . tackles the knot represented by the enigma of life from a particular vantage point; this point is determined by his attitude toward life and from there the singular structure of his system is formed." (My translation.) Cf. Also Dilthey, Vol. V, *op. cit.*: "They [moral-political sciences] are . . . essentially determined by causes which are external to our intellectual approach to the objects, by nature and the conditions of nations, the ideals of eras, the turmoil in societies and states, the forward pushing power of interests as voiced in public opinion. Here the will generates impulses to new theories which in turn react upon the will" (p. 32, my translation). Cf. also *Ibid.*, p. 413. Finally, see Dilthey, Vol. VII, *op. cit.*, pp. 290–291.

CHAPTER 9

EDMUND GUSTAV ALBRECHT HUSSERL
A Suspension of Belief

Edmund Husserl (1859–1938) is another German philosopher whose theories on the relationship of the conscious mind and objects—the basis of the system of phenomenology—have had great influence on the growth of the modern mentality.

Much like Husserl and probably under the influence of his ideas, Dilthey had proclaimed that man cannot grasp all of life and reality; the individual can only perceive life in its perspective variations.[1] While Dilthey left the problem there, while he went on to announce his particular solution to this impasse of thinking with the development of his theory of worldviews, Husserl made this very question one of his central concerns.

The Return of Ontological Realism

Dilthey had already seriously challenged the idealistic belief in an eternal, unchanging realm of truth when he conceived of thought as a function of life, of social reality.[2] Then a number of European philoso-

---

[1] For a discussion of this relationship see H. A. Hodges, *The Philosophy of Wilhelm Dilthey*, London: Routledge & Kegan Paul, 1952. Hodges states: ". . . the underlying conception of Husserl's 'phenomenology' is the same as that of Dilthey's 'reflection of self' (*Selbstbesinnung*), and both represent that 'transcendental point of view' which is one of Kant's great gifts to philosophy" (p. 35).

[2] This doubt in the superiority of ideas over the practical activities and interests of men is even more resolutely expressed in American pragmatism. The suspicion that ideas are not lofty entities or unchangeable qualities of the objects confronting the mind was first expressed in the pragmatist context by Charles Sanders Peirce and further developed by William James, who claimed that truth "happens to an idea." James' "radical empiricism" relegates "truth" to the rank of a descriptive term which characterizes certain practical ways in which we use ideas to serve our purposes. John Dewey expanded pragmatism into his theory of instrumentalism: now truth is seen as something evolutionary, not as an entity fixed or everlasting. According to him, the different forms of human activity and thinking must be understood as tools or instruments for the solution of problematic human conditions. These instruments *change* with the problems. In Dewey's thinking, Peirce's original statement of the pragmatist criterion—thoughts and beliefs are rules for action—thus

phers reintroduced the issue of ontological realism; they maintained that experience is an experience of objects. These objects derive their existence from conditions different from those conditions upon which they are dependent for their being known. The first among these neorealists was the psychologist Franz Brentano (1838–1917), who asserted that psychical activity mainly intends objects which may or may not actually exist. These objects derive their objective character from the fact that they are intended. These ideas were further developed by Brentano's student Alexius Meinong (1853–1920), who claimed that the objects perceived by the mind are in some way before, but not actually in, the mind.

Husserl, another of Bretano's students, gave to neorealism its most resolute expression in his realistic phenomenology which claims that our consciousness merely approaches objects; it does not constitute objects as Kant had maintained. In a general way, a course had been set that led to the subsequent developments of British and American realism culminating in the philosophies of Bertrand Russell (1872–), Alfred North Whitehead (1861–1947), and George Santayana (1863–1952). Husserl's central thesis that the mind intends its objects, but does neither constitute nor exhaust them invited the enmity of all idealists, and the attack was led by the Neo-Kantians who then dominated intellectual life in Germany.

The Neo-Kantian Road to "Truth"

The revival of Kant's ideas was spearheaded by a group of professors at the University of Marburg led by Hermann Cohen (1842–1918), a distinguished commentator of Kant's critiques, and his student and associate, Paul Natorp (1854–1924). While these critical idealists rejected the notion of the thing-in-itself and the metaphysical striving implied therein, they accepted the three dimensions of Kant's critiques: physical science, ethics, art. They conceived of their task as being twofold; on the one hand they strove to reveal the presuppositions of these three supersystems, on the other hand they felt the need to unify them more closely. To achieve this synthesis of logical, moral, and aesthetic activities, Cohen pointed to his "cultural consciousness" while Natorp suggested that the aspect of subjectivity or immediacy would show the unity of logic, ethics, and art.

The Southwest German School founded by Wilhelm Windelband

reached its fullest development. In the European intellectual tradition pragmatism finds its expression in the writings of Nietzsche—the admirer of Ralph Waldo Emerson; pragmatism is an important ingredient in Marx's thinking and forms part of Mannheim's political sociology.

(1848–1915) and continued by Heinrich Rickert (1863–1936) represents the other column supporting the edifice of critical idealism. Both were convinced that their ideas were the logical result of Kant's total philosophy as ultimately expressed in his three *Critiques*. Windelband is best known for his attack upon Dilthey's concept of the human sciences. He asserted that Dilthey's distinction between physical sciences and human sciences was wrongly drawn and set out to apply to the historical sciences Kant's analysis of the logical presuppositions of knowledge in the physical sciences. Windelband rejected Dilthey's solution which divided the two fields according to subject matter and pointed out that this procedure neglected the overlapping of subject matter. Consequently, Windelband had to discover a different criterion to draw the line of demarcation between the physical and human sciences; this he found in scientific method.

Windelband introduced the new distinction in his rectorial address, *Geschichte und Naturwissenschaft,* which he delivered at Strassburg in 1894: since historians have the task of describing *individual facts,* they must apply the *idiographic method* to any subject matter, whereas physical scientists who strive to *generalize* and establish *laws* will always bring the *nomothetic method* to bear on all phenomena they investigate. Any object can be viewed from either of the two methodological positions and the new line of demarcation cuts across any distinction that could be made on the basis of subject matter.

Windelband realized that the historian's interest in the nonrecurrent, individual aspects of life also reflects his fascination for values; he was convinced that values derive their existence from individual self-assertions and unique occurrences. His reduction of history to an inquiry on idiographic lines, however, led to the unforeseen but significant conclusion that all knowledge—except that of the physical scientist—is relative to the particular individuals or circumstances embodying a partial set of values.

Heinrich Rickert, who succeeded Windelband at Heidelberg in 1916, arrived at a position where an even greater significance is attached to meaning and value. Rickert vigorously limited the historian to the investigation of facts embodying cultural values since they alone are interesting and significant. The historian, furthermore, accepts the value-standards which the subjects of his study have entertained and investigates only those occurrences which are significant in the light of these standards provided by history itself.[3]

Rickert's philosophy has frequently been designated as "neo-Fichteanism" because both he and Fichte confirmed the "primacy of practical

[3] Cf. Heinrich Rickert, *Kulturwissenschaft und Naturwissenschaft.* 2nd edition, Tübingen: J. C. B. Mohr (Paul Siebeck), 1910, pp. 80–151.

reason" asserted by Kant. In this tradition Rickert worked out a thorough reduction of the "is" to the "ought." He maintained that we know the "is" (*Sein*) only as an object of judgement, but the ". . . peculiar logical essence of judgment is affirmation and denial, approval or disapproval, or an attitude to a value."[4] According to Rickert, then, we judge the "is" within a frame of reference established by the "ought." He, furthermore, believed that we were obliged to conform to this "ethical" principle which was, thereby, removed from all subjective bias, establishing an ideal objectivity equally unharmed by the limiting influences of either subjectivity or actuality.

The values guiding the historian's selection of facts must be those which the members of his society accept generally and over long periods of time; they represent, in other words, the basic heritage underlying his civilization. Rickert never doubted that all European readers of historical works, for instance, would recognize the values expressed by the Church, religion, the State, law, science, literature, art, economic organization, and so forth. Therefore, they would not think it arbitrary that these values should direct the selection of what is important, thereby limiting the historian's description to events which are significant to these values.

To escape the impasse of ideology Rickert introduced the notion that these widely accepted cultural values represent—despite their historical relativity—approximations to a galaxy of absolute norms. Rickert's philosophy of history in particular had the task of revealing the basic values determining both the meaning of history and the concepts guiding its interpretation. The great periods of history would then be revealed for us in the light of their highest values and these objective philosophical principles would show us true world history.[5]

His "idealistic" belief in the integrity of values prevented Rickert from pursuing the relativistic implications of his philosophy, but the next generation was soon to discover that Rickert's "objective" philosophical principles were nonexistent and that we are only left with partial, subjective perspectives and interest-bound ideologies.[6] This realization was furthered, however, by certain aspects of Husserl's philosophy.

---

[4] Heinrich Rickert, *Der Gegenstand der Erkenntnis*, 2nd edition, Tübingen: J. C. B. Mohr, 1904, p. 108. Here Rickert tries to show that purely logical reasons necessitate the assumption of objective or "transcendent" values.

[5] Cf. Heinrich Rickert, *Die Probleme der Geschichtsphilosophie*, 3rd edition, Heidelberg: C. Winter, 1924. For a more specific philosophical discussion of general and formal values underlying cultural change, cf. Rickert, "Vom Begriff der Philosophie," *Logos*, Vol. I, No. 1 (February, 1910), pp. 1ff.

[6] When convenient, however, Rickert displayed the "suspicion of ideology" quite forcefully. This is especially apparent in his "refutation" of the social democratic interpretation of history and in his attack upon the "ideologist" Lassalle. For this controversy see Rickert, *Kulturwissenschaft und Naturwissenschaft*, pp. 117–119.

A Philosophy Without Presuppositions

First of all, Husserl greatly contributed to the progress of modern thought because of his determination to examine critically all assumptions and to eliminate all presuppositions. To this end he submitted the structural elements of knowledge and reality to the crucial test of his phenomenological method which examines all assumptions including its own so that all objects may be constituted on the basis of "pure consciousness," which is consciousness freed from all beliefs in transcendent existence. Husserl's ideal of "presuppositionlessness" implies significantly that all investigations in the social and human sciences must proceed unbiased by worldview assumptions and prejudgements. Husserl's radical suspension of all traditional assumptions, both formal and nonformal, led to a view of mind, where mind stood divested of all bodilyness and all ideal and real conditions of thought and experience.[7]

Husserl demanded a mind purged of all beliefs and generalities accepted on trust or engrained by habit, because he suspected that all sciences rest on naive presuppositions of which their practitioners remain unaware. Therefore, the generalizations of science often lead to false pretensions and the physicists' mathematical facade is mistaken for reality, just as readily as is the cloak of idealizations cast over society by social scientists operating with complex typologies.

Husserl wanted to set himself apart from all traditional philosophy and science and since nearly all things and principles had become suspect, he had to begin with the most basic assertion that any idea is by intention an idea of some object. In analyzing experience, we are involved in considering the objects to which experience refers. Husserl applied the term phenomenology (*Phänomenologie*) to this descriptive study of our consciousness or, as it should rather be called, to this study of our consciousness of objects—since it is characteristic of our consciousness to have objects. Husserl believed that the phenomenologist was in a position to distinguish the subjective and objective aspects of experience. But in order to do so he had to develop a philosophical, reflective attitude in which the mind examines its own ideas as they refer to their objects. This peculiar attitude sets the phenomenologist apart from the "ordinary" scientist who has a different attitude; one in which the mind directly feels the objects of its ideas. Thus, Husserl contrasted the peculiar phenomenological attitude with the primary or "natural" conscious act, which is directed upon the object, and takes it to be real.

Husserl's philosophy had to begin with a "phenomenological reduction"

---

[7] Cf. Marvin Farber, "A Presuppositionless Philosophy," in Marvin Farber (editor), *Philosophical Essays in Memory of Edmund Husserl*, Cambridge: Harvard University Press, 1940, pp. 45–48.

which only accepts the observable character of our experiences, purely as experiences, since no statement about "real, objective" existence is beyond doubt. By way of immediate, intuitive acquaintance we only know one thing for sure—that we have experiences. This type of reflection, furthermore, "reduces" the naive attitude, and the phenomenologist achieves a detached standpoint from which objects simply appear as the objective aspects of the perceiving act—the phenomenologist no longer lives in the act, or sees objects through it. Husserl's reduction, finally, changed the objective world into a mere "phenomenon of consciousness"—something that neither exists nor does not exist, but which we presume to exist.[8]

The Fragmentation of the World

Husserl made his most important single contribution to the development of both the modern mentality and the sociology of knowledge when he elaborated the concept of perspective variation (*Abschattung*). Central to his philosophy is the claim that essences such as purely logico-mathematical forms and essentially necessary relations can be completely envisaged. Everyday physical nature, on the other hand, can only be grasped incompletely—the spatial properties of the physical thing present themselves only in one-sided shadings, that is, they can be grasped only partially in their perspective variations.[9]

The relation of the subject to the object is essentially one of seeing and intending and the object is approached in processes of active sensuous perceiving which contain a large measure of uncertainty and error. In Husserl's description, perception and the thing perceived, though essentially related to each other, are in principle and of necessity not really and essentially one and united.[10]

These problems become evident in the most basic acts of sensuous perception: in walking around a table I change my position in space continuously, but the table remains unchanged. What changes all the time, however, is my perception of it which is actually a continuum of changing perceptions.

> I close my eyes. My other senses are inactive in relation to the table. I have now no perception of it. I open my eyes, and the perception returns. The perception? Let us be more accurate. Under no circumstances does it return to me individually the same. Only the table is the same, known as identical through the synthetic consciousness which connects the new perception with

---

[8] Cf. Edmund Husserl, *Ideen zu einer reinen Phänomenologie und Phänomenologischen Philosophie, Erstes Buch: Allgemeine Einführung in die Reine Phänomenologie* (edited by Walter Biemel), Haag: Martinus Nijhoff, 1950, par. 46, pp. 106–110.

[9] Cf. *Ibid.*, p. 14.

[10] Cf. *Ibid.*, par. 41, pp. 91–94.

the recollection. The perceived thing can be, without being perceived, without my being aware of it even as potential only . . . and perhaps without changing at all. But the perception itself is what it is within the steady flow of consciousness, and is itself constantly in flux; the perceptual now is ever passing over into the adjacent consciousness of the just-past, a new now simultaneously gleams forth, and so on . . . One and the same shape (given *as* bodily the same) appears continuously ever again "in another way," in ever-differing perspective variations of shape.[11]

This example refers to a thing that appears unchanged in perception. Husserl proceeds in this manner for the sake of simplicity. Yet, according to him it is evident that the transfer to changes of any other sort is simple. Importantly, however, we must conclude that our consciousness of one and the same thing is fragmented into continuous patterns of appearances and perspective variations. These are part of what Husserl calls "sensory data." As he had already demonstrated in his *Logische Untersuchungen* it must be understood that these sensory data which exercise the function of presenting color, smoothness, shape, and so forth perspectivally, i.e. the function of exhibiting, differ wholly and in principle from color, smoothness, shape *simpliciter*.[12]

> *The perspective variation (the "Abschattung"), though verbally similar to the perspected variable (the "Abgeschattetes"), differs from it generically and in principle.* The perspective variation is an experience. But experience is possible only as experience, and not as something spatial. The perspected variable, however, is in principle possible only as spatial (it is indeed spatial in its essence), but not possible as experience.[13]

Thus Husserl means to prove the transcendence of the thing over against the perception of it. He, furthermore, argues that a thing cannot be given as really immanent in any possible perception or, generally, in any possible consciousness; only being as experience (*cogitatio*) is perceivable through immanent perception. This opposition between immanence and transcendence is accompanied by a further difference, i.e. a basic difference in the mode of being given: we can perceive a thing through its perceptive modifications. An experience, on the other hand, does not present itself in this manner, an experience has no perspectives. Only Being in space, only the thing, is intended by Husserl when he talks about standpoints and perspective variations: we see the thing from different standpoints with a changing orientation, we view it through

---

[11] Edmund Husserl, *Ideas: General Introduction to Pure Phenomenology* (translated by W. R. Boyce Gibson), New York: Macmillan, 1952, pp. 130–131 (emphasis in original).

[12] Cf. Edmund Husserl, *Logische Untersuchungen*, Vol. I, Halle: Max Niemeyer, 1913, pp. 128–130.

[13] Husserl, *Ideas*, p. 132 (emphasis in original).

varying appearances and perspective shadings. The thing presents continuously and endlessly its different sides and aspects.

Finally it is important to realize that the perception of things is necessarily characterized by a certain inadequacy. A thing can be given only in one of its aspects, only in perspective variations. A thing is given in mere modes of appearing and a nucleus of what is really presented is surrounded by a horizon of vague, marginal co-data. The latter come more clearly into the focus of real presentation as real data as the continua of actual perceptions are extended, but they also pass back into the unclear, the nonpresented. According to Husserl, it is an ineradicable essential of the correlation Thing and Thing-perception to be forever incomplete. A horizon of determinable indeterminacy will principally remain, however far we go along the path of observation and perception. No God can change this, any more than He can the equation $1 + 2 = 3$.[14]

Husserl's ideas did not remain limited to philosophy but exerted a wider influence upon other fields of human knowledge. The affinity of his hypotheses to modern theories in the physical sciences is fairly obvious. Max Planck's conclusions with regard to quantum mechanics and Heisenberg's uncertainty principle (*Unschärfebeziehung*) are just two examples which show the close relationship between Husserl's philosophy and modern physical science. Approaching the social sciences from the phenomenological position we find the individual naively existing within a social reality presenting itself for interpretation to him. This interpretation is possible only if the different aspects of the world are related to the practical interests forming part of the individual's concrete historical and social situation. "Furthermore, the life-world is arranged into fields (*Zentren*) of different relevance according to my current state of interest, each one of which has its own peculiar center of density and fullness, and its open but interpretable horizons."[15]

Husserl's assertion that the thing could only be perceived in perspective variations, in one-sided shadings, was of special importance for the formation of the radical sociology of knowledge. Mannheim adapted Husserl's thesis to the procedure and method of this field. Husserl had established the idea that our perception is bound to certain spatial standpoints; Mannheim applied this finding to historical-mental objects which then manifested themselves as partially and inadequately as physical things.

14 Cf. *Ibid.*, pp. 137–138.
15 Alfred Schuetz, "Phenomenology and Social Sciences," in Farber, *op. cit.*, p. 181.

PART THREE

CONCEPTUAL
PRESUPPOSITIONS

CHAPTER 10

HISTORICISM

The Oceanic Sense for Life

K ARL MANNHEIM in writing what could be called the "Manifesto of Historicism" declared that this intellectual force epitomizes the world-view of modern man: historicism is of extraordinary importance both in the social sciences and in everyday thinking. Today it is impossible to participate in politics, even to understand a person, without recourse to historicist principles. Modern man, be he social scientist or layman, must treat all realities confronting him as having evolved and as developing dynamically. For also in daily life people use concepts with historicist implications, such as cultural behavior, capitalism, social movement, and so forth. The modern mind copes with these phenomena as potentialities that are always in flux, moving from some point in time to another. Even in our everyday thinking we strive to locate our present situation within a dynamic field and to tell time by the "cosmic clock of history." The modern attitude to life is informed by sociological categories, and sociology belongs to those systems of interpretation that ". . . increasingly dominated by the principle of historicism, reflect most faithfully our new orientation in life."[1]

Historicism, in Mannheim's description, attains more than the rank of a fashionable intellectual current; it emerges as the fundament on which modern men construct their interpretations of social and cultural reality. Historicism is not something artificially contrived, but an organically developed basic pattern; it is the modern worldview which began to determine intellectual life after the religious, medieval picture of the world had fallen apart and when the Enlightenment, with its central idea of a supratemporal Reason, had lost its persuasive power.

The first approach to a historic mode of thought and living lies in the ability to experience every segment of the spiritual-intellectual universe as in a state of flux and growth. Men have become attuned to the doctrine of historicism only since there appeared books on the evolution of customs, institutions, psychic contents, etc. But as long as we are satisfied to just register the mobility of these forces, we cannot fully understand historicism; we can only grasp this theory completely if we succeed

---

[1] Karl Mannheim, "Historicism," in Karl Mannheim, *Essays on the Sociology of Knowledge* (edited by Paul Kecskemeti), New York: Oxford University Press, 1952, p. 84.

in extracting an "ordering principle" from the anarchy of historical transformation that first meets the eye. This achievement presupposes our
ability to uncover the ". . . *innermost structure* of this all-pervading
change."[2]

The historicist knows that reason may be regarded as static or dynamic,
that it is possible to endow the theory of knowledge with a structural
priority over the philosophy of history, and that we may argue the question whether the final concept of truth, that is, the distinction of the
absolute and the relative, is conceivable only in one single form. But for
the historicist these fundamental problems and the criteria which have
a bearing upon them all depend ". . . on the attitude one takes toward
reality and on the particular field of knowledge one prefers to invoke."[3]

The optic of extreme historicism significantly reveals the existence of
an inner link connecting human aspiration and knowledge. Modern man
wants to know only in order to clarify his suprarational aspirations; he
molds the present even as long as he seemingly persists in pure contemplation: even his contemplation is a kind of activity. This brings to
mind the earlier theory of historicism that Ernst Troeltsch developed;
it was also Troeltsch's central thesis—conceptualized in his "cultural
synthesis of the present"—that historical knowledge can only be obtained
from an ascertainable intellectual location and that this knowledge presupposes a subject which views the future with definite aspirations and
actively strives to realize them: the observation of the past is determined
by the interest which the presently acting subject has in the shape of
the future.

For Mannheim, historicism is a principle which pervades every phase
of our world experience; it implies a philosophy and a worldview which
does not attempt to do violence to the new element which moves us—
the dynamic—by treating it in the spirit of the old static system as a
residue to be relativized, but tries rather to place it right in the middle
and to make it the Archimedean lever which unhinges the old worldview
to make room for a new intellectual cosmos based on supratheoretical
realities, ". . . which the suprarational genetic process in whose element
we live, again and again places at the center of our experience."[4]

Philosophical Implications of Historicism

Already the early attempts of recreating the past revealed that the
historicist method had significant philosophical implications. The method
rested upon the assumption that it was possible for the historian to enter

[2] *Ibid.*, p. 86 (emphasis in original).
[3] *Ibid.*, p. 93.
[4] *Ibid.*, p. 133.

into genuine communion with the true spirit of the works and actions he studied. To establish this understanding, however, the historian had to abandon the concepts and value standards dominating his own time, and to replace them with the concepts and values of the age under examination.

Historicism implies a complete relativism as far as values are concerned, since none have timeless validity. Furthermore, the historicist is prohibited from the direct application of any value standard he may accept for himself as a private person, when analyzing and describing the past. Where the concept of historicism reigns supreme such direct application of personal values is viewed as the deadliest sin and those who commit this sin are no longer regarded as correct interpreters and scientific historians.

It is not without interest to note that the concept of historicism has implications not unlike those contained in what American sociologists frequently call the sociological frame of reference: moral and cultural relativity, cultural behavior, etc. It is equally interesting to observe that it were mainly anthropological findings that persuaded American sociologists to fashion this relativistic frame of reference, whereas, their European colleagues initially arrived at a similar position of moral and intellectual relativism after the execution of highly abstract methodological reflections in the realms of philosophy and history.

The earlier historicists, however, did not experience this relativism as a destruction pure and simple of the values thus relativized. Once a writer of the historical school had developed the antiquarian mood in which he could view cultural products not with his own eyes but with the eyes of the denizens of bygone cultures, he was capable of sensing a greatness, a human significance, which pervaded the entire historic process throughout its changing and perishable manifestations.

This sense of greatness, of glory, could be reached only by seeing things in historical perspective: there was no other possibility of escaping a feeling of futility connected with everything human. Paul Kecskemeti explains the historicist movement as a manifestation of the Protestant religious consciousness which was unable to renounce all crutches, which still had to cling to some experience of the Absolute, after all imaginable contents of an immediate, childlike belief had been dissolved by scientific and philosophical critique. Somehow history, the cemetery of values, granted them a ghostly afterlife, once they had passed out of empirical reality. The earlier historicists realized that their destruction of the immediate, whole perspective of the simple believer was making things impossible for a creative mind: for only he can create who is able to affirm something unconditionally. But they believed that the historical process would continue to create new values ". . . toward which they would again play the role of connoisseur. Historicism recognized that it could not create; but it claimed to be alone able to do justice to the creative spirit. This was its 'utopia.' "[5]

The position of the earlier historicists was not unusual; ever since Kant preferred to speak of practical reason instead of the catechism, ever since Hegel replaced God with the Idea, German thought was a process that transformed theology into idealist philosophy. The position of the historicist became much more uncomfortable and problematic in the 1870's when the advent of positivism denuded the movement of its transcendent sanction.

Mannheim, in developing his *extreme historicism*, was heir to both the idealist tradition and the positivistic appreciation of scientific fact-finding. Consequently he experienced the unmitigated effects of relativism as a scientist and the intellectual dilemma of the modern searcher for some kind of an absolute as a philosopher. In Mannheim's hands, historicism became "subtly transformed," says Kecskemeti politely. Mannheim increasingly stressed the element of commitment, of action, as the essence of the historic process. "For him, the basic impulse toward historicism was not the need to save some possibility of communion with the Absolute, if only as the after-glow of a defunct religious tradition— although some such yearning may have been present—but rather the need to endow a progressive political creed with depth, to save it from dogmatic shallowness."[6]

In a more general view, however, we recognize that the growth of historicism relates intimately with the intellectual current that essentially originates with Kant and—running its course—dialectically connects the thoughts of Hegel, Dilthey, Windelband, Rickert, and Husserl; in this development "mind" becomes epistemologically ever more dependent and ultimately "fragmented." Beginning with a view of mind that makes it sovereign, self-sustaining, and complete, modern philosophy and social science move toward a view that makes mind reflective of time and circumstance, a view that is suspicious of the sovereignty—even the very existence—of mind and of the independence of truth: both the development of historicism as a whole and Mannheim's extreme version of it are very much part of this movement.

To fully understand the development of historicism and the problems surrounding Mannheim's "subtle transformation" of it, we must examine three essential data:

1. Historicism in the idealist tradition (earlier historicism).
2. Historicism in the positivist mood (later historicism).
3. Twentieth-century historicism (extreme historicism).

[5] Paul Kecskemeti, Introduction to Karl Mannheim, *Essays on the Sociology of Knowledge*, pp. 6–7.
[6] *Ibid.*, p. 7.

Historicism in the Idealist Tradition

Historicism—to take up the first point—reached its full bloom in the thoughtful climate created by German idealist philosophy and social science: but it did not originate there. Historicism dates back further; it must be traced back to the *original growth of historical consciousness* which begins in seriousness with the Italian philosopher Giambattista Vico and the Scottish moral philosophers—especially Adam Ferguson— and which continues through Möser, Herder, and Goethe into the thought of Hegel. These *early historicists* discovered that an understanding of history had to be based on the concepts of *evolution* and *individuality*. The new emphasis on the individual worth of each historical epoch superseded the idea of immutable laws and terminated the rule of the one and timeless Reason; it also replaced the faith in a linear form of progress. The early historicists claimed that the *organic* growth of history imparts an unmistakable *meaning* to the succession of works and actions; they were calmly convinced that many different meaningful manifestations exist side by side. In this mood they accepted the worth of a *plurality of absolutes* and their enjoyment of manifold historic phenomena widened the perspective which now fully revealed the wisdom and beauty residing in the empirical world.

Of signal importance for this entire development was the French Revolution of 1789, which generated the specifically new awareness of the epochal importance of the times; this valiant and victorious attack upon the old world order also ignited the minds of most young intellectuals in the rest of Europe, and the youthful thinkers of Germany—among them Hegel—enthusiastically followed the progressive swell of political ideas; it was only the misery of political reality—particularly in Germany—that was soon to turn their thinking into sour reactionary ideology.

In this context it was above all the philosophy of Hegel which—to use the words of Karl Jaspers—formulated an ". . . historical consciousness of the epoch, giving expression to an unprecedented wealth of historical content in the extraordinarily supple and forcibly expressive dialectic method, which was charged with the effect of a conviction that the present had a unique significance."[7]

Hegel begins his intellectual labors with the Kantian assumption that the world is a unity conceivable only with reference to a knowing subject; but he adds a new idea of decisive magnitude: this unity is in a process of continual historic transformation. Philosophy in this key owes its existence to a pair of novel preoccupations: the concern with ideas reflecting the complex processes which determine the life of social groups and the desire to cope with historical and political currents of thought.

[7] Karl Jaspers, *Man in the Modern Age* (translated by Eden and Cedar Paul), A Doubleday Anchor Book, Garden City, N.Y., 1957, p. 8.

It is true that in the immediate view Hegel's philosophy appears as the definitive expression of the historical consciousness of a great epoch; but there is an undertow in his thinking which announces the coming of another, more relativist form of historicism:

> Whatever happens, every individual is a child of his time; so philosophy too is its own time apprehended in thoughts. It is just as absurd to fancy that a philosophy can transcend its contemporary world as it is to fancy that an individual can overleap his own age, jump over Rhodes. If his theory really goes beyond the world as it is and builds an ideal one as it ought to be, that world exists indeed, but only in his opinions, an unsubstantial element where anything you please may, in fancy, be built.[8]

Still, in revealing the unity of time and philosophy, Hegel consumed the desire of the early historicists to grasp the meaning and individual worth of each historical epoch: with him philosophy became epochal consciousness. The early historicists from Vico to Hegel shared a decisive assumption: the historic process possessed a deeper meaning.

This assumption still characterized the thinking of the *second generation* of historicists—men who are known as the pioneers of modern historical method, as the founders of historical schools in various academic disciplines.

It is a disciple of Justus Möser, Barthold Georg Niebuhr who is conventionally regarded as the creator of modern historiography; he was influenced by the founder of the historical school of jurisprudence, Friedrich Karl von Savigny, whose romaticism in the study of the evolution of legal and political institutions and brilliant application of the historical method to the exposition of the Roman law had a significant effect upon Niebuhr. Wilhelm von Humboldt called the Danish Niebuhr in 1810 to the newly established Friedrich Wilhelm University: in Berlin, Niebuhr published the first two volumes of his *Roman History*—the first book to combine the best of the newer critical methods with the constructive principles of basic institutional history. Niebuhr's work was the main source of inspiration for the historical labors of his famous successors, Leopold von Ranke and Theodor Mommsen.

Two of the fundamental characteristics in the historical methodology of Ranke are of special importance for the further development of historicism: first, his conception derived from the *romanticists* that every nation and era is under the spell of a dominant complex of ideas (the *"Zeitgeist"*) and, second, his postulate that the historian must view the past entirely freed from the prejudices of his own time and must portray the events of the past "as it truly was" (*"wie es eigentlich gewesen ist"*).

Together with strategically placed allies—such as Karl Ritter, the

[8] G. W. F. Hegel, *Philosophy of Right,* (translated with notes by T. M. Knox), London: Oxford University Press, 1953, p. 11.

founder of comparative geography, and August Böckh, who transformed philology into a useful tool for reconstructing the ancient cultures—these men brought historicism in the idealist tradition to its full bloom.

These *earlier historicists* taught that human activities could only be understood and explained by reference to the dynamic and ever-changing flux and flow of history—itself an outgrowth of the individuals' free will, the unique national heritage, and specific historic situations. In this climate of opinion Ranke pictured the nation-state as a living thing: an individual, a unique self.

In the field of economics the "timeless," abstract propositions of classical theory lost their hold over the imagination of men and thinkers like Leonard Simonde de Sismondi, Arnold Toynbee, Richard Jones, and Friedrich List initiated the movement that was to replace these static notions with the insight that the proper method was inductive and historical. Influenced by Hegelian philosophy and later by the theory of evolution, the members of the "older" historical school in Germany— Wilhelm Roscher, Bruno Hildebrand, and Karl Knies—substituted *"historical evolution"* for the allegedly universal concepts of the classical economists such as "economic man" and "economic law"; instead they emphasized the relativity of such generalizations and in general ridiculed the element of absolutism in the doctrines of Adam Smith and his peers and disciples. In the new view economic theories appeared as socially determined knowledge that must change with historical alterations in the socio-economic constitution of societies.

The work of the earlier historicists was above all dominated by the desire to understand the leading ideas behind the diversity of historic phenomena: Ranke portrayed men as the expressive agents of significant ideas; the philologist Böckh searched for the central idea governing the development of civilizations; and scholars like Savigny and Niebuhr joined in the ultimate endeavor to grasp the total spirit of a nation and to reveal the secret pattern of its organic growth. Wilhelm von Humboldt, whose philological studies were the first in this field to be based on history, philosophy, and the budding anthropological sciences, demonstrated the significance of the historian's creative imagination and, thereby, revealed the essential talent that sparked the labors of the entire group.[9]

Ranke's aphorism, *"Jede Epoche ist unmittelbar zu Gott"* (Every epoch is in immediate communion with God), finally showed that the pantheistic spirit of Goethe's interpretation of history was still very much alive in the thinking of the earlier historicists. Similarly Hegel had found the innermost secret of world history in the historical unfolding of the spirit: the progress of the spirit gave meaning to world events.

[9] Cf. Wilhelm von Humboldt, "Über die Aufgabe des Geschichtsschreibers," *Abhandlungen der Königlichen Akademie der Wissenschaft zu Berlin: Historisch-Philologische Klasse*, 1820–1821, Berlin: B. Behrs Verlag, 1822, pp. 314–321.

Hegel's very thesis provided the radical faction of his followers with the lever that was to unhinge the idealist worldview; the *Young Hegelians* tore down the walls surrounding the realm of absolutist metaphysics, thereby making possible its penetration with positivist philosophy and the further transformation of historicism. Reversing the position of their master, the Young Hegelians turned to world events to give meaning to the progress of the spirit. They simultaneously discovered the misery of world events and came to advocate moral, political, and social revolution. Suddenly philosophy moved to the beat of a new and nervous rhythm: revolution will give meaning to world events, thereby meaning to the progress of the spirit; concrete, empirical time now measures reason in history—and reason in history equals reason in revolution.

The destruction of Hegel's philosophy took place in three phases: first, Arnold Ruge and Ludwig Feuerbach transformed Hegel's philosophy in the realistic spirit of the new era, which was dominated by the materialistic interests of the physical sciences, commerce, and industry. Second, Bruno Bauer and Max Stirner (Johann Kaspar Schmidt) steered all of philosophy into the night of radical criticism and nihilism. Finally, Karl Marx and Sören Kierkegaard realized the extreme consequences of the changed situation: Marx demolished the bourgeois-capitalistic world and Kierkegaard dismantled the bourgeois-Christian universe.

The entire development of historicism up to this point found an interesting "personal history" in the intellectual career of Wilhelm Dilthey. This philosopher began his early work on religious grounds but went through an important transition during the years 1859–1861, which led to the replacement of God by the idea and the formulation of his life philosophy that viewed ideas as forces growing out of life.

Thus, Dilthey arrived at the proposition that the conditions which determine historical reality originate in the subject of cognition—in man. This attempt to approach thought from life was an important prerequisite for the idea that thought is existentially determined. Together with Marx —who added the thesis that modern life reveals itself most genuinely in social existence—Dilthey thus established the basis for extreme historicism and the sociology of knowledge.

From Positivist to Extreme Historicism

The earlier historicists had exposed the mind to the full impact of history; the problematic consequences of this exposure already registered during the later phase of this development. The advent of *historicism in the positivist mood*—to turn to the second major point— fully revealed these problematic ramifications. The positivist onslaught killed not only the remnants of the pantheistic and universalistic spirit of Goethe's era, where history had been understood as the unfolding of God in time, but all metaphysical presuppositions, and in the end—moving far beyond Comte's position—it even corroded the will to arrive at any kind of theoretical decision.

This *later historicism* reached its maturity in the 1870's; its exponents glorified the industrious gathering of empirical data and succeeded in flooding the human mind with unassimilated historical "knowledge." This development found an especially dramatic expression in the changes that took place in economics during that time. The "younger" historical school established its hegemony and its members zealously promoted the historically objective and statistically realistic method of research that was soon to lead to the production of an endless series of purely descriptive monographs. This new generation of intellectual workers openly declared that the formulation of generalizations by way of induction had to be postponed until the accumulation of an immense body of data was completed. In their enthusiasm for the compilation of exhaustive collections of economic and statistical facts the members of the younger historical school forgot more and more that meaningful scientific production calls not only for objective fact-finding but also for realistic theorizing.

The accumulation of material dragged on through the years and by 1900 even Gustav Schmoller—the leader of the school—lost his patience with what was finally deteriorating into a dusty display of historico-statistical curios; moving away from his disciples he declared that economics had to be more than a branch of historical knowledge: if the economist was to adequately treat the diverse aspects of the economic life of men, he needed a variety of methods as well as a judicious measure of theoretical imagination—a trait that the more outstanding members of the school such as Lujo Brentano had still possessed and that had enabled Karl Bücher to explain the evolution of the principal stages of economic organization; it was precisely this trait that empowered Max Weber to break through these limiting confines into the open space of the social scientific frontier.

This later historicism developed another defect: an aestheticism that was exemplified by the creation of a purely contemplative attitude toward history which prevented any kind of participation on the part of the observer and transformed historical interpretation into an aimless search for what had occurred in the past. All supertemporal values and truths were denied since all was seen as historically determined and changeable—the doors to relativism and pessimism swung wide open; Oswald Spengler took over the philosophy of history and announced *The Decline of the West*.

Reason itself—the element that supposedly linked all men—suffered a remarkable loss of status. The earlier historicists had organically related the diverse manifestations of history to a transcendent unity, thereby finding reason and meaning in the plurality of absolutes. The mechanistic thinkers of positivism renounced the idea of a universal, cosmic reason and experienced the same pluralism as a meaningless aggregate of phenomena, as a mere chaos of worldviews.

Our century opened with Spengler's fragmentation of historic reality into a series of disconnected events; shortly after the publication of his pessimistic work the three major expositions of *twentieth-century historicism* appeared: in 1919, Florian Znaniecki prepared his entrance into the sociology of knowledge with his book *Cultural Reality*, a resolute philosophical presentation of historico-cultural relativism. Three years later Ernst Troeltsch developed his theory of historicism which bound historical interpretation to the socio-historical standpoint, present activity, and future aspirations of the observer.[10] In 1924, Karl Mannheim formulated his *extreme historicism* as the expression of a new attitude to the world which leads to the sociological attempt of building up an intellectual cosmos centered around such supratheoretical realities as biological generation, social class, historical time, economic striving, religious outlook, and political commitment.[11]

Mannheim's discussion of his central principle—extreme historicism—is also a document which reveals the frustration that he experienced when faced with the inevitable result of the march of ideas and reality factors: relativism. Mannheim knew that relativism was there in all its stark reality, but as a typical product of the idealist social science tradition he could not fully rid himself of the yearning for an absolute. What he did not know was that modern man would have to start living with relativism as the logical product of intellectual and social evolution. Thus the promoter of extreme historicism came to battle relativism—the consequence of his own position. What Mannheim did know, however, was the fact that this issue cannot be solved theoretically: he abandoned the arena of thought and philosophical argumentation and adopted an activistic, atheoretical attitude. Irrationally, his ultimate criterion of "truth" was that of the pragmatists—action: ". . . only a philosophy which is able to give a concrete answer to the question 'what shall we do?' can put forward the claim to have overcome relativism."[12]

---

[10] Cf. Florian Znaniecki, *Cultural Reality*, Chicago: University of Chicago Press, 1919. Ernst Troeltsch, *Der Historismus und seine Probleme. Erstes Buch: Das logische Problem der Geschichtsphilosophie*, Tübingen: J. C. B. Mohr, 1922.

[11] Cf. Karl Mannheim, "Historismus," *Archiv für Sozialwissenschaft und Sozialpolitik*, Vol. 52, No. 1 (June, 1924), pp. 1ff.

[12] Mannheim, *op. cit.*, pp. 128–129.

CHAPTER 11

IDEOLOGY
The Twilight of Ideas

Since the dawn of Western intellectual history the idea, which is something we see in the mind's eye, has figured prominently. The Greeks and their intellectual heirs saw the idea, or the intelligible, as the real, the perfect; the particular was considered deficient, only apparent. From its start in *Pythagorean mathematics* and *Socratic thought* the theory of ideas has been suspicious of immediate, actual reality—the sensible. Thus Pythagoras found the proof of his theorem not in any "real" physically manifest triangle; any actual drawing is no more but an approximate copy of the mental image, of the perfect triangle as seen with the mind's eye, of the *idea* of the perfect triangle.

The theory of ideas was not left unchallenged and even Plato did not always stick to its implications. But despite this early uncertainty the dominance of ideas continued and even the critical renegade Aristotle asserted that forms are more important than matter, which is merely raw material. But forms are unchanging, eternal entities which exist as creative substances independent of particular things.

Everyday language places the word "idea" close to the world "ideal." The history of thought shows that for a long time there existed a similar proximity in the intellectual realm. The theoreticians of ideas for once were simultaneously preoccupied with ideals. This holds true for the Greeks and the medieval philosophers. As explained in the simile of the cave, the light which gives us truth stands for the idea of the Good. For the ideal man—the philosopher who rules the ideal state—this *idea* is also the ultimate *ideal* which governs his life. Moreover, in philosophy, the word idealism applies to those systems of thought in which all nature and experience are explained with the help of ideas, or products of the mind. Plato conceived of a universe of immutable ideas as the only reality. Medieval realists postulated a similar world in their concept of universals. In all these philosophical systems, however, the proximity to ethics is apparent: the epistemological and ontological propositions intimately connect with ethical propositions and ideals.

The Preparation of Ideology

Classical idealism placed ideal reality outside and transcendent to the world of experience. The central assumption was: *ideas determine reality* (the world of sensory experience, the sensible). Premonitory rumblings of the intellectual revolution which was to reverse this proposition can be heard throughout history but the decisive turn came with the *philosophy of consciousness*. The *modern* idealist philosophers placed ideal reality in the consciousness of man.

In John Locke's *Essay Concerning Human Understanding*, begun in 1671, we have the first outright attempt at setting forth the limitations of the mind. In this first "manifesto of doubt" Locke critically discusses what inquiries it is possible for man to pursue. The optimism of the rationalists is thus severely challenged. The terms idea and idealism take on a new meaning.

Locke based knowledge strictly on experience and consequently he had to reject the recollected or innate ideas of the theoreticians of ideas from Plato to Descartes and Leibniz. According to Locke the mind is to begin with like a clean sheet of paper. It is experience that provides the mind with contents and Locke calls these mental contents ideas, employing the term in a very wide sense. He furthermore divides ideas into two basic types, according to their objects. Ideas of the first type are derived from the observation of the external world through our senses and they are known as *ideas of sensation,* whereas the other kind are called *ideas of reflection* and these arise when the mind observes itself. Up to this point Locke had hardly left the traditional premises of philosophy: already an old scholastic formula maintained that nothing is in the mind unless it has come through the senses, and Leibniz had added a qualification excepting the mind itself from the general formula. Of importance and startling novelty, however, was the claim made by the empiricists that the senses constitute the sole sources of knowledge. It is the essential assertion of empiricism that in the course of our thinking and speculation we can never transcend the confines of what we have gathered through sensation and reflection.

Then the eighteenth-century English philosopher George Berkeley introduces the idea that the objective or natural world has its existence in the consciousness of individuals. In the *Principles of Human Knowledge*, published in 1710, Berkeley claims that for something to exist is the same as its being perceived. Reality is now coextensive with what can be experienced.

David Hume was led to inquire into the scope and limitations of man's mental apparatus by a prospective science of man. Hume denied the rationalists' assumption that there are close connections between things which can be known. He seriously doubted the existence of such connections and argued that, even if there were, we could never know them. All man can know, Hume maintained, are successions of impressions or ideas, and it is, therefore, idle even to consider the question whether there are other, deeper connections or not.

So the arguments of Locke, Berkeley, and Hume give rise to a wave of doubt that reaches its crashing climax in the philosophies of Kant, Hegel, and the historicists. With the development of a philosophy of consciousness the objective ontological unity of the world is rapidly demolished. The new unity is one imposed by the perceiving subject. In the place of the classical, and medieval-Christian objective ontological unity of the universe, there came forth the subjective unity of the absolute subject of the Enlightenment: *consciousness in itself*.

Now the world exists only with reference to the knowing mind, and the mental activity of the subject determines the form in which the world appears. When Kant relates the world to a fictitious "consciousness in itself" we witness the conclusion of the first stage in the dissolution of an ontological dogmatism regarding the world as existing independently of us, in a fixed and definitive form. Henceforth, the terms idea and ideal no longer suffice to characterize the storm of events. With Kant the conception of ideology emerges. His forerunners had already broken the classical notion that ideas determine reality: Locke, Berkeley, and Hume taught that ideas were determined *by* reality. Then Kant introduced his subject, consciousness in itself, which in the course of his experience with the world evolves the principles of organization that enable him to understand it. The second stage in the development of the conception of ideology is attained when the supertemporal notion of ideology is seen in historical perspective: this is largely the accomplishment of Hegel and of the *Historical School*.

We have seen the close connection between ideas and ideals in classical idealism. For Plato ideas, being eternal and unchangeable, are outside space and time; they are the object of all longing and aspiration, the object of all real knowledge, and they are also the forms in which the one final and absolutely real Being, the supreme Idea of the Good, manifests itself. The world of Plato's ideas is a world of values and Plato's teaching aimed mainly at defining the good life for the individual and for society.

We have seen how the emerging philosophy of consciousness reverses the proposition: ideas determine reality, into, reality determines ideas. From here we reach the concept of ideology; ideologies have been provisionally defined as ideas which are determined by reality.[1]

The relationship between ideas and ideologies is a complex story. We

[1] Cf. Raymond Aron, *German Sociology* (translated by Mary and Thomas Bottomore), New York: The Free Press of Glencoe, 1957, p. 52.

will therefore defer the analysis of this relationship till later and first ask: How do ideologies connect with ideals?

Ideologies and Ideals

In a general way, the term "ideologies" denotes complexes of ideals that channel behavior toward the maintenance of the existing social order. Historical and sociological analyses have shown that practically all societies try to indoctrinate their members, especially the young, with ideologies: systems of belief that express a particular worldview; ideologies can energize a society, make it cohesive, and give it a fighting strength. In an equally general way, the companion term "utopias" refers to complexes of ideals which inspire desires and activities that aim at changes of the existing social order: revolutionary groups, trying to subvert and overthrow the prevailing social order indoctrinate their followers with utopias.

Sociologists know that the real or overt behavior of people is most of the time different from their ideal or professed behavior; the ideological analyst is equally aware of the frequency of ideological distortion. We have a case of ideological distortion in the attempts to overcome frictions ". . . and anxieties by having recourse to absolutes, according to which it is no longer possible to live. This is the case when we create 'myths,' worship 'greatness in itself,' avow allegiance to 'ideals,' while in our actual conduct we are following other interests which we try to mask by simulating an unconscious righteousness, which is only too easily transparent."[2]

Technicians of power-politics, well aware of the fact that men may possess ideas but are possessed by ideals, have always advocated the exploitation of this dichotomy in human behavior. Long before the days of Machiavelli the ruling groups used and discarded ideals in the same way they used and discarded weapons. Gibbon informs us that the ruling elite in the Roman Empire were entirely sceptical and cynical of emperor-worship, yet in their overt behavior the members of the ruling group went through the forms of the religious ritual. They realized that the maintenance of the existing social order, so beneficial to the elite, was only possible as long as the mass of the population continued to believe in the faith.

The modern world is permeated with ideologies: its totalitarian half consists of cultures where the underlying population is divided into those who have been thoroughly indoctrinated with a particular ideology and

[2] Karl Mannheim, *Ideology and Utopia: An Introduction to the Sociology of Knowledge* (translated by Louis Wirth and Edward Shils), 7th impression, London: Routledge & Kegan Paul, 1954, p. 86.

others who are forced by state power to make an overt show of acceptance. The other half of the world is dominated by a few (technologically) developed nations whose ruling economic groups are sceptical of majority rule; abroad, the economic elite favor, more often than not, conservative regimes of an undemocratic nature that are engaged in and permissive of socio-economic exploitation. At home, the elite make only the most unavoidable concessions to the underlying population by providing a minimum of economic security. For the rest, the ruling groups employ the opinion and entertainment industries to manipulate and channel the thought processes of the masses.

With the widespread acceptance of Functionalism, sociological theory now offers a view of society that narrows our vision to the ideas of order, stability, and integration. In this simplified analytical frame all social systems consist of elements contributing to the maintenance of the fragile equilibrium of social structure. A conservative mood already permeated the limited axioms of Social Action Theory prepared by Max Weber in Wilhelminian Germany, and further developed by American sociologists as an expression of the dominant mood of American society.

With the subsequent appearance of the Functional School, however, the suspicion has definitely arisen that ". . . sociology, instead of pointing to alternatives of development, revealing the imperfections of the present, and insisting on the reality of change, has become an ideology of complacency with the *status quo*, and a (however involuntary) tool of the powers that be."[3]

In similar fashion the so-called empirical sociologists operate within a field which is as narrow and fragmented as the interests of the bureaucracies and foundations paying for their expensive and inflated research apparatus. Here research problems are for the most part initiated by the commercial or administrative concerns of outsiders and independent scholars are replaced by research technicians for hire. Nothing could better document the exhaustion of the intellectual attitude than the growing practice to clothe safe $100 ideas in $100,000 grants.

The understanding of the modern "ideological climate" will be aided by the further question: How do ideologies connect with ideas?

Ideologies and Ideas

Regarding their relationship with ideas we may initially distinguish two meanings of the term ideology:

[3] Ralf Dahrendorf, "European Sociology and the American Self-Image," *European Journal of Sociology*, Vol. II, No. 2 (Fall, 1961), p. 343. Reprinted from the *European Journal of Sociology*, II (1961), pp. 324–366.

1. Ideologies can be regarded as (false) ideas which serve as the weapons of a society or a social class.
2. Ideologies can be the manifestation of false consciousness or the refusal to see reality as it is.

The first meaning of the term ideology is usually applicable to a historical situation, where a ruling elite attempt to maintain the prevailing social order and the exploitation of an underlying population through the deliberate creation and dissemination of misleading ideas; a false picture of reality is suggested to the masses. The ruling elite employ usually a specialized group of professionals who are experts in ideological distortion; historically these professional ideologists have appeared in a great variety of disguises: from Hindu priests to public relations men.

False consciousness, on the other hand, is most blatantly manifest in the attitudes of individuals who belong to the less successful groups and social classes; here persons tend to incorrectly interpret their own self and their roles to cover up their "real" relations to themselves and to the world and to falsify to themselves the basic facts of human life by romanticizing, idealizing, or deifying them. Unable to face up to disappointing, often unbearable, life situations, persons resort to the device of escape from themselves and reality, thereby conjuring up false interpretations of experience. Historically this escapist weakness ranges from the attempts of the mystic to find release from misery in the beyond to the self-destructive blindness and dishonest conceit of the underprivileged office hireling who refuses to join a union because he imagines himself to be part of the status whirl of management.

In a concrete case the two variants of ideology typically combine to create an ideological climate: the ruling elite are able to successfully suggest a false, misleading picture of reality because of the willingness of the underlying population to exchange reality for antiquated and inapplicable norms, modes of thought, and conceptions of life which have the function of obscuring and hiding the actual meaning of conduct rather than of revealing it.

Advanced ideological analysis has, however, discovered that ruling groups can in their thinking become so intensively interest-bound to a situation that *they* are simply no longer able to see certain facts which would undermine their sense of domination. This discovery leads from the simple theory of ideology with its emphasis on patterns of fraudulent dominance and self-deceptive submission to the sociological method in the study of intellectual phenomena.

Essentially, the concept of ideology emerged from political struggle; as we now turn to the history of the concept—as we must to reveal the transition from simple ideological theory to sociological method—we shall notice that the suspicion of ideology grows more formidable with increasing bitterness of political conflict.

The Unfolding of Ideology

When the word ideology first appeared it was nothing more than a term denoting the subject matter of the theory of ideas. It was Destutt de Tracy who founded a school of thought in French philosophy which was dedicated to the science of ideas; according to this school "ideology" was the generic term applicable to the science of ideas.[4] In 1801, Destutt de Tracy set forth his theory of ideas in a book entitled, *Les éléments de l'idéologie* . . .

Napoleon found that the men of this school were opposing his imperial ambitions and reacted by giving a new meaning to the term ideology: he used the word sarcastically and contemptuously to ridicule the ideologists around Destutt de Tracy as impractical, unrealistic, and foolish idealists. The political, derogatory meaning of the term ideology had been born. Initially, then, the defamation was hurled at the men of scholarly theory and contemplation and the attackers were political men of action representing that practical irrationality which has so little understanding for ideas as instruments for the mastery of reality.

The study of the theoretical implications of this contempt shows that the depreciation concerns the validity of the opponent's thought because it is regarded as unrealistic. Since the accusation is that of the irrational politician, this means that it is "unrealistic" in contrast to practice and the activities of the political sphere. Here the politician, the man of practical affairs, labels all thought, especially when dangerous to his power, "ideology," and claims that reality can only be grasped through practical activity.

After Napoleon's days the term ideology, used in this derogatory fashion, gained wide acceptance: the political criterion of reality with its implicit pragmatism pushed aside the scholar's contemplative modes of thought and life. Increasingly, the problem concerning reality was solved by recourse to practice and to the propositions of pragmatism and, more and more, the concept of ideology was used as a weapon to demolish the ideas of an enemy.

More importantly, the history of the concept ideology shows that the Enlightenment represents a major source of origin. The French philosophers of the Enlightenment viewed "ideological" distortion of thought— or prejudice as they actually called it—as a *psychological* problem: man deceives himself when he permits prejudices and superstitions to penetrate his reason. They distinguished three causes of prejudice: idols, interests, and priestly fraud. These they considered the causal determinants creating a psychological sphere of error that clouds man's perception and his grasp on reality.

[4] Cf. Picavet, *Les idéologues: essai sur l'histoire des idées et des théories scientifiques, philosophiques, réligieuses en France depuis 1789*, Paris: Alcan, 1891.

The concept of *idols* has an even earlier origin; it stems from Francis Bacon's theory of the *Idola Mentis;* the idols are "illusions," "phantoms," or "preconceptions" that hinder the attainment of true knowledge. Bacon, therefore, figures prominently as a precursor of the conception of ideology. The theory of idols, however, was a minor strand in the thought of the French Enlightenment movement. Here much greater emphasis was placed on the theory of priestly fraud and the analysis of vested interests.

The antecedents of this analytical frame date back to the *Renaissance* where the close observation of political life stimulated a new critical awareness of the "ideological" element in human thinking. In his *Discourses*, Machiavelli relates that the people of the Renaissance began to use a common sense adage which distinguished critically between the thought of the *palace* and that of the *public square*. This distinction reflects the mood of a public that was beginning to "find out" the secrets of politics. Here we are already confronted with the beginning of the process in the course of which, what had formerly been merely an occasional outburst of suspicion and scepticism toward public statements developed into a systematic investigation of the ideological element in all utterances. This process was greatly advanced by the French philosophers who transformed the naive distrust and suspicion which men everywhere evidence towards their adversaries, at all stages of historical development, into a systematic *particular notion of ideology*, which, however, remained on the psychological plane: in their "ideological" theory the philosophers accused the adversary of conscious or unconscious falsification; in their attempts to reveal the source of error, distortion was uncovered only on the psychological plane by pointing out the personal roots of intellectual bias. The philosophers still considered the adversary capable of thinking correctly; they did not discredit the total structure of his consciousness; their attack did not yet extend into the cognitive sphere.

The psychological theory of the Enlightenment found a curious "afterlife" in the irrationalistic theory of ideology as developed by Nietzsche, Pareto, and Sorel. These writers also assumed that vital interests obscure true knowledge, but, in contrast to the Enlightenment thinkers, they did not propose to remedy this situation. Quite the opposite, the authors of the irrationalistic theory of ideology claimed that men are condemned to a twilight existence: they must live *with* ideological distortion, deception, lies.

The falsest judgements are most significant; without the constant falsification of the world, man could not exist; error and illusion maintain and foster life: this is Nietzsche's position from where the elimination of ideology appears suicidal, a position that helps us to understand the fictionalism of Vaihinger's "philosophy of as if." In Pareto's view man exists thanks to his ability to deceive himself and others. Sorel's values are error and illusion: the myth; all historically significant actions emerge from errors and deceptions; the masses will only respond to a myth, never to scientific truth.

Suddenly the political men of action, these masters of practical irrationality, discovered the intellectual world; the practitioners of political and ideological totalitarianism, in particular, had found their cerebral heroes. There was, of course, Freud—a lonely man in dimly lit, almost empty lecture halls, who set out to counterattack the spiritual regimentation oozing from the irrationalistic theories of ideology. Regarding ideology Freud returned to the position of the Enlightenment. Investigating the powerful motivating forces of the individual which operate beneath the surface, he came to view this surface not only as revealing but also as concealing and "masking" reality. Freud debunked the significance of what can easily be perceived; he demolished the facade of the merely extant and all the time he was driven by the desire to penetrate into the hidden uniformities of human existence. His aim was also therapeutical: to restore man to his full stature as a healthy human being. During the larger part of his career Freud investigated the world in the optimistic, humanitarian spirit of the Enlightenment; up to his final years—which, however, were overshadowed by the dark pessimism of the cancer patient—Freud studied reality in order to improve it. This devotion to the future brought the spirit of the Enlightenment back into the life of the twentieth century.

The psychological theories of ideology from Bacon to Holbach, Sorel, and Freud have two elements in common: they are all ahistorical and they all imply, as we saw, that it is basically possible (not necessarily desirable) to perceive truth. The *ahistorical* element is first of all, part and parcel of the conception of Enlightenment: Enlightenment is not the result of a unique historical constellation, it is a timeless postulate.

The intellectual leaders of the movement saw the past in the main as a nonhistorical, static darkness and did not visualize any historical movement of significance for the future.[5] Once man jumps from the past darkness of error and superstition into the light of truth and reason the climax has been reached and history "ends." With the irrationalist reversal of all values—within the psychological theory—even this momentary flash of historical significance vanishes and all that remains is the totally ahistorical concept of *eternal recurrence* (Nietzsche) or the unending meaningless *cycle of elites* (Pareto). Similarly, the representatives of the Enlightenment accepted the idea that human nature was everywhere and at any time the same. In man there is always the struggle between a psychological depth-layer of interests and willings and a rational super-

[5] The thinkers of the Enlightenment, however, produced significant historical writings of which examples can be found in Hume's *History of England*, Gibbon's *Decline and Fall of the Roman Empire*, and Voltaire's *Essai sur les moeurs*.

structure of intellectual mastery. Enlightenment means the victory of the intellect over our basic drives and appetites. In a final analysis the psychological theorists never questioned the possibility of a science which could reveal and eliminate all ideological distortions. In this respect the psychological concept of ideology never cast the shadow of doubt over the logic and method of science itself. In the terminology of Karl Mannheim the psychological concept of ideology was, therefore, only "particular" and never "total."

The Reign of Ideology

It is, however, the total concept of ideology which makes possible the sociological method in the study of intellectual phenomena—a method that, in principle, was first discovered by politics. Essentially, it was political conflict that led men to an awareness of the unconscious collective motivations which had always guided the direction of thought. Political argumentation is at all times more than theoretical discussion. Political argumentation demolishes disguises, and unmasks the unconscious motives that connect the existence of the group with its cultural aspirations and its theoretical arguments. To the extent, however, that modern politics fought its battles with theoretical weapons (such as those furnished by Hegel and Marx), the process of unmasking penetrated to the social roots of theory.

The further development of ideology is, then, also a result of political and social conditions: the suspicion of ideology grows more formidable, the more groups are drifting apart. Only in a world of upheaval, in which fundamental new values are being created and old ones destroyed, can intellectual conflict go so far that antagonists will try to annihilate not merely the specific beliefs and attitudes of one another but also the intellectual foundations upon which these beliefs and attitudes rest: the total concept of ideology implies a more thoroughgoing annihilation since the attack extends into the cognitive sphere, discredits the total structure of the adversary's consciousness, and undermines the validity of his theories by showing that they are merely a function of the generally prevailing social situation.

It is only after the flowing together of two powerful currents that this decisive stage in the history of modes of thought is reached. The *psychological theories of ideology* constitute one of these currents; the other current consists of the *historical theories of ideology* and can be traced back to the Christian dogma asserting the omnipotence of God.[6] God is omnipotent and determines human thinking and action to the fullest extent; man is not a free agent but a tool in the hands of God. This

[6] Cf. Ernst Grünwald, *Das Problem der Soziologie des Wissens*, Wien-Leipzig: Wilhelm Braumüller, 1934.

reasoning suggests the important conclusion that human error and human wrongdoing are also part of God's plan of salvation (G. E. Lessing). In contrast, most psychological theories pictured ideology as the result of deliberate or unwitting deception which had really no place in the scheme of things. The French philosophers, furthermore, believed that ideology so conceived, could be eliminated. The historical type of theory, on the other hand, rests anciently upon the assumption that error and deception, that ideology, are an outgrowth of God's will, and therefore, inevitable, irremovable.

The Christians possessed a transcendent guarantee of truth: God. He, or rather his self-appointed representatives on earth, decided whether a judgement was true or false; they also pronounced individuals and groups as being in error. Once God had cursed a person or group with blindness, all the utterances of this person or group were false and no earthly power could eliminate the "ideological" distortion. In this Christian universe, there was no room for doubt; everybody could easily orient himself, as long as he accepted the authoritarian decree of truth.

The important change occurs in Hegel's philosophy. Hegel secularizes the old religious conception of the "planned universe" and replaces the Christian God with *reason*. Also man changes roles: he is no longer the tool of God, but the agent of reason. Now it is the cunning of reason that operates behind the backs of men. In the new scheme of things all human activities have only one purpose: to make it possible for reason to fulfill its historical mission, which is the attainment of full consciousness for itself. As this process takes place in history, *historical consciousness* now enters the picture.

It is this current of thought that makes it possible for Hegel to replace Kant's abstract concept "consciousness in itself" with his less inclusive and *historically* differentiated concept "national consciousness" (*Volksgeist*). It is the same current of thought that eventually makes it necessary for Marx to see the world with the eye of an even less inclusive and *socially* differentiated concept: "class consciousness."

Marx actually reverses Hegel's philosophy: the meaning of history is no longer to be found in the "process of absolute spirit" but in the "real life-process." This real life-process is nothing but the *modes of production*. The modes of production, then, take the place of Hegel's reason; their development constitutes the content of history. The modes of production, or more generally, social existence, are the ontically most real substructure and everything that exists *qua superstructure*—above this substructure—is less real. The content of the superstructure, or to put it bluntly, all ideas, have been reduced to a mere manifestation of the substructure. In Marx's view, human thought floats above the concrete existential level and it is, therefore, *ideological*.

With Marx the *concept of ideology has become total:* all ideas are inevitably ideological since they are fatefully suspended in mid-air, floating "above" the ontically real level of social existence. Ideas merely reflect the thinker's position in the "process of production" or his class position; the *entire* mind is ideological.

In Marx's case, the relationship between ideological analysis and political argumentation is especially close. Political discussants try not only to be in the right but also to demolish the basis of the opponent's social and intellectual existence; they do not merely weigh the theoretical relevance of an argument: they seek to penetrate into the existential foundation of thinking. Political conflict is a struggle for special predominance and in this struggle we assault the enemy's social status, his public prestige, and his self-confidence. Political argumentation reflects the will to psychic annihilation and attacks the entire life-situation of the opponent, hoping to corrode his social position along with the demolition of his theories. In political conflict attention is aimed not only at the adversary's utterances but also at his group connections and his potential actions. Political discussants view thought in connection with the mode of existence to which it is bound.

Marx used the new, the total method of ideological analysis as an intellectual weapon in the interest of the group he believed to represent: the working class or, as he preferred to say, the proletariat. This political commitment arrested the development of the concept of ideology in Marx's thinking. For him ideological analysis was in the main a strategic device in the class struggle. Therefore, he had to limit the destructive effects of this analysis so that it would only hurt the enemy: the middle class or *bourgeoisie.*

Again, Marx uses and transforms Hegelian thoughts; where Hegel had insisted on a *personal* guarantee of truth, Marx claims a *collective* guarantee of truth: the group that is on the "right side of history," the group that is in tune with the economic process, is not subject to the charge of ideology. At the close of the Middle Ages, the bourgeoisie had functioned as the collective guarantor of truth—advancing history, understanding and mastering the economic process; today the bourgeois is as uncomprehending and blind to his fate as the feudal lord he once carted to the guillotine. Today, says Marx, only the interests of the proletariat coincide with the real life-process of history; now the working class is the agent of history and, therefore, the ideas of proletarian thinkers are not ideological but "true."

Such was the state of ideological analysis: the concept of ideology was total; Marx used it to accuse the entire mind of being ideological— he sensed in the enemy's total behavior an unreliability which he regarded as a function of the social situation in which the adversary found himself. Yet, Marx's concept was limited or "special" since it was aimed at the thought of a specific group only: the bourgeoisie.

During the twentieth century we have reached a stage in which this weapon of the radical unmasking of the hidden sources of intellectual existence has become the property of all parties and groups. But in their attempts to corrode their enemies' confidence in their thinking, the various groups have also destroyed man's confidence in human thought in general. As all positions eventually were subjected to analysis, as the process of exposing the social roots of thought which had been latent since the dissolution of the Middle Ages continued, there emerged during our century the awareness that confidence in thought in general had been dissolved.

The twentieth century had hardly reached its third decade, when Karl Mannheim realized that the *concept of ideology had become total and general:* the thought of *all* groups is ideological. At this decisive stage the simple theory of ideology develops into the sociology of knowledge; what was once the intellectual armament of a fighting group is transformed into the sociological method in the study of intellectual phenomena. "To begin with, a given social group discovers the 'situational determination' (*Seinsgebundenheit*) of its opponents' ideas. Subsequently the recognition of this fact is elaborated into an all-inclusive principle according to which the thought of every group is seen as arising out of its life conditions."[7]

Mannheim was prepared to investigate without consideration for special interests all the forces in social reality which are likely to affect the intellectual process. But he also knew of the problematic consequences of this analytical stance and asked: "How is it possible for man to continue to think and live in a time when the problems of ideology and utopia are being radically raised and thought through in all their implications?"[8]

The answer to this question will to a large extent depend upon a full understanding of the many-faceted intellectual history that led to the development and eventual blending of the psychological and historical theories of ideology; to advance such understanding is the purpose of the remainder of this essay.

[7] Mannheim, *op. cit.*, p. 69.
[8] *Ibid.*, p. 38.

CHAPTER 12

FRANCIS BACON
The Idols of the Mind

W HEN BACON equated the practical and theoretical with his announcement, whatever is most useful in practice is most correct in theory, he not only voiced an early pragmatism but also expressed the new spirit of the Renaissance which transformed the ideas of the Middle Ages.[1] His pragmatic assertion reflects the will to lord it over nature and to make its forces serve man's wants. In this he becomes the spokesman of the English Renaissance, the bold theorist of the Elizabethan Age. Bacon, peer of brazen navigators, adventurers, and daring scientists, wanted men to abandon the medieval wasteland of empty words and phantasies and to turn to the study of *things;* born in London in 1561, he labored to show men what power and advantage they could gain from a true knowledge of nature and worked out a method for the acquisition of this knowledge. A scholar to the end, he died in 1626, when an experiment to test the preservative properties of snow proved too much for his already feeble health.

Bacon explained the method by means of which he believed true knowledge of nature could be gained in his *Novum Organum,* first published in 1620. Aristotle's logical works had long borne the title of the *Organon* and Bacon chose his title to announce the end of the Aristotelian influence, which he blamed for what *he* considered the barren landscape of medieval intellectual life. In the *Novum Organum,* man is exhorted to interpret nature to discover the laws of nature. Bacon disdains the vain attempts to extract truth deductively by the use of syllogistic forms and advocates induction, the employment of systematic observation, experimentation, and reasoning about things and their modes of behavior. In brief, he sets out to analyze the inductive method and demonstrates what conditions must be fulfilled so true knowledge can be obtained.

In the course of this work—the analysis and illustration of the method of inductive research—Bacon "discovered" obstacles in the path of true knowledge: the *"idols,"* or fallacies to which the mind is especially subject in the attempt to reach truth. He believed that man must reduce himself to a blank tablet, ·if he wants to understand nature correctly.

[1] Cf. Francis Bacon, *Advancement of Learning and Novum Organum,* New York: Wiley, 1944, p. 370.

The observer of nature must enter this realm free from all prejudices which distort reality; but man is hindered by various illusions, both native and acquired (*idola mentis*).

A Typology of Intellectual Fallacies

The idols and false notions which have already preoccupied the human understanding, and are deeply rooted in it, not only so beset men's minds that they become difficult of access, but even when access is obtained will again meet and trouble us in the instauration of the sciences. To counteract their influence men must be warned so that they can guard themselves with all possible care against the idols. Bacon distinguishes four species of idols which beset the human mind and he calls the first *Idols of the Tribe,* the second *Idols of the Cave,* the third *Idols of the Market,* the fourth *Idols of the Theater.*

The idols of the tribe (*idola tribus*) are inherent in human nature and the very tribe or race of man; this Bacon attributes to the false claim that human intelligence is the measure of things. Actually *mankind* suffers from serious intellectual inadequacies, exemplified by the tendency to believe only what is pleasing and to disregard what is not.

The idols of the cave (*idola specus*) reflect *individual* prejudices and intellectual shortcomings. Errors arise because we are particular kinds of beings with limited ranges of experience and knowledge. We all interpret the world around us from the restricted, provincial viewpoint of the particular "cave" we happen to occupy: all thoughts are affected by the personal situation of the thinker.

Other distortions stem from associated living and from the failure of language to properly communicate ideas. These twin problems find their conceptualization in the idols of the market (*idola fori*) which show that language and thus thought are socially determined: words are shaped by the aspirations and will of the majority which render them inexact and faulty. Therefore, men are endlessly plagued by confusion, vain controversies, and fallacies.[2]

Bacon ascribes the idols of the theater (*idola theatri*) to the influence of traditional theories. Aristotelianism is his hated example; but errors arising from received opinion and systems of philosophy are as general as all others. Without exception philosophers have failed to advance knowledge—they merely created "fictitious and theatrical worlds." In the exact sciences, as well, many theories and axioms gained acceptance simply because of the human tendency to set tradition and majority opinion above critical, independent inquiry. This is an early complaint about "group think"—it is also an early announcement of a fundamental distrust of the intellectual attitude:

[2] Cf. *Ibid.,* pp. 319–320.

The human understanding resembles not a dry light, but admits a tincture of the will and passions, which generate their own system accordingly; for man always believes more readily that which he prefers. He, therefore, rejects difficulties for want of patience in investigation; sobriety, because it limits his hope; the depths of nature, from superstition; the light of experiment, from arrogance and pride, lest his mind should appear to be occupied with common and varying objects; paradoxes, from a fear of the opinion of the vulgar; in short, his feelings imbue and corrupt his understanding in innumerable and sometimes imperceptible ways.[3]

The Origin of Idols

The idols of the tribe are caused by a number of elements; they arise from the alleged uniformity of the constitution of the human mind, from man's prejudices, and the limited intellectual faculties of man. Furthermore, they arise from the interference of human passions, from the incompetency of the senses, or the mode of their impressions.

The origin of the idols of the cave is seen in the particular nature of each individual's mind and body, and in education, habit, and personal circumstance. They are furthermore caused by some predominant pursuit, or by an excess in synthesis and analysis, by a bias in favor of certain periods, and by the scope of a researcher's subject matter.

The distortions caused by the idols of the cave call for the greatest caution. Here we are confronted by influences which exert formidable power in polluting our understanding: extreme specialization in scientific pursuits is a case in point. The bias in favor of certain periods was of special interest to Bacon, who himself was battling the rule of Aristotelianism, the authoritarian intellectual system of his own time. He argued that some scientists and philosophers betray an unlimited admiration for antiquity; others, however, make their mistakes by going too far in the opposite direction because of their uncritical and eager acceptance of novelty.[4]

The idols of the market are the most troublesome of all. Their distorting influence stems from the rule of words and names over reason —undoubtedly Bacon had an early semantic awareness concerning the tyranny of words over philosophy and science. The idols of the market are subdivided: one type stems from the practice to invent names for things which have no existence outside the fanciful imagination of certain thinkers. The *primum mobile* is such an empty word derived from false and futile theories. The second type is represented by the names of actual, ontically real objects which are, however, confused, badly defined,

[3] *Ibid.*, p. 322.
[4] Cf. *Ibid.*, p. 323.

and hastily and inaccurately abstracted from things. The first type can be destroyed with relative ease by the refutation of the phantastic theories which gave rise to it. The idols of the second type, derived from faulty abstraction, are more deeply rooted in man's mind.[5]

The idols of the theater are numerous and Bacon foresees that there will even be more of them as time goes on. He derived the term from a comparison between the stage of philosophical speculation and the poetical stage; the plots enacted upon the stage of philosophy resemble those of the poetical and dramatic theater since both are invented for the sake of consistency, elegance, pleasure, and both differ from the less glittering but more accurate plots of real history. Along with the term "idols of the theater" Bacon uses the more obvious synonym "idols of theories" to indicate that these obstacles in the path of knowledge originate in the fictitious theories and corrupted rules of demonstration of "false philosophy." Actually there are three sources of error giving birth to three types of false philosophy: the *sophistic*, the *empiric*, and the *superstitious*.

The "sophistic" or "theoretic" philosophers err by taking for the groundwork of their philosophy either too much from a few topics, or too little from many; their philosophy has an insufficient experimental basis and never attains to the certainty of results that only repeated observation can achieve.[6] Essentially their systems are founded on vulgar notions —the commonplace.

Similarly distorted are the systems of the empiric philosophers who have diligently and accurately attended to a few experiments. They left the path of realistic knowledge when they set out to deduce and invent systems of philosophy on this scanty basis. They did violence to the facts when they furthermore presumed to form everything to conformity with their insufficiently empirical systems of philosophy.

Faith and religious veneration have persuaded the superstitious philosophers to rely on theology and tradition; some of them have gone so far as to "derive the sciences from spirits and genii."

Aristotle affords the most eminent example of the first species of false philosophy—the sophistic, or theoretic. The Greek corrupted natural philosophy by logic; he ". . . imposed innumerable arbitrary distinctions upon the nature of things; being everywhere more anxious as to definitions in teaching and the accuracy of the wording of his propositions, than the internal truth of things." Bacon dismisses Aristotle's physics as a collection of mere logical terms and debunks his metaphysics as a rehash of the same topic under a more impressive title. His recourse to experimentation fails to impress Bacon; Aristotle ". . . drags experiment

[5] Cf. *Ibid.*, p. 325.
[6] Cf. *Ibid.*, p. 326.

along as a captive constrained to accommodate herself to his decisions; so that he is even more to be blamed than his modern followers (of the scholastic school) who have deserted her altogether."[7]

The members of the empiric school produced even more deformed and monstrous dogmas than the sophistic philosophers whose theories were at least conceived in the light of common notions which, however insufficient and superstitious, still possessed some kind of universal and general tendency. The dogmas of the empiric school lack even this element—they are founded in the confined obscurity of a few experiments that corrupted the scientific imagination of the experimenter: the alchemists are a prime example of this form of intellectual decadence.

The superstitious school of philosophy has been corrupted by the admixture of theology and superstition—this is most injurious both to philosophy and theology. The fanciful, bombastic claims of these "poetical" philosophers flatter the human understanding so that men will fall into their idealistic trap. The Pythagorean superstition is coarse, overcharged, and therefore, rather obvious. More refined and consequently more dangerous are the superstitions spread by Plato and his school; but the evil of superstitious and fanciful argumentation is found whenever abstractions such as final and first causes are introduced into philosophy. Some modern writers have extended this madness to the point of deriving natural philosophy from various parts of the Bible ". . . seeking thus the dead amongst the living."[8]

Bacon concludes that we must renounce all idols to completely free the understanding which alone will give us access to the world of men which is based on the sciences.

The Instauration of the Sciences

If an analysis of traditional philosophy and science can show their weaknesses, an important step has been made in the extirpation of the idols. First of all, we must realize that the sciences have been mainly derived from the ancient Greeks. The additions of the Roman, Arabic,

---

[7] *Ibid.*, p. 327. The disdain for logic reappears in twentieth-century philosophy. Notably Heidegger is suspicious of traditional logic which parades ". . . as a court of justice, established for all eternity, whose rights as first and last authority no rational man will impugn. Anyone who speaks against logic is therefore tacitly or explicitly accused of irresponsibility." The German existentialist enlarges the attack, however, by the inclusion of scientific thought: both logic and science become suspect as strongholds of narrow philistine ostentatiousness and rigidity; only the philosopher and the poet have the abundance of "world space" that frees all things from the stifling embrace of commonplaceness and indifference—they cleanse them from the "cheap acid" with which a merely logical intelligence had soiled them. (Cf. Martin Heidegger, *An Introduction to Metaphysics* (translated by Ralph Manheim), A Doubleday Anchor Book, Garden City, N.Y., 1961, pp. 21–22.)

[8] Bacon, *op. cit.*, p. 328.

and modern writers are in Bacon's view of small importance and, anyhow, based on Greek discoveries and inventions; but what kind of basis did the Greek philosophers provide for scientific development? Their wisdom was professorial and disputatious, therefore most adverse to the discovery and investigation of true knowledge.[9] So far, then, scientific pursuits have been dominated by vanity and superficiality and their practitioners have always had their eyes on the multitude desirous of its applause.

Two factors in particular explain the slow and unsatisfactory development of science: the goal of science has been ill defined and men have chosen an erroneous and impassable direction in their scientific pursuits; so far ". . . everything has been abandoned either to the mists of tradition, the whirl and confusion of argument, or the waves and mazes of chance, and desultory, ill-combined experiment."[10] The progress of natural philosophy—that guiding force in scientific advancement—has also been impeded by religion through the fanaticism of some and the ignorance of others.

Along with religion Bacon charges the institutions of education and government with faulty performance. The practices and rules in schools and universities hinder the advancement of the sciences; instructional procedures are geared to the commonplace. The occasional innovator who dares dissent from majority opinion and the prevailing intellectual tradition is quickly put down as a ". . . turbulent and revolutionary spirit." In the sphere of government ". . . even a change for the better is suspected on account of the commotion it occasions, for civil government is supported by authority, unanimity, fame, and public opinion, and not by demonstration."[11]

An intellectual weakness which seriously hinders the progress of science and the rate of innovation arises from the timid, despairing attitude of men who quickly reject novel ideas and procedures as impossible. The original thinker is rebuked as unbridled and immature; dire consequences are predicted for his activities.

These were the errors of past generations; their problems, however, arose not from the nature of things but from the human understanding which is open to corrective measures. This is significant and there are further grounds for hope: orderly, empirical methods will greatly accelerate scientific progress. Numerous useful discoveries have occurred to mankind by chance or opportunity, without investigation and attention on their part. Therefore, the rate of discovery will be vastly accelerated as soon as regular and orderly scientific investigation and attention replaces the hasty and interrupted approach of our predecessors. Bacon

[9] Cf. *Ibid.*, p. 333.
[10] *Ibid.*, p. 339.
[11] *Ibid.*, p. 347.

also foresaw the need for a bold, pioneering, and progressive spirit in the sciences. He was hopeful that the realm of scientific discovery would provide the best breeding-ground for a modernistic mentality.[12]

The Significance of Bacon's Philosophy

Bacon was not content with depicting the past and heralding the future; he also contributed to the advancement of science. First of all, he showed that man is the interpreter of nature, that truth is not derived from authority, that knowledge is the product of experience. He gave to logic the method of *ampliative inference* which employs analogy to infer from the properties of a single *datum* the characteristics of the larger group to which that *datum* belongs, leaving to subsequent experience the correction of evident errors. This technique constituted an advance over the older method of induction by simple enumeration, whereby general conclusions were derived from a number of particular data. The new technique of *ampliative inference* promoted greater boldness in the formulation of hypotheses—an important step in the direction of scientific progress had been taken.

In his *Novum Organum,* Bacon promulgated a new scientific spirit of more objective and exact observation and experimentation. His postulate to free the mind from all prejudices and preconceived attitudes— embodied in the various species of idols—represents an important milestone in the development of modern scientific method.

The English philosopher did not question the ability of the human mind to perceive the phenomena of nature. On the other hand, man has failed to utilize this perceptive potential because of a number of obstacles that have so far obscured his knowledge: the deductive method, the syllogism, and the *idola mentis* which dominate the human understanding.

Bacon accuses the Greek and medieval philosophers of having sacrificed the study of nature by wasting their energies on mere words and concepts. Against the deductive and syllogistic logic of the past he pits induction and experimentation. His critique of the human understanding is contained in his theory of idols which is to safeguard our understanding of nature. This precaution is necessary because of the properties of the human mind which Bacon compares to an "uneven mirror" that changes the reflection of the objects because of its peculiar shape.

Bacon assumes that certain species of idols are learned while others are innate. In the first case, their destruction is difficult, but possible. In the second instance, however, the idols cannot be annihilated—man can only hope to bring the innate idols into his consciousness so that their hidden power may be known and overcome.

[12] *Cf. Ibid.,* p. 354.

Our understanding is furthermore endangered because of the powerful influence of the human will. For Bacon the human mind is "not a dry light" but subject to the influence of our will, our affections and feelings which sway the intellect in many different and often imperceptible ways; the idols are to a large extent products of the human will and of human feelings. Bacon's critique of the human understanding is, therefore, basically aimed at the analysis of the psychological preconditions of intellectual operations. He hopes to bring into consciousness the subjective elements of feeling and the social factors which hinder our understanding of nature. Once man knows the obstacles in the path of true knowledge he will be able to attack and remove the sources of error. Bacon's concept of truth is based on the idea that man is able to establish an adequate relationship between existence and consciousness.

Our understanding is also endangered by superstition. Bacon arrived at this argument probably under the impression which the religious struggle of the sixteenth century had made upon him. He favored a clear division between philosophy and theology, between knowledge and faith, to avoid the corruption of philosophy as evidenced by *scholasticism*. In the first book *Of the Proficience and Advancement of Learning*, Bacon attributes to superstition and religious fanaticism the same pernicious influence that he attributes to the *idola mentis* in his *Novum Organum*. The four species of idols are thus augmented by superstition—by perverted religion. Superstition mainly results from the vested interests of the clergy, which pits itself as a social class against the rest of society.

The philosophers of the French Enlightenment were quick to realize the dynamic potential of the theory of idols; because of the close connection between this theory and Bacon's critique of (religious) superstition, they could use it as a weapon in their attack upon religion.

Basically the theory of idols was only applicable to the physical sciences. But this limitation could not be maintained for very long.[13] Soon the philosophers of the eighteenth century were to develop Bacon's critique of idols into the *theory of prejudice*. Especially the philosophers of the French Enlightenment widened Bacon's theory by intensifying the critique of religion and by radically expanding the theory of idols that was henceforth to encompass state and society. Now all sciences were subject to the suspicion of ideological distortion. It must be realized, however, that Bacon had viewed the social order as something that was hopelessly subject to authority, tradition, and irrational opinions. In this realm, innovations could only endanger the existing balance.

In contrast, the philosophers of the Enlightenment maintained a far more optimistic view of the social world. They believed in a social order based on reason and natural law and interpreted the absence of such a

---

[13] Cf. Hans Barth, *Wahrheit und Ideologie*, Zürich: Manesse Verlag, 1945, p. 52.

rational order in state and society by reference to the prejudices which tend to obscure its existence. They were, however, intent upon the discovery of this rational order; the theory of idols assumed a definitely political character, as soon as it had been transformed into the theory of prejudices. The irrational basis of the existing state and of religion was now exposed as an idol, as a prejudice, that had to answer the summons of the tribunal of reason. We shall soon see how the judgment of this high court exposed the irrational nature of the social order as the villainous creation of certain interested parties.

The powerful significance of Bacon's *Instauratio Magna* for the philosophy of the French Enlightenment extended into the "ideology" of Destutt de Tracy. The *ideologues*—in developing the *science des idées*, which was to discover the origin and formative principle of ideas— continued Bacon's endeavor to prevent the formation of false ideas.

Condillac, who represents the link between the Enlightenment and the *ideologues*, has eulogized Bacon in a statement that was later reprinted in the Great French Encyclopedia: "Personne n'a mieux connu que Bacon la cause de nos erreurs; car il a vu que les idées qui sont l'ouvrage d l'esprit, avaient été mal faites et que par conséquent pour avancer dans la recherche de la vérité il fallait les refaire."[14]

Bacon's influence continued into the nineteenth and twentieth centuries, where his attempts to safeguard the interpretation of nature from the idols and the interventions of theology were further expanded to develop sciences that were far more exposed to the influence of special interests: ideological analysis was brought to bear on the subject matter of the social sciences.

Following the trail that Bacon left behind, Herbert Spencer claimed that sociology in particular suffered from difficulties to a much larger extent than any other science. The sociologist is expected to develop a certain scientific attitude which represents an impossibility for the average man and an achievement that the exceptional individual can only attain very imperfectly. As a thinker the sociologist must sever the umbilical cord which connects all men with their ". . . race, and country, and citizenship—to get rid of all those interests, prejudices, likings, superstitions, generated in him by the life of his own society and his own time—to look on all the changes societies have undergone and are undergoing, without reference to nationality, or creed, or personal welfare. . . ."[15]

Spencer's *Study of Sociology* is largely devoted to the analysis of the various difficulties besetting the discipline; he describes in detail all the

---

[14] Condillac, "Essai sur l'origine des connaissances humaines." Quoted in Hans Barth, *Ibid.*, p. 41.

[15] Herbert Spencer, *The Study of Sociology* (Introduction by Talcott Parsons), Ann Arbor Paperbacks, Ann Arbor: The University of Michigan Press, 1961, p. 67.

psychological and social factors hindering the scientific interpretation of society and discusses the different sources of error as well as their influence upon theorizing. In this manner Spencer (1820–1903) hopes to free sociology from the charge of being merely a reflection of the political and economic interests of groups and nations and to safeguard sociological knowledge as such. He addresses himself especially to the biases of education, patriotism, social class, politics, and theology to investigate the possibility of their elimination and to safeguard scientific objectivity.

CHAPTER 13

THE FRENCH
ENCYCLOPEDISTS

Subversion of the Established Order

T<small>HE</small> YEAR 1751 marks the beginning of the publication of the *Great French Encyclopedia*. It was not until 1772 that this great achievement of the French Enlightenment had been completed with the appearance of the 28th volume. With Diderot as editor and d'Alembert as coeditor until 1758, the work entitled *Encyclopédie ou Dictionnaire raisonné des sciences, des arts et des métiers* mirrors the intellectual dynamics of the period, as well as the features of the bourgeoisie of prerevolutionary France.

According to d'Alembert's *Discours préliminaire* the work fulfills, as an encyclopedia, the philosophical task of establishing a *science universelle* and, as a dictionary, the informative function of spreading knowledge about all the different spheres of culture. In the first instance the encyclopedic spirit proclaims to fuse all the different forms of intellectual activity into one unified system, to reduce the various sciences to relatively few basic principles which are to establish a general and universal science. In the second instance the pragmatic undercurrent of the French Enlightenment comes to the surface: to instruct the people in all the areas of knowledge and to help them master the practical problems of their daily lives.

Two less obvious features of the encyclopedia are, however, of greater importance. First, as demanded by Diderot, the *Encyclopédie* became a platform for progessive ideas about religion and political and social relations. Second, a democratic tendency is manifest in the appreciation of the importance of crafts and mechanics and in the conception of the work as an introduction to the sciences to be used by the layman to initiate self-education.

In 1752, Voltaire composed the first articles of his *Dictionnaire philosophique* at the court of Prussia's Frederick II. This polemical tract, which is probably the most mature philosophical work of this belligerent enemy of Christian civilization, was published in 1764, and soon all copies of the first edition were seized and burned upon orders of the governing bodies in Geneva, The Hague, and Paris. Voltaire answered the defenders of the established order by launching a second, enlarged edition of the *Dictionnaire* to turn his savage irony even more strongly against what he considered the expression of fanaticism and stupidity—the foe of humanity and decency.

The work was a sensational success that stimulated a lively "subterranean" traffic of the first edition on the part of the reading public and frantic activity on the part of ecclesiastics who immediately started to write anti-philosophical dictionaries to refute Voltaire, the "wild beast." Events had confirmed Voltaire's hope that the *Dictionnaire* would effectively combine small size with big explosive force.

Like most of the philosophers of the French Enlightenment, Voltaire contributed to Diderot's *Encyclopédie;* he defended this gigantic undertaking but he did not expect much from it, fearing that the propagandistic effect would be buried beneath the sheer size of this clumsy and expensive work. Voltaire knew that Diderot also intended to bring about a change in the minds of men, but at the same time he believed that the Church, that prime defender of the established order, was a powerful edifice, solidly built on rock. *L'infâme* ". . . could be blasted loose only with simplicity, clarity, brevity, and rage: as he composed his articles for Diderot, he inevitably thought of his own, one-man *Encyclopédie*."[1] In 1766, he expressed this fear in a letter to d'Alembert: " 'Twenty folio volumes will never make a revolution: it's the small, portable books at thirty *sous* that are dangerous. If the Gospel had cost 1,200 sesterces, the Christian religion would never have been established.' "[2]

The Destruction of Metaphysics

The philosophers of the French Enlightenment—the *philosophes*—who made the Great French Encyclopedia a reality were to a large extent the intellectual heirs of Bacon, the progenitor of English materialism. Bacon, whose thinking anciently connects with the *homoiomeriae* of Anaxagoras and the atoms of Democritus, hypostatized the physical sciences and especially physics. With Bacon, all science rests upon experience and consists in subjecting the data furnished by the senses—the infallible source of all knowledge—to a rational method of investigation which has observation, experimentation, comparison, induction, and analysis for its instruments.

[1] Peter Gay, *The Party of Humanity: Essays in the French Enlightenment,* New York: Alfred A. Knopf, 1964, p. 36.
[2] Voltaire to d'Alembert, April 5 (1766). *Correspondence,* LXI, 8. Quoted in Gay, *Ibid.,* p. 36.

With Hobbes, knowledge based upon the senses becomes the abstract experience of the mathematician who reduces the movement of matter to mechanical or mathematical processes thereby losing track of the vital spirit which Bacon had emphasized in his description of the qualities inherent in matter movement. Hobbes' systematization of Baconian materialism, furthermore, failed to establish Bacon's thesis concerning the origin of all knowledge in the senses on firm grounds.

It was not until John Locke investigated the nature and validity of human knowledge in his *Essay Concerning Human Understanding* (1690) that Bacon's and Hobbes' fundamental principle was provided with a firmer basis. Locke's ideas were to have special importance for the course of events on the other side of the English Channel: they provided the final blow to the metaphysical tradition which still held the seventeenth century spell-bound. Thus, Locke gave the signal for the attack of the *philosophes* upon all metaphysics, especially that of Descartes, Malebranche, Leibniz, and Spinoza, and the resulting fight against the extant political institutions and their supposed ally: theology and religion.

Locke's work came to the French at an opportune time. "Locke had established the philosophy of *bon sens*, of healthy common sense, that is, to express it in a roundabout way, that there are no philosophers other than those of the understanding which is based upon the healthy human senses."[3] The victory of the antitheological, antimetaphysical, materialistic movement that has one of its important sources in Locke—Descartes' physics constitutes the other—must, furthermore, be explained by reference to the fact that metaphysics had lost all credit in practice: the educated Frenchmen already subscribed to a secular life-style evolving around the enjoyment and mastery of the present. With the weapon of scepticism Pierre Bayle, whom religious doubt drove to question the metaphysics supporting his faith, was already destroying metaphysics from within when he subjected its entire evolution to criticism, and when he announced the atheistic society which was casting its shadow over the historical horizon.

Thus France, where the old order of things had reached a greater degree of contemptuous definiteness than in England and Germany, was revolutionized *pace* English ideas. After Voltaire's and Montesquieu's visits to England the island's philosophical, political, religious, scientific, and aesthetic thought-styles found their way into France and the continent generally. In 1734, the hangman burned as irreligious and subversive Voltaire's just-published synthesis of his English experience, the *Lettres philosophiques*. But after that Voltaire frequently based his

[3] Karl Marx, *Selected Essays* (translated by H. J. Stenning), New York: International Publishers, 1926, p. 190.

sarcastic criticism of the Church's theology and the established order of things on English notions, such as Locke's principle that all our ideas proceed from experience, Hume's psychological approach to the history of religion, the critical deism of men like Woolston, and above all Newton's discovery of the uniformity of nature and his "refusal to make hypotheses." Montesquieu, enamored with the English form of constitution, criticized the French conditions incisively in his *Esprit des lois*, which he published in 1748.

The immediate follower and interpreter of Locke, however, was Condillac, who did not hesitate to turn the sensationalism of the English physician upon the metaphysics of the seventeenth century.

Condillac referred conscious experience to passive sensations when he tried to simplify Locke's epistemology in his *Traité des sensations* (1754). Furthermore, he augmented Locke's position in his *L'Essai sur l'origine des connaissances humaines*, in as much as he conceived of the senses and the apparatus of sensual receptivity as themselves being dependent upon experience. Now man's development was subject to external circumstances and education. Although Condillac, who was a priest and an abbé, never openly doubted theology, he, nevertheless, accepted Locke's scepticism as to the power of the mind to reveal the real nature of outer objects. Moreover, his *Traité des Systèmes* clearly rejects the metaphysical assumptions of Descartes, Leibniz, Spinoza, and Malebranche. Helvétius demonstrated in his *De L'Esprit* that all the operations and contents of the mind originated in sense-perception and proceeded to establish an ethical and political theory that viewed moral ideals and norms as the outgrowth of the basic sensations of pleasure and pain. In Helvétius' *De L'homme*, English materialism, then, found its application to social life; the foundation of morality was now seen in sensual qualities and egotism, enjoyment and enlightened self-interest.

In 1770, Holbach (1723–1789) published his *Système de la Nature*, where materialism found its most systematic elaboration in the synthesis of English and French materialism as derived from Cartesian physics. Holbach's discussion of morals is based essentially on the ethics of Helvétius (1715–1771).

Philosophy and Revolution

The influence of the *philosophes* upon the Great French Revolution is subject to scholarly discussion and disagreement. Carl Becker's influential Yale lectures on the philosophers were certainly in the nature of an ironic attempt to debunk their intellectual position on several counts. This American historian set out to show that the philosophers were no philosophers in the first place, that they were not nearly as modern as they thought they were: that their ties with medieval thinkers were quite intimate and that they were essentially Christians in disguise—never mind the antireligious fireworks. Debunking Becker's own dubious implications, however, we note that he arrives at a rather direct connection between the philosophers and the revolution. The philosophers were after the hide of the merchants of ignorance. They were also searching for a special truth that would be on their side. The philosophers, furthermore, could not view error with detachment because they themselves were too recently emancipated from error and thus they were eager to "spread the light." These emancipated philosophers were convinced that they played a messianic role in the world historical struggle for freedom, justice, knowledge, and the liberation of mankind; their enthusiasm for this role grew from year to year and reached its delirious climax ". . . in that half admirable, half pathetic spectacle of June 8, 1794, when Citizen Robespierre, with a bouquet in one hand and a torch in the other, inaugurated the new religion of humanity by lighting the conflagration that was to purge the world of ignorance, vice, and folly."[4]

Crane Brinton of Harvard University views Jacobinism as a "sect" of the "wider faith of Enlightenment," which "held some form of the cosmology of the Enlightenment." He summarizes the Jacobin teleology as "progress, with reason doing the work of grace" and points to the article *philosophe* in the *Encyclopédie* to indicate the ideological connection. In a sense the faith of the *philosophes* found its church in the Jacobins' republic, and if the philosophers were enemies of traditional religion, there emerges another connection since Jacobinism was ". . . one of the first and one of the most important of the efforts made in modern times to supplant Christianity, to root it out and replace it."[5]

Peter Gay of Columbia University starts out with the opposite assumption that philosophical ideas held a rather modest place in the daily actions of the revolutionaries, but in his own writings there is sufficient evidence to show that the connection between the philosophers and the revolution was more than coincidental. Gay admits that they became the spokesmen for a revolutionary society in need of interpreters and that the philosophers—although they were not Jacobins themselves— ". . . helped to prepare the way for the Jacobins. . . ."[6] The philosophers completed the intellectual revolution that led men out of the "social primitivism" of the Middle Ages. The articles in the *Encyclopédie* had

[4] Carl L. Becker, *The Heavenly City of the Eighteenth-Century Philosophers,* New Haven: Yale University Press, 1932, p. 43.

[5] Crane Brinton, "Comment on Gay," *American Historical Review,* Vol. LXVI, No. 3 (April, 1961), p. 681. Cf. also Crane Brinton, *A Decade of Revolution, 1789–1799,* New York and London: Harper & Row, 1934, and *The Jacobins: An Essay in the New History,* New York: Macmillan, 1930.

[6] Gay, *op. cit.,* p. 119. Cf. also p. 213 where Gay says with reference to Rousseau: "The Jacobins defended the Terror in his name."

a single purpose: "to reinterpret the world and by reinterpreting it, to change it."[7]

The French historian Roustan asserts that the *philosophes* had a direct and strong influence upon the revolutionary development that exploded in 1789. Poverty, despair, and mistreatment inflamed the masses but without the intellectuals there would have been no revolution: the men of 1789 were not merely escaping starvation which had been an integral part of the national tradition. In 1753, eight hundred people died of hunger in one small community alone—more died in other cities. There were riots, but no revolution—the military won the day. It took almost forty years of education and propaganda on the part of the philosophers before the French could stand up and demand their rights and human dignity: " 'The spirit of the *philosophes* was the spirit of the Revolution.' "[8]

This notion is equally prominent in Taine's history of eighteenth-century France. But far from hailing the philosophers as champions of liberty, Taine condemns them as irresponsible salon-intellectuals who provided "brutal force" with a "radical dogma," thereby infecting the French mind with the sickness of revolutionary ideas.[9]

The task that the *philosophes* had chosen was dangerous. A few years after the military action against the people, the clergy—in alliance with Parliament and the king—set out to organize the intellectual counterattack. This move was based upon a law dating back to 1563, which condemned all authors of antireligious writings to death by hanging.

The work of the *philosophes* was facilitated, however, by the lack of unity among their enemies as well as by their mediocrity. Many members of the aristocracy were impoverished by debts, living a meaningless existence without virtue, power, and repute. The nobles of the court were viewed by the *philosophes* as titled flunkeys whom they despised and whose vicious ill-will they braved. On the other hand, the philosophers were in close, friendly contact with some nobles of genuine distinction such as the Marquis d'Argenson and the Comte de Segus.

The magistrates in the 14 provincial *parlements* and in the *Parlement* of Paris, who represented the chief judiciary body until 1789, were counted among the enemies by the *philosophes* themselves. Diderot attacked the *Parlementaires* in his *L'Histoire du Parlement de Paris* in terms even sharper than those employed by Voltaire, who had already dismissed them as a pack of "little black-gowned scoundrels," the mercenary enemies of reason and philosophy.

[7] *Ibid.*, p. 129.

[8] M. Roustan, *The Pioneers of the French Revolution* (translated by F. Whyte, edited by H. J. Laski), Boston: Little, Brown, 1926, p. 24.

[9] Cf. Hippolyte Taine, *Les origines de la France contemporaine*, Vol. I, *L'Ancien régime*, 28th edition, Paris: Librairie Hachette, 1917, p. 311.

How did the *philosophes* view French monarchy? The relevant articles of the *Encyclopédie* blame the governmental practices of Louis XIV for the misery of France and call for the replacement of the outmoded divine-right monarchy by a more representative form of government with the Third Estate finding its appropriate place in the new political order. The attack upon the political system and the person of Louis XIV was addressed to Louis XV as well. The *Encyclopédists* feared that France was headed for a revolutionary change and hoped that the successor to the *Roi Soleil* could still be motivated to forestall the catastrophe. The *philosophes* foresaw the revolution but did not view it as something to be hoped for; rather they looked upon the approaching upheaval as a danger which might be avoided through peaceful reforms.[10]

The prevailing political corruption was, furthermore, seen as the direct result of the deplorable connection between throne and altar. Since the institution of monarchy was still to be retained as the source of social and political reform, the brunt of the attack fell, therefore, upon the Church. Consequently, the *philosophes* supported contemporary attempts to subordinate the Church to a national monarchy. When the order of the Jesuits was dissolved in France in 1761, the *philosophes* were wholeheartedly on the side of the State. Absolved from what they considered their most dangerous enemy, they revealed an attitude that showed itself also on other occasions: to strive for an alliance with the Crown, whenever the royal powers seemed to realize vital points of the philosophers' program. Thus, the *philosophes* accepted the claim of the modern state for absolute sovereignty; an idea that they inherited from Hobbes and that they in turn passed on to Rousseau and the revolution. These attitudes coalesce in Voltaire's political relativism which permeates his relevant writings such as the *Henriade*, the *Lettres philosophiques*, and his correspondence with statesmen.

The Great French Revolution was essentially a middle-class movement. This economic group had risen to a position of financial, technological, and professional importance which contrasted glaringly with its lack of political influence and social prestige. The educated and affluent bourgeois was belittled and insulted by a parasitic, frivolous nobility which monopolized the highest honors and all political privileges of consequence. Emboldened by success, the new class displayed a growing irritation with social and political discrimination; its transformation into a revolutionary force became complete when the desire of its industrial, commercial, and financial leaders for an equilibrium of economic and political power changed into the determination to act. The revolutionary class found its intellectual leaders among the philosophers—men of predominantly bourgeois extraction, sympathy, and taste. The socio-economic

---

[10] Cf. Eberhard Weis, *Geschichtsschreibung und Staatsauffassung in der französischen Enzyklopädie*, Wiesbaden: Franz Steiner Verlag, 1956, p. 170.

standpoint of the intellectuals explains both their cautious, pragmatic-opportunist attitude toward the king and their success in attracting a large number of middle-class followers.

Notwithstanding their position in the bourgeoisie, the philosophers found their best friends in the working class. The laborers, artisans, and peasants admired them as men who were united in a generous task, who were feared and at times respected by the wealthy and the powerful, and they greeted them as men who behaved as thinkers by rousing and guiding public opinion. The philosophers' writings could not fail to attract followers: they reflected the talent of these men to make ideas come to life and convince. Artisans capable of reading could grasp what the intellectuals had to say and since they said it well and clearly, their ideas could be expounded to the illiterate—in this way the *philosophes* reached the masses and became their real educators.

The question of the masses received the philosophers undivided attention: Should simple men, mostly lacking in even basic education, be permitted to play a role in political life? Should the masses be given the true picture of religion and be trusted to handle themselves with moral self-restraint or would it be better to control them with the time-honored device of the politic lie? "The balance of opinion was in favor of telling the truth, not in favor of organized deceit."[11]

Voltaire, who had long maintained that the masses were hopelessly steeped in superstition and unworthy of self-government, changed his thinking as he grew more politically experienced and came to exhibit considerable faith in the rationality of the poor. The shift toward radicalism, toward belief in the possibilities of universal Enlightenment, became a general characteristic of the philosophers and in the second half of the eighteenth century more and more of them accepted the principle of universal Enlightenment that Voltaire had discovered for himself in Geneva and that Montesquieu had already extolled in 1748, when he proclaimed in the Preface to his *Esprit des Lois* that the people had to be enlightened.

As the leaders of polite society, the women of the eighteenth century formed an influential circle that strategically encompassed such significant segments of society as the financiers, the nobility, and the royal court. The focal point of this feminine influence was the *salons*. There were, for example, the receptions of Madame Necker, wife of the Swiss-born financier and statesman Jacques Necker, which were attended by the chief personalities of the bourgeois society of Paris. Intellectuals, financiers, and nobles mingled in the *salon* of Madame d'Épinay, the friend of Diderot and Grimm and until 1757, a benefactress of Jean Jacques Rousseau. Equally respected by the sovereigns, princes, states-

[11] Gay, *op. cit.*, p. 277.

men, and intellectuals of Europe was Madame Geoffrin, whose famous "Wednesdays" completed the philosophical education of Madame d'Étoiles, who was later to become royal mistress and to enter the books of history as the Pompadour. Madame de Pompadour had first been exposed to the intellectual currents of the time when she frequented, as Mademoiselle Poisson, the *salon* of Madame de Tencin, where she had met Fontenelle, Montesquieu, Marivaux, Piron, and Duclos. Already Mademoiselle Poisson had been delighted by these bold thinkers without clearly realizing whither they led. As Madame d'Étoiles she had not been able to form a *salon* of her own due to her husband's attitude. As Marquise de Pompadour, however, she could fulfill her desire to entertain the audacious intellectuals and reformers who had already impressed her in her youth. "The Marquise neglected no opportunity of manifesting publicly her sympathy for the *philosophes.*"[12]

Voltaire's intellectual career also shows the influence of a woman: Madame du Châtelet, who was not only his mistress during fifteen long years but his intellectual companion and collaborator as well, helping him to consolidate his knowledge and encouraging his desire to strike out in new directions. She was an unusual woman who consumed men and new ideas with equal intensity. Madame du Châtelet read tirelessly and wrote constantly. Some of Europe's most brilliant intellectuals, like the mathematical genius Maupertuis, ". . . improved her algebra and warmed her bed."[13]

Thought and Existence

The question concerning the relationship between thinking and being is increasingly becoming a major concern of modern intellectual pursuits. This disturbing question dates back to medieval *scholasticism*, where the primacy of nature and mind was debated. At the close of the Middle Ages, the question appeared in sharper formulation: Did God create the world or did it always exist?

Those philosophers who maintained the primacy of mind over nature assumed ultimately that the universe had somehow been created and, thus, formed the various schools of *idealism*. Other thinkers, however, claimed the primacy of nature and initiated the varieties of *materialism*.

According to a radically materialistic position—such as the one held by Holbach—man is born into the world with nothing but the capacity to register sensations. His intellectual abilities are only an outgrowth of these basic sensory capacities. Some sensations that man receives from the objects will be to his liking; others will cause him pain. Thus, man

[12] Cf. Roustan, *op. cit.*, p. 87.
[13] Gay, *op. cit.*, p. 21.

will call everything that causes pleasure, good, and everything that results in pain, he will call bad. From this materialistic position it follows that, should a person be the source of pain, he would be called bad. Or differently worded: a person who hurts his fellow creatures is bad; another, who does good for them is good. These simple relationships in the epistemological as well as in the ethical realm are, however, disturbed and distorted through the operation of a number of factors. First of all, as Holbach teaches, man is only bad because he has an *interest* in being bad.

The philosophers worked with the conception that three *prejudices* operate to cause errors and deceptions which distort men's relations to the objects constituting their world: *idols, interests, priestly fraud.* They largely accepted Bacon's theory of idols as a conceptual model for dealing with the problems of distorted perception and error. They did not signally contribute, however, to the further advancement of the theory. The main contribution of the *philosophes* must be seen in the elaboration of the third source of error: priestly deceit. The emphasis upon the cunning of the priests is probably a result of the antireligious program of the French Enlightenment, which sets this strand of the European Enlightenment apart from the English and especially German movements which were less radical in their approach to religion. The attack upon religion is, furthermore, the only motive that the different representatives of the French school really share. In many other respects, especially with regard to methodology and philosophical outlook, one philosopher was often the worst antagonist of another. Holbach and Helvétius, for example, were actually *encyclopédists* by mere association. They found no admirers among their associates for their cut and dried methodological premises and they contributed little to the *Encyclopédie*. But in their criticism of religion they reflected the position of their contemporaries, although in its most radical and outspoken manner. Drawing upon these two men, therefore, means to get at the strongest statement of the Enlightenment attitude toward religion, which amounts to a declaration of open warfare. Driven by Voltaire's battle cry, *écrasez l'infâme*, the Encyclopedists accused ". . . religion, of having been an eternal hindrance to intellectual progress and of having been incapable of founding a genuine morality and a just social and political order."[14]

This antireligious theory divides mankind into two groups: a small elite, with access to truth, and the mass of people living in the darkness of superstition and error. The priests know truth but they deliberately keep it from the masses to maintain their powerful grip over them. Simultaneously, the *philosophes* inform the masses that they have exposed the cunning and deceit of the priests and encourage the people to rebel

[14] Ernst Cassirer, *The Philosophy of the Enlightenment* (translated by F. C. A. Koelln and J. P. Pettegrove), Boston: Beacon Press, 1955, p. 134.

against the fraudulent rulers that have subjugated them for so long with the help of religion, metaphysics, and pseudoscientific dogmas.

The theory of priestly deceit has rarely been used in this pure form. Most of the time it made its appearance in combination with the "interest theory." The priests were accused of exploiting their knowledge and power to advance their economic interests. In this combination the theory charged the ideological adversary with deliberate lying: the enemy was pictured as using the weapon of ideas to consciously falsify reality.

This, however, was only one variant of the interest theory. First, it must be understood that this theory constituted the probably most important thesis of Enlightenment philosophy. Basically, the interest theory represented the stubborn epistemological optimism of this intellectual movement, in as much as man was credited with the ability to conceive truth. The problem of distorted or ideological knowledge entered as a *psychological* phenomenon: man is able to see truth, but he rejects it because it conflicts with his interests. Thus man may block his own path to truth in following his interests. The source of ideology in this case is man's will. The therapy consists of making this voluntaristic element conscious. Once we are *conscious* of the falsifying power of our *will* we are able to hinder and paralyze it. This is the other variant of the interest theory which still credits man with good faith; it goes back into antiquity and also finds an appropriate formulation in the Hobbesian proposition that man will go against reason, as soon as reason goes against man.

The first-mentioned variant of the interest theory, however, does no longer credit the falsifier of truth with good faith; it indicts him as a *deliberate liar.* In this instance, man, principally equipped to see truth, keeps it away from others to further his selfish interests. Here the therapy must come from outside forces: enlightening education of the victims of the falsifiers of truth. In this connection the *philosophes* saw themselves as therapists. Their major target was the priests as falsifiers of truth; their patients were the people deliberately kept in superstition and ignorance by the representatives of religion. The plot against truth assumed even more sinister forms through the alliance between throne and altar. In the opinion of the philosophers, the priests were seeking additional power by drawing the representatives of the political order into their antitruth conspiracy; the intellectuals, therefore, constantly tried to drive a wedge between the monarch and the priests.

Among the philosophers, two especially stand out for their religious, political, and social criticism: Helvétius and Holbach. Throughout their writings we find the complaint that the prejudices work against man's attempts to realize his personal happiness and a rational social order.

The Radicalism of Helvétius and Holbach

Bacon meant to safeguard our understanding of *nature* from the pernicious influence of the idols. Helvétius and Holbach wanted to establish the objective and independent understanding of *social reality*. The rational reconstruction of the social order begins for these authors with a "sociological" interpretation of the ideas which guide men in their behavior and actions; ideas which men mistake for an objective reflection of social reality. This approach implies the analysis of society's influence upon the formation and the content of ideas.

Helvétius argues: ". . . our ideas are . . . of necessity the consequences of the societies we live in . . ."[15] The reactions of people to different occurrences and facts change as we move from one standpoint to another. Men accept only the ideas and conceptual perspectives that correspond to their particular social position and occupation; they are products of society and their minds are quite passive. Consequently, the importance of education is paramount: *"L'éducation peut tout."*[16] The progress of education, however, presupposes political progress. Under an enlightened and constitutional government, there develops a human type that is upright, courageous, frank, and loyal. A despotic government, in contrast, breeds men that are ". . . vile, without spirit and courage." Helvétius attributes this difference in the character of people to the ". . . different education received under one or the other of these governments."[17]

Ethical ideas are also socially determined. "The sentiments of father-love, mother-love, and child-love merely result from reflection and habit. All ideas, all the concepts of men are acquired."[18] What, then, is virtue? "He is virtuous who does good for his fellow citizens. The word virtue always includes the idea of some public usefulness." Saints therefore are not virtuous. They have done no good for the earthly life. They are as dishonest as the scoundrel who ". . . converts at the moment of death, he is saved; he is quite happy; but he is not virtuous. A person merits this name only through habitually just and noble conduct."[19]

The ethical sphere is, furthermore, dominated by the relativism which characterizes all social action. The centuries lead, ". . . in both a physical and moral sense, to revolutions which change the face of Empires . . . in great confusion . . . the same actions can become successively useful

[15] Claude Adrien Helvétius, *Oeuvres Complètes*, Vol. I: *De L'esprit*, Paris: Lepetit, 1818, p. 104 (my translation).

[16] *Ibid.*, Vol. II: *De L'homme*, Paris: Lepetit, 1818, p. 566.

[17] *Ibid.*, pp. 566–567 (my translation).

[18] Claude Adrien Helvétius, *Neunundzwanzig Thesen des Materialismus*, Halle a. S.: Verlag von A. Erlecke, 1873, p. 14 (my translation).

[19] Claude Adrien Helvétius, *De L'homme*, Vol. I. London: Société Typographique, 1774, p. 76 (my translation).

and detrimental and consequently, can be called in turn both virtuous and vicious."[20] Therefore, each nation ". . . esteems in others only
those ideas which are analogous to its own; all contrary opinion is therefore a germ of contempt between them."[21]

Holbach also claims that *existence determines thought:* "Our ways of
thinking are necessarily determined by the circumstances of our existence."[22] Most philosophers have been unable to see the important influence which the environment exerts upon man's thinking and behavior,
because of their one-sided fascination with the alleged freedom of the
will.[23]

Ideas and values are socially determined, because thinking and acting
are determined by interests which are always shaped by social conditions
and needs. According to Helvétius, it is always personal interest which
produces the astonishing diversity of opinion.[24] The different moral,
political, and philosophical beliefs result from the fact that it is against
man's interest to see things as they really are: ". . . the Public never
takes advice unless to its interest;" it never esteems intellectual and
artistic achievements with regard to quality but only with regard to the
". . . advantage which it reaps from them."[25] In other words, we do not
judge objects, ideas, or human actions by their inherent value but by
the utility that they possess for ourselves or our group.[26]

In *De l'esprit,* Helvétius taught that self-love is the essence of man,
the driving force behind his actions, and that it is necessarily one with
love of power, since man can only fulfill his desires if he possesses the
means to reach his goals. From here important political consequences
follow:

Tyrants and fanatics have always ". . . felt that their power had only
human ignorance and imbecility as its foundation: thus, they have always
imposed silence on whoever, in uncovering the true principles of morals
to the nations, would have revealed all their misfortunes and all their
rights to them, and would have armed them against injustice."[27]

Similarly, persecutions of defenseless people are triggered off by egotis-
tical interests. "*L'intérèt est toujours le motif caché de la persécution.*"[28]

On this basis Helvétius developed his psychological theory and practice of unmasking and debunking. Now it becomes clear that the socially

[20] Claude Adrien Helvétius, *De L'esprit,* Paris: Durand, 1776, p. 107 (my translation).

[21] *Ibid.,* p. 169 (my translation).

[22] Paul Henri Thiry Holbach, *Système de la Nature,* Part One, London, 1770, p. 200
(my translation).

[23] Cf. *Ibid.,* pp. 200–203.

[24] Cf. Helvétius, *De L'esprit,* p. 75.

[25] *Ibid.,* p. 97 (my translation).

[26] Cf. *Ibid.,* p. 96.

[27] *Ibid.,* pp. 180–181 (my translation).

[28] *Ibid.,* p. 182n.

determined ideas, i.e. the prejudices, result from the love of power. The prejudices hide the love of power. The philosopher of the Enlightenment has the supreme task of unmasking this fact.[29]

Similarly, in the view of Holbach, man has remained a child without experience, a slave without courage, afraid of reason, and unable to find his way out of the labyrinth, in which he has so long been wandering.[30]

The enslavement of men, Helvétius adds, is largely the result of the actions of the priests whose interests are contrary to the general good.[31] "The priests have duped the people, and made of the Roman Church an instrument of their own selfish aggrandizement."[32] Holbach's ideas are the fundament upon which the theory of priestly deceit rests. He begins with the basic question: What is the origin of religion? How has it been possible to persuade reasonable beings that the thing, the most impossible to comprehend, was the most essential to them? "It is because they have been greatly terrified . . . Ignorance and fear are the two hinges of all religion."[33]

How was religion established? It was to gross, ignorant, and stupid people that the founders of religion have in all ages addressed themselves, when they wished to give them their Gods, their modes of worship, their mythology, their marvelous and frightful fables.[34]

The doctrine of a future life is an important element in the deceitful practices of the priests and the rulers of the people who are their worldly allies. "If futurity is of no real utility to mankind, it is, at least, of the greatest utility to those, who have assumed the office of conducting them thither."[35] Political expediency demands that religion be founded on mysteries. The unknown, the hidden, the fabulous attract a mass following more easily than the clear and the simple; "the vulgar ask no better than to listen to fables; priests and legislators, by inventing religions and forging mysteries, have served them to their taste."[36] The rulers also serve their own interests better in not explaining themselves too clearly: "Princes and their ministers make a mystery of their projects, for fear their enemies should discover and render them abortive."[37]

Holbach is convinced that in religion the evidence of interested parties becomes irrefragable and incontestable: God's miracles ". . . are prob-

---

[29] Cf. Helvétius, *Oeuvres Complètes*, Vol. II, pp. 211–212.

[30] Cf. Paul Henri Thiry Holbach, *Good Sense: Or, Natural Ideas Opposed to Supernatural* (translated by H. D. Robinson), Boston: J. P. Mendum, 1856, pp. IV–V.

[31] Cf. Helvétius, *Oeuvres Complètes*, Vol. II, p. 396.

[32] Quoted in Charles Hunter van Duzer, *Contribution of the Ideologues to French Revolutionary Thought*, Dissertation, Baltimore: The Johns Hopkins Press, 1935, p. 54.

[33] Holbach, *Good Sense*, p. 8.

[34] Cf. *Ibid.*, p. 10.

[35] *Ibid.*, p. 93.

[36] *Ibid.*, p. 100.

[37] *Ibid.*, p. 101.

able tales, related by suspected people, who had the greatest interest in giving out that they were the messengers of the Most High."[38] Central to the theory of priestly deceit is the conspiracy argument maintaining that throne and altar are in alliance against the freedom and welfare of the people: ". . . *the true religion is always that on whose side are the prince and the hangman*. Emperors and hangmen long supported the gods of Rome against the God of Christians; the latter, having gained to his interest the emperors, their soldiers, and their hangmen, succeeded in destroying the worship of the Roman gods."[39] Everywhere men are ". . . governed by tyrants, who use religion merely as an instrument to render more stupid the slaves, whom they overwhelm under the weight of their vices, or whom they sacrifice without mercy to their fatal extravagancies."[40]

The doctrine of "the divine right of kings" is an ideological facade hiding the exploitive tactics of the aristocracy and clergy.[41]

The alliance between kings and priests, however uneasy it may be, also serves the interests of the religious party: ". . . Christianity, at first weak and servile, established itself among the savage and free nations of Europe only by intimating to their chiefs, that its religious principles favored despotism and rendered them absolute."[42]

Helvétius follows Holbach in his version of the theory of priestly deceit: religious opinions are the true source of all the suffering afflicting mankind. Man's ignorance of natural causes resulted in the creation of Gods. These Gods became man's terror through the addition of the element of deceit.[43]

Statesmen and priests thrive on prejudices; this brings them inevitably into conflict with philosophers who are interested in the destruction of prejudices and the discovery of the rational social order which they believe to be rooted in the law of nature. The problem of philosophy becomes a political problem: religious intolerance ". . . is the most dangerous. Love of power is the motive of it, and religion the pretext."[44] Political and moral questions ". . . are determined by the strong and not by the reasonable, and . . . if opinion governs the world, it is . . . the powerful who governs opinion."[45]

Truth is the only weapon against the prejudices which always hide the interests and the power of individuals or groups. The reign of truth, however, presupposes the reign of freedom; the battle against the preju-

---

[38] *Ibid.*, pp. 117–118.
[39] *Ibid.*, p. 133 (emphasis in original).
[40] *Ibid.*, p. 138.
[41] Cf. *Ibid.*, pp. 139–140.
[42] *Ibid.*, p. 142.
[43] Cf. Helvétius, *Neunundzwanzig Thesen des Materialismus*, p. 26.
[44] Helvétius, *De L'homme*, Vol. I, p. 67 (my translation).
[45] Helvétius, *Oeuvres Complètes*, Vol. II, p. 541 (my translation).

dices is also a battle against the forces of oppression: State and Religion. "But what are the matrices of truth? Contradiction and dispute. The liberty to think bears the fruit of truth."[46] Therefore, education must be wrestled from the hands of the clergy and rebuilt on a secular basis.[47]

Thus Helvétius and Holbach view religion, first, as a peculiar form of intellectual exercise which creates imaginary entities and an unreal world wherein man finds substitute gratification for his desires, thwarted, as they are, by social and political reality. Second, they suspect religion as an instrument of power, created and used by the rulers to sanction a given order as the expression of divine reason and will.

Prejudices blocking our understanding of true virtue originate at throne and altar and serve the preservation of power. "Authority believes itself commonly interested in maintaining the recognized opinions; the prejudices and mistakes that it judges necessary in order to assure its power, are sustained by force, which never reasons."[48]

The prejudices can be recognized and overcome as soon as freedom from arbitrary authorities gives full sway to rational truth as contained in the lawful order of nature. Likewise, true morality as guaranteed by the laws of reason will then become the fundament of the social and politico-legal order. Religion will be replaced by this true social morality which is ". . . the only natural religion for man."[49]

Similarly, Diderot's "unorthodox articles" in the *Encyclopédie* aimed ". . . to expose certain widespread prejudices, which meant, so far as religion was concerned, the undermining of Christianity and its replacement by a new faith in natural morality which would establish bonds of mutual esteem and tolerance."[50]

---

[46] *Ibid.*, p. 525 (my translation).

[47] Cf. Claude Adrien Helvétius, *De L'homme*, Vol. II, p. 402.

[48] Holbach, *Système de la Nature*, p. 153 (my translation).

[49] Paul Henri Thiry Holbach, *Letters to Eugenia: On the Absurd, Contradictory, and Demoralizing Dogmas and Mysteries of the Christian Religion* (translated by H. D. Robinson), New York: H. M. Duhecquet, 1833, p. 233.

[50] J. E. Barker, *Diderot's Treatment of the Christian Religion in the Encyclopédie*, New York: King's Crown Press, 1941, p. 12. Diderot thought that the "unnatural" moral restrictions imposed by Christianity must of necessity make people miserable and criminal: "People will no longer know what they ought or ought not to do." (Denis Diderot, "Supplement to Bougainville's 'Voyage'" in Denis Diderot, *Rameau's Nephew and Other Works* (translated by Jacques Barzun and Ralph H. Bowen), Garden City, N.Y.: Doubleday & Company, 1956, p. 209.

It was, however, Rousseau who took up what Ernst Cassirer has called the signal problem of eighteenth-century ethics: the justification of the cosmos independent of the traditional Christian explanation. Rousseau approached this problem with his great principle that claims in the final formulation used in his *Rousseau juge de Jean Jacques:*

". . . nature has made man happy and good, but society depraves him and renders him miserable." More important than this verdict, however, is Rousseau's companion assumption that man has been endowed with the moral energy to overcome the evils of a society resting on unnatural principles. At the center of Rousseau's vision resides the conviction that, although natural man cannot live outside society, he can never-

The *philosophes* knew that this undermining of Christianity spelled war with the defenders of the established order; but this was a consequence they were willing to accept: "As self-appointed knight errants of truth, they found the makers of myth and the forces of privilege planted like grim-faced guardians before a precious hoard. And the identity of the enemy was, as it were, emblazoned on their shields: it was Christianity."[51]

Against the common enemy Holbach hurled the philosophers' battle cry when he exclaimed, liberty, truth, utility: there are all the characteristics of the philosophical spirit—the trinity of philosophical reason, destined to replace the Christian Trinity.[52]

---

theless recreate society to recreate himself. At this point the philosophy of the Enlightenment announces a theme that is to reappear even more strongly in Marx's attempt to establish a philosophical anthropology evolving around the desire to "make man into man." (Cf. Ernst Cassirer, "Das Problem Jean Jacques Rousseau," *Archiv für Geschichte der Philosophie,* Vol. XLI, No. 1/2 and No. 3 (1932), pp. 177–213 and 479–513. See also Jean-Jacques Rousseau, *Oeuvres complètes,* (edited under the direction of Bernard Gagnebin and Marcel Raymond), Vol. I, Paris: Gallimard, 1959, p. 934).

[51] Gay, *op. cit.,* p. 44.

[52] Cf. Paul Henri Thiry Holbach, *Essai sur les préjugés,* London: M. M. Rey, 1777, p. 267.

CHAPTER 14

KARL MARX
Exponent of Total Suspicion

$\overline{}$

THE SEEDS of doubt and suspicion, contained in the great debate of the *philosophes*, matured considerably in the work of Helvétius and Holbach. Yet, they only suspected ideological distortions of the truth in some part of the opponent's assertions and then merely with regard to the content of these statements. The theory of prejudices contains the assumption that ideas are socially determined: the reflection of group interests, however, does not exhaust the function of ideas; they also contain truth.

With the arrival of Karl Marx (1818–1883) upon the intellectual scene the world experienced the full impact of systematic doubt and suspicion. In historical perspective Hegel's work was the intermediary between Holbach and Marx: it provided Marx with the sophistication that he needed to elevate materialism to the rank of a scientific instrument capable of revealing significant interconnections in socio-economic and political reality.

Marx crystallized one aspect of the world: the economic structure of society, constituted by the material "relations of production" which form the real foundation, on which develop legal and political superstructures and to which correspond definite forms of social consciousness. This historical materialism is at the center of Marx's system of thought, which is essentially a theory of social revolution.

Marx conceived of history as a process of the self-creation of man. This notion he derived only partially from Hegel, for whom the historical process was, after all, a movement and conflict of abstract categories, enacted in the heaven of pure thought; Marx found the "sociological" thesis that social institutions change in the process of historical development in the political and historical works of late eighteenth-century authors; among them are the Scottish historian Adam Ferguson, whose *Essay on the History of Civil Society* appeared in 1767; the Scotsman John Millar, who published *The Origin of the Distinction of Ranks* in 1771; and the Frenchman S.N.H. Linguet, whose *Théorie des lois civiles* was first published in 1767. Marx, who was bent on writing an empirical work when he started his *Capital*, was a "sociologist" largely opposed to Hegel's philosophy of history and political theory: his criticism of

Hegel reveals the strong influence of the Scottish and French writers along with that of Saint-Simon.

Marx's work is also a new historiography: his earliest and dominating interest was in historical and social change. From his account he eliminated, however, ". . . any reference to forces or agencies beyond those of human beings living and working in society. . . . His intention . . . was to give a scientific account of social change. . . ."[1]

To begin with, Marx reversed Hegel's philosophy when he put *matter before mind*. Already in Paris, while writing for the *Deutsch-Französische Jahrbücher*, he concluded that ". . . legal relations as well as forms of state . . . are rooted in the material conditions of life, which are summed up by Hegel . . . under the name 'civil society'; the anatomy of that civil society is to be sought in political economy."[2] Marx continued the study of political economy—begun in Paris—after his expulsion to Brussels. There he arrived at a general conclusion which continued to serve as the leading idea in his further studies:

> In the social production which men carry on they enter into definite relations that are indispensable and independent of their will; these *relations of production* correspond to a definite stage of development of their material powers of production. The sum total of these *relations of production* constitutes the *economic structure of society*—the *real foundation,* on which rise legal and political *superstructures* and to which correspond definite forms of social consciousness. The mode of production in material life determines the general character of the social, political, and spiritual processes of life. *It is not the consciousness of men that determines their existence, but, on the contrary, their social existence determines their consciousness.*[3]

What exactly is the meaning of Marx's concept "relations of production" (*Produktionsverhältnisse*)? They include the forces of production (*Produktivkräfte*) such as technology, existing skills, both mental and physical, inherited traditions, and ideologies. But it would be erroneous to identify the relations of production with the forces of production. The relations of production, furthermore, are not the same as the conditions of production (*Produktionsbedingungen*) consisting of such elements as population, climate, and the natural supply of raw material. Marx's central concept describes the way of economic production—the *entire* economic life of a society, the manner in which men's *social* activity *organizes* both the forces and conditions of production. These relations

---

[1] T. B. Bottomore and Maximilien Rubel, Introduction to Karl Marx, *Selected Writings in Sociology and Social Philosophy* (edited with an introduction and notes by T. B. Bottomore and Maximilien Rubel; texts translated by T. B. Bottomore), second impression, London: Watts & Co., 1961, p. 21.

[2] Karl Marx, *A Contribution to the Critique of Political Economy* (translated from the second German edition by N. I. Stone), Chicago: Charles H. Kerr & Company, 1904, p. 11.

[3] *Ibid.*, pp. 11–12 (my emphasis).

of production find their legal expression in property relations. Therefore, only productive or property relations may be called feudal or capitalistic. "For Marx it is the relations of production, not the forces of
production and not the conditions of production, which are the basis of
the cultural superstructure."[4]

Alienation: The Loss of Man

The *philosophes* had already realized that man's opinions and his education are determined by the social milieu. In the nineteenth century,
the German idealist philosophers taught that the historical development
of public opinion as all of history constitutes a lawful process. Now
Marx declares in partial opposition to the idealist philosophers that the
historical process is not determined by the "spirit of the world" but solely
by the material relations between men.

The *philosophes* meant to explain human history by reference to "human nature." They also used this concept to describe the qualities which
an ideal state and society had to possess. The concept *human nature*,
however, is settled with logical inconsistencies. If human nature is constant, we cannot refer to it in order to explain historical variation and
cultural differences. If human nature, on the other hand, is variable, we
have to ask what causes its changes?

The German idealist philosophers fully recognized this logical problem
and located the hidden force behind the historical process outside of man,
who consequently became a puppet in the hands of the spirit of the
world. The spirit of the world, as the power behind the historical process,
is, however, nothing else but one aspect of human nature which has
been forced through the filter of logical abstraction.

Marx saw human nature as variable and combined this notion with
the idea of a *meaningful* historical process, set in motion by man's intentions and activities. While man through his labor has important effects
upon nature outside himself, he simultaneously causes changes in his
own nature. The important difference between man and animal derives
from the fact that man "produces his life." In contrast to animal species,
man has to create the means of his subsistence and is always the product
of his own activity. This "production," however, can only be carried out
by a creature that sets its own goals and knows in advance what it
wants to create. "At the end of every labour-process, we get a result that
already existed in the imagination of the labourer at its commencement."[5]

[4] Sidney Hook, *Towards the Understanding of Karl Marx: A Revolutionary Interpretation*, New York: The John Day Company, 1933, p. 134.

[5] Karl Marx, *Capital: A Critical Analysis of Capitalist Production*, Vol. I (translated from the third German edition by Samuel Moore and Edward Aveling, edited
by Frederick Engels), Fourth Edition, New York: D. Appleton & Co., London: Swan
Sonnenschein, 1891, p. 157.

Significantly man projects himself outward, relinquishes what he designed—a part of himself: the products of his imagination and labor assume an independent existence.

This basic fact of human life begins to threaten man when a new element is added: the division of labor which establishes the mutual dependence of individuals and thus introduces the contradiction between the interests of the individual or the individual family and the common interest of all individuals. The collective work develops powers transcending those of man and finally ". . . each man has a particular, exclusive sphere of activity, which is forced upon him and from which he cannot escape."[6] The division of labor in its complete form creates a situation where nobody any longer disposes over the means of his subsistence: now the relations of production and trade completely replace human relations; men no longer confront one another as men but as mere exponents of the anonymous and all powerful relations of production which separate and alienate one human being from the other.

This situation finds its expression in the writings of political economists who conceive of men's social life as forms of exchange and trade: Adam Smith views society as a commercial enterprise; every one of its members is a salesman. Political economy establishes, therefore, an alienated form of social intercourse as the true and original form of active human life.

On the nontheoretical level, human alienation finds its most striking expression in money. Money as such has no qualities; it is the indifferent power that makes everything and everybody available as an object of purchase. Since nobody has what he needs, everybody needs money to have anything: money ". . . is therefore the most eminent *object*."[7] The other person becomes for all others whatever he can be in relation to money. What I am not, I can become through money which ". . . is the universal whore, the universal pander between men and peoples."[8] It turns love into hate and hate into love, virtue into vice and vice into virtue, nonsense into reason and reason into nonsense. Money reflects the complete alienation of man from his true nature: from his nature as man.

While commodities relinquish their ultimate qualities in money, man relinquishes his in becoming a commodity: he becomes one as soon as his power of labor becomes useless unless it is sold. In society the worker is not a human being but merely the exponent of an abstract commodity —in selling it, he sells himself: the self-alienation of man has reached

[6] Karl Marx, Friedrich Engels, *The German Ideology*, Parts I & III (edited with an introduction by R. Pascal), New York: International Publishers, 1939, p. 22.

[7] Karl Marx, *Nationalökonomie and Philosophie* (with an introduction by Erich Thier), Köln und Berlin: Verlag Gustav Kiepenheuer, 1950, p. 227 (my translation; emphasis in original).

[8] *Ibid.*, p. 229.

its ultimate form. The economic theorists of capitalism, therefore, view the proletarian—the man who, without capital or ground rent, lives entirely by his labor—as a mere worker, but not as a human being.[9]

The alienation of labor appears not only in its product but also in the process of production—in productive activity: here the worker experiences his labor as an external process which, instead of fulfilling him, makes him miserable; he does not develop a feeling of well-being but a nausea of physical exhaustion and mental debasement. For the worker the alienated character of labor ". . . shows itself in the fact that it is not his work but work for someone else, that in labor he does not belong to himself but to another person."[10]

Marx rejected a human being which was nothing but a self-alienated producer of commodities and informed his collaborator Ruge that he had decided to "make man into man." The realization of man's true purposes, however, necessitated the liberation of life from its subservience to "alien powers." Man was no longer to be a product of the relations of production—these were to become a product of man; their power over man had to be terminated so that he could become the highest being for himself, his conduct toward others and toward himself motivated by nothing but his character as man. Only after his liberation from the external and alien conditions of his existence which adulterate all his true potentialities, as money does for example, can man fulfill his human possibilities: only then his ears will be free to receive music and his eyes will behold the beauty of form. Man must be freed from his slavery under the needs of material life to fulfill his real character: a being that determines himself.[11]

Marx's entire lifework was oriented around this central idea: the realization of man's true character and purpose. He crystallized it out of his differentiation from Hegel and Feuerbach; it motivated him to concentrate all his energies on the task of identifying the forces in the processes of reality that dissolve the contradiction between idea and reality. Consequently, Marx had to discover those elements in social activity that possessed the power to effect the breakdown of the existing relations and that would because of their own inner contradiction negate the general self-alienation in social life.

These elements, however, had to be found in the relations of active life itself; they were present in the relations which dominate as a nameless force the relations between men—that is in the economic relations wherein all self-alienation originates. The discovery of the laws of politi-

[9] Cf. Karl Marx, "Ökonomisch-Philosophische Manuskripte aus dem Jahre 1844," in Marx, Engels, *Historisch-Kritische Gesamtausgabe*, Vol. I/3 (edited for the Marx-Engels-Institute Moscow by V. Adoratskij), Berlin: Marx-Engels-Verlag, 1932, pp. 45–46. (Referred to hereafter as MEGA.)

[10] *Ibid.*, pp. 85–86 (my translation).

[11] Cf. Marx, *Nationalökonomie and Philosophie*, p. 191.

cal economy was, therefore, at the same time the discovery of the conditions which had to be met in order to achieve the self-realization of man. This is the reason for Marx's tireless analysis of economic laws and their development as reflected in his *Capital* and similar writings.

Revolution and Ideology

Like Hegel, Marx meant to embrace all of reality to offer a final answer to the question about the meaning and the course of human history. He combined this passion for totality with a ruthless determination to completely change the world: the material foundations of the world that he was born into had to be blown up in the grand revolution that he worked for; all the nonmaterial forces that were emanated by this doomed fundament had to be exploded along with the *economic* order. The destruction of nonmaterial culture was inevitable since all ideas were nothing but reflections of human existence as determined by the relations of production. The unavoidable overthrow of the economic order would automatically cause a change in intellectual reality.

Marx developed this theory of social and cultural change in his *Economic and Philosophical Manuscripts*, written in 1844, and immediately designated communism as the instrument that was to effect the radical transformation of economic, social, and cultural reality. First, however, "true communism" had to be distinguished from "false communism." For true communism the expropriation of private property constituted merely one aspect of the general and overall appropriation of the world. Adherents of false communism, on the other hand, attacked the existing property relations in vain since they merely advocated a levelling of differences in property through raised wages or the equal distribution of wealth. These theoreticians—notably Proudhon—fostered only partial reform. In Marx's opinion they could neither effect a thorough change in human behavior nor could they halt the pernicious process that transformed the world of things into values by devaluating the world of man into things. False communism, if ever realized, would destroy everything that did not lend itself to be owned by all as private property. Instead of terminating the determination of man as a "worker," false communism would expand it over all of mankind, while capital would remain the general power dominating society. In contrast, true communism or humanism would lead to a repossession of man on the level of civilization attained under capitalism while simultaneously abolishing private property and thus human self-alienation.[12]

Fully comprehended communism would change, therefore, not only the social and economic relations but also the political, legal, moral, reli-

[12] Cf. MEGA I/3, p. 114.

gious, and scientific behavior of man. Socialist man would own the world of objects not by having private, capitalistic possessions but by transforming all things into positive and concrete realizations of himself. In a world totally changed by communism—which is neither the aim nor the final form of human development—man produces man, himself, and then other men; his object which is created by the direct activity of his personality is his existence for other men, and their existence for him. Socialist man through his action makes the world his own since his mode of production does not lead to alienation but to self-assertion.[13]

Since Marx was convinced that the revolutionary overthrow of the existing order was the unavoidable consequence of the march of history, he immediately debunked all conservative ideas as false, as hopelessly out of tune with reality or the actual social configuration.[14]

To begin with, the relationship between existence and consciousness, that Marx postulates as basic, is destroyed as soon as the division of labor separates material and mental work. Now consciousness loses its connection with life; the fictitious idea arises that consciousness is no longer determined by existence. The division of labor, thus, causes our consciousness to replace life with its own creations. At this point man becomes unable to recognize that consciousness is nothing else but conscious existence. This development is aggravated through a further consequence of the division of labor: the producer loses his control over the product of labor which confronts him, henceforth, as an independent alien force in the shape of the automatism of the economic and political order. On this basis the ideological misinterpretation of existence arises: the world-market is confused with the spirit of the world.[15]

Traditional philosophy and theology explain law, political power, ethics, etc. as the manifestations of metaphysical principles, only because we can no longer grasp that such suprahuman powers, as God or the universal spirit, merely express man's self-alienation.[16] Thus man "ideologically" deduces socio-political reality from omnipotent otherworldly forces because of his inability to control the relations determining his life. Against this background of the division of labor, Marx debunks as ideological the entire history of philosophy from Plato to Hegel and his followers.[17]

For Marx, Plato's ideas represent ghosts as much as Hegel's spirit. In Hegel's system men and their circumstances actually appear upside down, as in a *camera obscura.* "To Hegel . . . the real world is only the external, phenomenal form of 'the Idea.' With me, on the contrary, the ideal is

---

13 Cf. *Ibid.,* pp. 115, 119, 126.
14 Cf. Marx, *A Contribution to the Critique of Political Economy,* p. 12.
15 Cf. Marx, Engels, *The German Ideology,* p. 27.
16 Cf. *Ibid.,* p. 21.
17 Cf. *Ibid.,* p. 1.

nothing else than the material world reflected by the human mind, and translated into forms of thought."[18]

The Young Hegelian philosophy is rejected as mere boasting which mirrors nothing but the "wretchedness of the real conditions in Germany." These philosophers interpret the relationships of men as products of their consciousness. Consequently, they want to bring about social change by demanding men to exchange their present consciousness for another kind of consciousness. This demand amounts to the postulate to *interpret* reality differently, i.e. to accept it by means of another interpretation which according to the various exponents of this school could be anything from human, to critical and egoistic. During this battle of phrases not one of these philosophers ever thought of inquiring ". . . into the connection of German philosophy with German reality, the relation of their criticism to their own material surroundings."[19]

Ideology as False Consciousness

Apart from its allegedly communistic beginning, history has so far been the history of human alienation. The economic basis of this development which separated the idea of man from the reality of man was found in the involuntary division of labor leading to forced labor and private property. Simultaneously, society split into warring classes; the state as the organized expression of the will of the upper class emerged. With the loss of his freedom man developed false consciousness—the consciousness of the individual in *alienation* which creates ideologies or systems of beliefs and ideas that are object-inadequate and, therefore, without effect upon reality. They merely act upon man's imagination.

Man's false or ideological consciousness creates religion as an otherworldly realm of fancy which offers substitute satisfactions and escape from this-worldly misery. Along with this system of beliefs man creates a system of ideas which does no more than to justify the *status quo*.

So far we have been confronted by philosophers who imagine to understand history when they view it as a process, wherein ideas or spirit find their realization.[20] To understand the historical changes in man's thinking we must, however, turn to the analysis of the production and reproduction of *real* life. In his attack on Proudhon's *La Philosophie de la Misère*, Marx tries to expose the illusions that are in his opinion typical for "speculative" philosophy. He accuses the French philosopher of transforming the economic categories in his imagination into "eternal ideas," existing before any reality, instead of interpreting them as the theoretical

[18] Marx, *Capital*, Vol. I, p. xxx.

[19] Marx, Engels, *The German Ideology*, p. 6.

[20] Cf. Karl Marx, Friedrich Engels, *Die Deutsche Ideologie*, Berlin: Dietz Verlag, 1953, p. 186.

expressions of the historical relations of production, corresponding to a given stage in the development of material production.

Economic categories are only the ". . . theoretical expressions, the abstractions, of the social relations of production." Proudhon, however, as a "true philosopher" sees things upside down. He sees in the real relations only the incarnation of theoretical principles which slumbered in the bosom of the ". . . impersonal reason of humanity."[21] Actually, new productive forces change the mode of production, the manner of earning a living, and all social relations: "The windmill gives you society with the feudal lord; the steammill, society with the industrial capitalist."[22]

But the bourgeois philosophers cannot grasp these basic connections; their false consciousness cannot penetrate reality. Consequently they do not possess an adequate understanding of history, or social and economic life: social philosophy, history, philosophy, religion, etc. are devoid of truth.

False consciousness characteristically mistakes outward appearances for inner essences. It is, therefore, doomed to remain unscientific, since we have science only when surface phenomena are successfully reduced to actual inner processes. The false philosophers teach that the essence of things resides in the allegedly independent development of ideas and thus mistake outward appearances for reality. They forget that ideas merely reflect the alien hypostatized power that was generated by the totality of human labor: the essence of historical change can only be found in the economic process; therefore, false consciousness is barred from the understanding of history. False consciousness is mad consciousness; it distorts reality by transforming the material world into a mere idea and mere ideas into material entities. The fancies of our brain assume bodily form; in the mind a world of "ghosts" materializes. "This is the secret of all pious visions, this is at the same time the general form of madness."[23] Against this "madness" Marx pits his interpretation of ideas which sees them as the "expression," the "ideological echo," the "mental reflection," or the "symptom" of the material relations of production.

Kant's *Critique of Practical Reason*, for instance, "reflects" completely the political and economic conditions that prevailed in Germany at the close of the eighteenth century. At this time the French bourgeoisie came to power through the world's most colossal revolution and conquered the continent of Europe; the politically emancipated English bourgeosie revolutionized industry and gained the commercial mastery over India

[21] Karl Marx, *The Poverty of Philosophy* (translated by H. Quelch), Chicago: Charles H. Kerr, 1910, p. 119.

[22] *Ibid.*, p. 119.

[23] Karl Marx, Friedrich Engels, *Die Heilige Familie*, Berlin: Dietz Verlag, 1953, p. 330 (my translation). Cf. also Marx, Engels, *Werke*, Vol. 2, 4th edition, Berlin: Dietz Verlag, 1962, pp. 195–196.

and the rest of the world. But the impotent German bourgeoisie merely achieved "good will." Kant was satisfied with this mere good will, remained disinterested in practical results, and ultimately expected the realization of this good will in the other world. Kant's good will echoes the impotence, suppression, and misery of the German citizens who were never able to develop their narrow interests into the common, national interests of a class. Therefore, the German bourgeoisie was constantly exploited by its counterpart in other nations. The bourgeoisie of a country as small as Holland was more powerful—thanks to advanced class interests—than the numerically superior German bourgeoisie which suffered from its lack of common interests and the diversity of its pitiful preoccupations. The disunity of political organization corresponded to the disunity of interests. Yet where should political concentration originate in a country devoid of all economic presuppositions for political concentration? Neither the German bourgeoisie nor its ideological spokesman Kant understood that liberalism, the theory of the French bourgeoisie, was based on material interests and a common will generated by the material relations of production. Hence, Kant separated the theoretical expression from the interests which the theory expresses. He transformed the will of the French bourgeoisie motivated by the material relations of production into the pure self-determination of "free will," into will in and for itself, and arrived at purely ideological definitions of concepts and moral postulates. Therefore, the German *petit bourgeois* also recoiled from the practices of energetic bourgeois liberalism as manifest in the Reign of Terror and the insolent forms of bourgeois profiteering.[24]

Undoubtedly, the German middle class lagged far behind the middle classes of other, more advanced European nations.[25] The retarded German bourgeoisie was also rejected by the Young Hegelians. The philosophical anarchist Max Stirner, for example, reduced bourgeois humanism to the egoistic "I" that transforms everything in his reach into property. With Stirner the concept of man is completely devaluated: the stage is dominated by the eternal declensions of "I, me, and myself." With his concept of the "only one" Stirner felt superior to any social commitment; his "I" was not subject to any determination, whether bourgeois or proletarian. Marx, however, reveals Stirner's glorification of hardboiled egoism as the social defense-mechanism of a *petty bourgeois* soul desiring to save "its own"; his social truth of the only one is nothing but the decadent bourgeoisie.[26]

---

[24] Cf. Marx, Engels, *Die Deutsche Ideologie,* pp. 196–199.

[25] Cf. Karl Marx, "Moralising Criticism and Critical Morality: A Polemic against Karl Heinzen," in Karl Marx, *Selected Essays* (translated by H. J. Stenning), New York: International Publishers, 1926, p. 159.

[26] Cf. Marx, Engels, *Die Deutsche Ideologie,* p. 433.

Ideological, as well, were the ideas of the "true socialists," mainly represented by Karl Grün, Moses Hess, Georg Kuhlmann, R. Matthäi, and F. H. Semmig. Against their claim that a movement of social reform had to be based upon absolute ethical principles like "social love" and justice, Marx held his own that every realistic social movement must be a class movement.[27]

Abroad, Marx found similar problems: classical economics was an ideological system reflecting the capitalistic relations of production; its major fault was the assumption that its economic categories were valid for any historical system. In opposition to this ahistorical orientation, Marx claims that economic categories are not Platonic Ideas, but that they are as transitory as the historical relationships which they express. The theory of the labor-fund expresses both the rigidity of the English economists and their ideological function in the defense of the status quo.

> The facts that lie at the bottom of this dogma are these: on the one hand, the labourer has no right to interfere in the division of social wealth into means of enjoyment for the non-labourer and means of production. On the other hand, only in favourable and exceptional cases, has he the power to enlarge the so-called labour-fund at the expense of the "revenue" of the wealthy.[28]

The same shortcomings characterize Jeremy Bentham's version of the theory of utility; again the concept is handled in a rigid, ahistorical fashion, betraying the class interests of the bourgeoisie.

> With the dryest naiveté he takes the modern shopkeeper, especially the English shopkeeper, as the normal man. Whatever is useful to this queer normal man, and to his world, is absolutely useful. This yard-measure, then, he applies to past, present, and future. The Christian religion, e.g., is "useful," because it forbids in the name of religion the same faults that the penal code condemns in the name of the law . . . With such rubbish has the brave fellow . . . piled up mountains of books.[29]

Marx was always keenly suspicious of the ideological character of theories and concepts. In 1848, he warned his audience at the Democratic Association of Brussels not to be taken in by the standard slogans of the bourgeoisie: "To call cosmopolitan exploitation universal brotherhood is an idea that could only be engendered in the brain of the bourgeoisie."[30]

The German revolutionist incorporated Helvétius' psychology of inter-

---

27 Cf. Marx, Engels, *The German Ideology*, p. 79.
28 Marx, *Capital*, Vol. I, p. 623.
29 *Ibid.*, p. 622n.
30 Karl Marx, *Free Trade: An Address delivered before the Democratic Association of Brussels, Belgium, January 9, 1848* (translated by Florence Kelley, preface by F. Engels), New York: New York Labor News Company, 1921, p. 41.

ests into his theory of ideology: ideas are the expression of human interests; they are always modified by the class position of those who produce
them. Like the philosophers of the Enlightenment, Marx also used the
term prejudices: "Law, morality, and religion have become . . . so many
bourgeois prejudices, behind which bourgeois interests lurk in ambush."[31]
Philanthropists serve their own interests by turning charity into play:
human misery, the bottomless depravity of having to accept alms, must
serve to satisfy the self-love of the aristocracy of money and education
that wants games, amusement, and laughter. The numerous charitable
organizations in Germany, France, and England, all the concerts, balls,
shows, and dinners for the poor have one meaning: the organization of
charity in the interest of entertainment. The hidden reasons behind his
charitable activities were revealed by that ". . . Dandin of Paris who—
after the dance—invited his lady to dinner with the following words:
'Ah, Madame, it is not enough to have danced for the well-being of these
poor Poles . . . let us be philanthropists to the last . . . let us now *eat
dinner* for the *benefit of the poor!*' "[32]

Interests have, of course, exerted their decisive influence upon larger,
more vital questions as the study of revolutionary movements and political upheavals shows. "One ruling minority was . . . overthrown; another
minority seized the helm of state in its stead and refashioned the
state institutions to *suit its own interests*."[33]

So far intellectuals have been suffering from the illusion of ideologists.
Historians, as well as jurists, politicians, and practical statesmen, etc.,
have taken every epoch at its word and believed that everything it says
and imagines about itself is true. This ideological illusion can be explained if we recall the actual position of intellectuals in life, the nature
of their job, and the role played by the division of labor. Marx starts with
the basic assumption that the ideas of the ruling class are in every historical period the ruling ideas.[34] The class which acts as the ruling material force of society is, simultaneously, the ruling intellectual force of
society; the class that controls the means of material production also
controls the means of mental production. Consequently, the ideas of
those members of society who lack the means of intellectual production
are subject to the ideas of the ruling class which merely express the

[31] Karl Marx, Friedrich Engels, "Manifesto of the Communist Party," in *The Communist Manifesto of Karl Marx and Friedrich Engels* (edited by D. Ryazanoff, translated by Eden and Cedar Paul), New York: Russell & Russell, 1963, pp. 39–40.

[32] Marx, Engels, *Die Heilige Familie*, p. 343 (my translation, ellipsis and emphasis
in original). Cf. also Marx, Engels, *Werke*, Vol. 2, p. 206.

[33] Karl Marx, "The Class Struggles in France, 1848 to 1850," in Marx, Engels,
Selected Works, Vol. I, Moscow: Foreign Languages Publishing House, London:
Lawrence and Wishart, 1950, p. 113 (my emphasis).

[34] Cf. Marx, Engels, *Manifesto of the Communist Party*, p. 50.

dominant material relationships in the disguise of ethical and theoretical systems. These systems, therefore, only express the relationships which establish the power of the ruling class: they are the ideas of its dominance. The division of labor appears in the dominant class as the division of material and mental labor: the ruling class divides its functions; some of its members work as the thinkers of the class, as active ideologists who make their living by perfecting the illusion of the class about itself; others develop a merely receptive attitude to the ideas and illusions produced by their ideological spokesmen. This lack of intellectual commitment and interest stems from the particular role of these members of the ruling class which demands great practical activity; the active members of the ruling class simply have less time to invent illusions and ideas about themselves.

Historians have failed to grasp this vital connection between ideas and the dominant relations of production; instead, they erroneously assumed that abstract and universally valid ideas dominate history. They arrived at this interpretation of history by detaching the ideas of the ruling class from that class and by attributing to them an independent existence. They never bothered to analyse the relations of production and their connection with the producers of ideas. In this manner they made it easy for each new class which replaced the previous ruling class to establish its power. The new rulers simply had to represent their interest in an ideal form as the common interest of all the members of society. In this ideal formulation the new ruling class embellished its ideas as the only rational and universal ones.[35]

From here it is an easy step to deliberate deceit; on this ground misleading and fraudulent idea-systems flourish: this is the other, the politically decisive side of ideology: "Indeed, holy missions are always bound up with the holy beings who pursue them."[36] Marx illustrated the use of ideas and intellectual currents by political strategists in one of the articles on the Crimean War which he contributed to the *New York Tribune* between 1853 and 1856: the period of the Protestant Reformation initiated a process of decay of religious authority; the upper classes in every European nation and especially the diplomats, lawyers, and statesmen, began to abandon individually all religious belief, and turned into so-called free-thinkers. Marx calls this period the era of aristocratic revolt against ecclesiastical authority and quotes approvingly Comte, who in his opinion has unmasked the ideological reasons for the tolerance of Enlightenment philosophy on the part of the authorities: ". . . this system of hypocrisy has been more and more elaborated in practice, *permitting the emancipation of all minds of a certain bearing*, on the tacit condition

---

[35] Cf. Marx, Engels, *The German Ideology*, pp. 42–43.
[36] *Ibid.*, p. 181.

that they should aid in protracting the submission of the masses. This was eminently the policy of the Jesuits."[37]

Equally useful was the notion of primitive accumulation, first introduced by Adam Smith under the name of previous accumulation. The economic theoreticians asserted the existence of this form of accumulation which is not the result but the starting point of the capitalistic mode of production in order to ideologically justify the existence of considerable masses of capital and of labor power in the hands of the producers of commodities. They had to explain to the have-nots why they were have-nots and not capitalists. Instead of telling the story of "brutal force" and "enslavement," the economists invented the deliberately misleading ideological illusion of primitive accumulation.

> In times long gone by there were two sorts of people; one, the diligent, intelligent, and, above all, frugal elite; the other, lazy rascals, spending their substance, and more, in riotous living . . . Thus it came to pass that the former sort accumulated wealth, and the latter sort had at last nothing to sell except their own skins. And from this original sin dates the poverty of the great majority that, despite all its labour, has up to now nothing to sell but itself, and the wealth of the few that increases constantly although they have long ceased to work.[38]

The political strategists of the ruling class found one of their most powerful weapons in jurisprudence which is the will of their class made into a law for all, ". . . a will whose trends are determined by the material conditions . . ." governing the existence of their class.[39] On March 1, 1813, Lord Palmerston stated in the House of Commons: ". . . the legislation of a country has the right to condemn part of the community to . . . a political loss of rights when it considers this necessary to safeguard the security and well-being of the whole . . . This is part of the fundamental premise upon which a civilized government rests." He cynically admitted that the masses had no rights at all; they were only to enjoy that measure of freedom that the legislation, i.e. the ruling class, was willing to grant them.[40]

Marx, then, was convinced that property relations which legally express the relations of production are supported by extra-economic power: the state which the ruling class turns into its tool to provide the ultimate protection for the existing property relations. The class that wants to control production and the division of its fruits must of necessity control

---

[37] Karl Marx, "The Decay of Religious Authority," in Emile Burns (Ed.), *A Handbook of Marxism*, London: Victor Gollancz, 1935, p. 174 (emphasis in original).

[38] Marx, *Capital*, Vol. I, pp. 736–737.

[39] Marx, Engels, *Manifesto of the Communist Party*, p. 47.

[40] Karl Marx, "Palmerston," in Karl Marx, *Politische Schriften*, Vol. III/2 (edited by Hans-Joachim Lieber), Stuttgart: Cotta Verlag 1960, p. 589 (my translation).

the state which represents, as Engels put it, ". . . the first ideological power over mankind." Higher ideologies—still further removed from the economic basis—appear in the shape of religion and philosophy where ". . . the interconnection between the ideas and their material conditions of existence becomes more and more . . . obscured by intermediate links."[41]

Religion appears to be furthest removed from material life. The opposite, however, is true: it is nothing but the ". . . fantastic reflection in men's minds of those external forces which control their daily life, a reflection in which the terrestrial forces assume the form of supernatural forces."[42] The close relation between religion and material life is constantly asserted by Marx. In 1844, he states in the *Deutsch-Französische Jahrbücher:* "Man makes religion, religion does not make man. . . . Religion is the moan of the oppressed creature, the sentiment of a heartless world, as it is the spirit of spiritless conditions. It is the opium of the people."[43] In 1867, he reaffirms: "The religious world is but the reflex of the real world." The same close connection between religion and material life holds true for the primitive and ancient societies; religion will vanish ". . . when the practical relations of everyday life offer to man none but perfectly intelligible and reasonable relations with regard to his fellowmen and to nature."[44]

Under existing conditions, however, the connection between religion and material life is either not recognized or not admitted. Therefore, religion dominates man's thinking as part of the ideological superstructure. As in philosophy, law, history, political economy, etc., so also in the ". . . mist-enveloped regions of the religious world" the fantastic productions of the human brain ". . . appear as independent beings endowed with life, and entering into relation both with one another and the human race."[45]

Marx's antireligious sentiments are already evident in the foreword to his doctor's thesis, where he shows the incompatibility of Epicurus' *materialistic* philosophy with religion. The young Marx asserts that as long as materialistic philosophy still has a ". . . drop of blood left in its world-conquering, absolutely free heart . . ." it will make Prometheus' hatred of all gods its own battlecry against ". . . all gods, heavenly and earthly,

[41] Frederick Engels, *Ludwig Feuerbach and the Outcome of Classical German Philosophy* (edited by C. P. Dutt), New York: International Publishers, 1934, pp. 64–65.

[42] Frederick Engels, *Anti-Dühring: Herr Eugen Dühring's Revolution in Science,* Moscow: Foreign Languages Publishing House, 1954, London: Lawrence and Wishart 1955, p. 438.

[43] Karl Marx, "A Criticism of the Hegelian Philosophy of Right," in Marx, *Selected Essays*, pp. 11–12.

[44] Marx, *Capital*, Vol. I, p. 51.

[45] *Ibid.*, p. 43.

who do not acknowledge the consciousness of man as the supreme divinity. There must be no god besides it."[46]

In the company of the Young Hegelians, Marx was also exposed to religious criticism. Bruno Bauer went against Hegel's Protestant orthodoxy when he wrote a study of the Bible which saw Jesus as a revolutionist, Arnold Ruge's System meant to substitute Humanity for Christianity, and Ludwig Feuerbach developed a radically atheistic doctrine "unmasking" God as the pathological reflection of man's sickly character. In *The Essence of Christianity*, Feuerbach claimed that religion represented the inverted picture and imaginary satisfaction of man's real interests, and demanded that a *religion of man* replace the religion of God. The ideas of the Young Hegelians, however, did not satisfy Marx; he felt that his associates were merely trying to exchange one kind of belief for another. Against Feuerbach he asserted: "The philosophers have only *interpreted* the world differently, the point is, to *change* it."[47]

Marx wanted to reveal the actual roots of religion, its *raison d'être*. He assumed that in earlier stages of human development religion stemmed from the primitive's helplessness in the struggle with the forces of nature; later the social oppression of the peasants and workers explained the acceptance of religious beliefs and the trust in heavenly rewards for sufferings in this world.[48] "The mortgage that the peasant has on heavenly possessions guarantees the mortgage that the bourgeois has on peasant possessions."[49] Furthermore, education was often ". . . in the hands of the Catholic priesthood, whose chiefs, in the same manner as the large feudal landowners, were deeply interested in the conservation of the existing system."[50] On the basis of such observations, Marx characterizes the social principles of Christianity as an ideological front defending ". . . all vile acts of the oppressors . . . to be . . . the just punishment of original sin. . . ."[51]

The Death of Truth

With the exception of the findings of the physical sciences all existing knowledge has now been debunked as ideological. Marx's total concept

[46] Karl Marx, "Differenz der demokritischen und epikureischen Naturphilosophie," (Ph.D. Thesis) in Marx, Engels, *Historisch-Kritische Gesamtausgabe* I/1 (edited for the Marx-Engels-Institute Moscow by D. Rjazanov), Frankfurt/Main: Marx-Engels-Archiv Verlagsgesellschaft, 1927, p. 10 (my translation).

[47] Karl Marx, "Theses on Feuerbach," in Marx, Engels, *The German Ideology*, p. 199 (emphasis in original).

[48] Cf. Karl Marx, "The Communism of the Paper Rheinischer Beobachter," in Marx, Engels, *On Religion*, Moscow: Foreign Languages Publishing House, 1957, p. 81.

[49] Marx, Engels, "The Class Struggles in France, 1848 to 1850," *Selected Works*, Vol. I, p. 171.

[50] Karl Marx, "Austria," in Marx, *Revolution and Counter-Revolution* (edited by Eleanor Marx Aveling), London: Swan Sonnenschein, 1896, p. 35.

[51] Marx, "The Communism of the Paper Rheinischer Beobachter," pp. 82–83.

of ideology has suspiciously invaded truth and declared it dead: all existing ideas are *formally* parts of an ideological superstructure and *materially* the expression of a social reality mainly characterized by domination and oppression—by class struggles. Since Marx maintains that man's social existence determines his consciousness, he implies that his *total* worldview is conditioned by the all-important criterion of interest-bound class position: the total concept of ideology calls into question man's total *Weltanschauung*—including his conceptual apparatus—and interprets it as a product of the collective life of which he partakes as a member of his class. Marx's forerunners did not expand the suspicion of ideology to the point of excluding the opponent—the victim of ideology —from intellectual discourse on the basis of a common theoretical frame of reference. The case, however, is different with the *total suspicion of ideology*. When we attribute, as Marx did, to almost all of history one intellectual world debunked as false and to ourselves another one, or if we assume that the bourgeoisie thinks in categories other than those of the proletariat, we refer not to the isolated cases of thought-content, but to fundamentally divergent thought-systems and to widely differing modes of experience and interpretation.[52]

Mannheim has pointed out that it was Marxist theory which first fused the particular and total conceptions of ideology.[53] Marx emphasizes the role of class position and class interest in thought. His approach, however, reflects at times the particular conception of ideology, i.e. a scepticism toward the ideas and representations of the ruling class which are viewed as more or less conscious disguises of reality, the true recognition of which would be harmful to the interests of this class. The distortions of reality which Marx suspects in the thought systems of the ideological spokesmen of the ruling class range all the way from deliberate lies to half-conscious and unwitting disguises—from calculated attempts to dupe the masses to self-deception.

In this light the ideological advocates of the existing social system appear as the fighting representatives of a certain political-social position and are accused of conscious or unconscious falsification of the true situation. As long as Marx operates with this particular conception of ideology, he uncovers distortion only on the psychological plane by pointing out the personal roots of intellectual bias. Hegelianism, however, enabled him to transcend this plane and to posit the problem in a more comprehensive, philosophical setting. Consequently the notion of a "false consciousness" took on a wider meaning, implying the existence of the totally distorted mind that falsifies everything which comes within its range.

[52] Cf. Marx, Engels, *The German Ideology*, pp. 14–15.
[53] Cf. Karl Mannheim, *Ideology and Utopia: An Introduction to the Sociology of Knowledge* (translated by Louis Wirth and Edward Shils), 7th Impression, London: Routledge & Kegan Paul, 1954, p. 66.

On the basis of his theory of the *division of labor,* Marx begins to suspect that *inevitably* man's *total outlook* as distinguished from its details must be *distorted.* At this point the *particular conception of ideology merges with the total conception of ideology* and Marx discredits the total structure of man's consciousness, considering him no longer capable of thinking correctly.

Marx's total conception of ideology, however, was still limited or "special" because of his decision to elect a collective guarantor of truth: the proletariat. Since Marx considered himself the spokesman of the proletariat he believed his particular philosophy safe from the charge of ideology. He, furthermore, limited his attack upon ideas to the "prehistory of man." For the utopia that he sketched in his philosophy he assumed a reign of truth. The seriousness of his attack, however, must not be underrated as this prehistory of man covers almost all of history prior to Marx's utopia. As soon as the belief in the saving powers of the proletariat and in the possibility of Marx's utopia are not shared, the destruction of truth remains as the one stark fact.

We have to remember, however, that Marx's concept of truth differed greatly from that of traditional philosophers who defined a true idea as one that corresponds with the external environment. Marx was much closer to the American pragmatist thinkers than to his European speculative predecessors. What he represented may be described as a *political pragmatism:* "In order to discover whether our ideas are true, we must act on them . . . Whatever cannot be tested in action is dogma."[54]

Marxism is both the theory and practice of social revolution; it is the class theory of the proletariat. The alleged nature of the historical process—an inevitable movement from capitalism through the dictatorship of the proletariat to a classless society—establishes the interests of the proletariat, however, as the interests of mankind. Here the hidden claim toward universality and absoluteness becomes obvious.

Marx's attempt to guarantee the truth and objectivity of his theory rests upon a syllogism: the premise that history is an inevitable process leads to the next that the class which accepts and carries this process knows truth. The reality of this historical process, however, is deduced from the assumptions that the proletariat has access to true reality and that consequently Marxism is true.

Marx expresses his communistic faith in the messianic role of the proletariat for the first time in his article "A Criticism of the Hegelian Philosophy of Right," where he depicts the proletariat as the agent that will achieve "true" human relations and solve the problems of philosophy.[55] This article appeared in the *Deutsch-Französische Jahrbücher* in 1844, and shows that Marx's decision to adopt the proletariat as the guar-

---

[54] Hook, *Towards the Understanding of Karl Marx,* pp. 103–104.
[55] Cf. Marx, "Zur Kritik der Hegelschen Rechtsphilosophie," MEGA I/1, p. 620.

antor of the truth of his philosophy was an early one. Already in the years of his Parisian exile, then, Marx decided to transform speculative philosophy into a critical "true" social theory which would be of use to men overcome by misery and poverty. In Paris, Marx had the chance to observe the proletariat and contact its leaders and thus came eye to eye with a scene of miserable poverty and revolt. "He realized that there was some connection between his own experience as a thinker and writer, whose free exercise of his profession had been forbidden by an authoritarian government, and the condition of the proletariat."[56]

The proletarian is the member of a class in "radical chains" which develops as a consequence of capitalistic production; its poverty does not result from natural circumstances but is artificially created.[57] After its victory over the feudal ruling class, the bourgeoisie begins with a proletariat which is a relic of feudal times. "In the course of its historical development, the bourgeoisie necessarily develops its antagonistic character, which at its first appearance was found to be more or less disguised, and existed only in a latent state. In proportion as the bourgeoisie develops, it develops in its bosom a new proletariat, a modern proletariat . . ."[58] This new proletariat, the modern working class, develops in the same proportion as capital—it consists of laborers who live only so long as they have work, and who have work only ". . . so long as their work increases capital."[59] The workers, who must sell themselves, are a commodity, and like every other article of commerce they are subject to the laws of the market. The price of a commodity, and therefore also that of labor, is according to these laws equal to its cost of production. Hence the cost of production of a workman is limited to ". . . the cost of the means of subsistence he needs for his upkeep and for the propagation of his race."[60] The proletariat grows steadily as the lower strata of the middle class are reduced to nothing in their hopeless competition with the large capitalists.

This opposition of interests originates in the economic conditions of bourgeois life, which has a double character. In the same relations ". . . in which wealth is produced, poverty is produced also." Capitalistic relations of production are a development of productive forces as well as a productive force of repression; they produce ". . . the wealth of the bourgeois class, only in continually annihilating the wealth of integral members of that class and in producing an ever-growing proletariat."[61]

[56] Bottomore and Rubel, Introduction to Karl Marx, *Selected Writings in Sociology and Social Philosophy*, p. 27.

[57] Cf. Marx, "A Criticism of the Hegelian Philosophy of Right," *Selected Essays*, p. 38.

[58] Marx, *The Poverty of Philosophy*, p. 133.

[59] Marx, Engels, *Manifesto of the Communist Party*, p. 34.

[60] *Ibid.*, p. 34.

[61] Marx, *The Poverty of Philosophy*, p. 134.

Toward the end, when revolution draws near, a portion ". . . of the bourgeoisie goes over to the proletariat," and in particular, a portion ". . . of the bourgeois ideologists, who have achieved a theoretical understanding of the historical movement as a whole."[62] Engels saw the German working class as the "inheritor of German classical philosophy" and claimed that Marx provided the world outlook ". . . corresponding to the conditions of the life and struggle of the proletariat; only lack of illusions in the heads of the workers could correspond to their lack of property. And this proletarian world outlook is now spreading over the world."[63]

[62] Marx, Engels, *Manifesto of the Communist Party*, p. 38.
[63] Engels, *Ludwig Feuerbach and the Outcome of Classical German Philosophy*, p. 70 and "Juristic Socialism," in Marx, Engels, *On Religion*, p. 270.

CHAPTER 15

FRIEDRICH NIETZSCHE
Panegyrist of the Lie

W HILE FRIEDRICH ENGELS applauded the lack of illusions among the workers and the spread of the proletarian world outlook, another critic of modern society was applauding the *presence of illusions* in the human mind; in the estimate of Friedrich Nietzsche (1844–1900), the world was chilled, however, by the spread of a different worldview—that of the bourgeoisie which establishes the reign of mediocrity, hypocrisy, dishonesty.[1]

Strange as it may seem Nietzsche shares an important antecedent with the Marxists: the philosophy of the Enlightenment. His *irrational theory of ideology* begins with the contradiction "truth versus ideology" which the ideological analysts of the Enlightenment used as *their* point of departure. In his interpretation of this basic contradiction, however, Nietzsche introduces a new criterion which completely reverses the conclusions reached by the *philosophes* and their followers: ideological falsehood does not devaluate thoughts or as he technically words it "judgements." The important question is whether or not judgements *further life*, whether they maintain groups and further the breeding of a better race.[2] The falsest judgements, Nietzsche claimed—with an eye upon Kant's synthetic judgements *a priori*—are the most necessary judgements for man. Man cannot exist without logical fictions. In giving up the illusory world of the absolute, we would give up life; error, falsity, the lie are the basic conditions of human life. Nietzsche, then, mounts a determined attack upon traditional values and ". . . a philosophy which dares this much finds itself immediately beyond Good and Evil."[3] Modern

---

[1] Cf. Friedrich Nietzsche, *Gesammelte Werke*, Vol. XVIII, München: Musarion Verlag, 1926, p. 225. All future references to this *Musarion* edition of Nietzsche's *Gesammelte Werke* (23 vols., 1920–29), will be to volume and page numbers only. All translations from the German original are mine. A list at the end of the chapter shows the content and chronological rank of each volume.

[2] Nietzsche was basically *not* a racist, advocating the breeding of a "pure race." Although he shared *Lamarck's* erroneous belief in the heredity of acquired characteristics, Nietzsche realized and emphasized the advantages of race mixture; turning against the nationalists and racists of his own time, he denied the value of preserving nations and called for the creation of a European race mixture. (Cf. VIII, 337.)

[3] XV, 10.

165

man must accept untruth and transform error into the lie which is a life necessity.[4]

In the tradition of the Enlightenment, Nietzsche thus experiences the conflict between truth and ideology as a basic problem. In principle, man can know truth, as the use of the terms "true" and "false" indicates, but two human attributes prevent man from the realization of his cognitive potential: vital interests and the will to power which Nietzsche initially explains as a craving for mundane success and later as a psychic drive. His revaluation of the intellectual situation elevates *error* and *illusion* to life-enhancing factors: it opens the door to the irrationalistic theory of ideology as continued by Pareto and Sorel.

The Making of a Philosopher

Nietzsche was not a systematic philosopher; he, furthermore, had an exasperating tendency to contradict himself. Still it is not impossible to distinguish three major stages in his philosophical career.

His early activities were in the realm of classical philology, where he acquired considerable expertness in the language, literature, philosophy, and art of Roman and especially Greek antiquity. His uncritical admiration of the aristocrat might well have originated during this period since he was deeply impressed with what he considered the aristocratic spirit in Hellenism: noble, open, active, subtle, trusting, and happy—these were the attributes of the high-born Greek.[5] Similarly inspiring were the examples of the great man of this culture who led Nietzsche away from his early infatuation with Schopenhauer's *will-to-live* so that he finally contrasted the pessimistic philosopher's ascetic doctrine of salvation with his own call for the heroic affirmation of the will in the face of life's tragic demands. "Only heroes are truly alive as individuals" Nietzsche says in *Homer's Contest*, "in them the present recognizes itself and in them it lives on."[6]

As a philosopher Nietzsche aimed at a novel affirmation of life based upon the historical facts of civilization; he took Greek art for his starting point to reveal the vital sources of life and reality which are eternally justified only as aesthetic values and other values the *Birth of Tragedy* does not recognize.[7]

In Greek culture, Nietzsche discovers the interplay of two conflicting forces: the furiously passionate assertion of the will-to-live—which finds its orgiastic consummation in the ritual of *Dionysos*, the god of formless frenzy—battles *Apollo*, the deity of harmonious beauty who lent

[4] Cf. XI, 170.
[5] Cf. XV, 297.
[6] II, 382.
[7] Cf. XXI, 224.

Greek genius its form-giving force. Mastery of this dialectical tension between Apollonian reason and measure and the limitless passion and drunken frenzy of Dionysian instincts, which threaten to consume all forms and norms in a fiery orgy of life, empowers Greek genius to give birth to tragedy.

Nietzsche entered the second stage of his philosophical career as the implacable enemy of Wagner and everything he stood for. The *Birth of Tragedy* had been dedicated to Wagner but in *Human, All Too-Human* Nietzsche challenges his old masters Wagner and Schopenhauer with the battle standard of the Enlightenment: he has become heir to the sceptical social-philosophical tradition of Petrarca, Erasmus, and Voltaire.[8]

Classical philology is replaced by a new intellectual emphasis; free scientific inquiry into the secrets of reality is the new road leading to an heroic mastery of life; artistic creation is of lesser importance. *The Gay Science* attacks religion and morality as dishonest creations of the great liars: the conservatives.[9] Against the "superficial" Greeks Nietzsche pits his mature scepticism: he is resigned that truth will never reveal itself to man.[10]

In 1883, *Zarathustra* proclaimed the *will-to-power:* the central concept of Nietzsche's final philosophy had at last reached its full maturation. The philosopher with the hammer was now in his third stage, which had the "will-to-power" for its single, unifying principle. Nietzsche overcame the division which had so far characterized his philosophy when he permitted this principle to direct his thought—now ". . . all the dualistic tendencies which had rent it previously could be reduced to mere manifestations of this basic drive. Thus a reconciliation was finally effected between Dionysus and Apollo, nature and value, wastefulness and purpose, empirical and true self, and *physis* and culture."[11]

The same principle fused Nietzsche's ideals of creative art and his anti-religious naturalism into a valiant philosophy of life which only recognized the importance of heroic men propelled by the will-to-power.

Now all of nature and especially all of human life and society is seen as a battlefield where this dominant will drives ever new cohorts into the struggle for mastery—and thinking is interpreted in pragmatic fashion: thinking aims at action, where it receives its ultimate test. Turning against the traditional goal-definitions of extant ethical and religious systems, Nietzsche describes "the real philosophers" in *Beyond Good and Evil* as commanders and lawgivers who determine: "Thus *shall* it be." These real philosophers ". . . grasp at the future with a creative hand,

[8] Cf. VIII, 43.
[9] Cf. XII, 68.
[10] Cf. *Ibid.*, pp. 8–9.
[11] Walter Kaufmann, *Nietzsche: Philosopher, Psychologist, Antichrist*, New York: Meridian Books, 1959, p. 152.

and whatever is and was, becomes for them thereby a means, a tool, a hammer. Their 'knowing' is *creating*, their creating is a lawgiving, their will to truth is—*will-to-power*."[12] The established ideals of society appear for what they are: the goals which valiant and masterful men have set for themselves. The will-to-power, however, is more than a will-to-live —it is a force driving those who possess it to transcend, to perfect themselves; life, says Zarathustra, ". . . *must always overcome itself.*"[13]

Nietzsche's preoccupation with the idea that only a life of heroic affirmation is worth going through stems mainly from his interpretation of the world as a gigantic mechanism in which every event results from a combination of energy factors. His belief in the law of conservation of energy led him to assume that the universe consists of a finite sum of elements, and that consequently the number of combinations of these elements must likewise be finite. Once the number of combinations has been exhausted the same course of evolution must of necessity begin all over again. Nietzsche already encountered the idea of repetition or recurrence in his philological studies. His "Lectures on the Pre-Platonic Philosophers" contain references to the Pythagorean exposition of the idea.[14] In *Ecce Homo* he mentions Heraclitus as a possible and the Stoics as a definite early source of the doctrine of the "eternal recurrence," which teaches the unconditional and endlessly repeated circulation of all things.[15]

Unlike the Pythagoreans, Nietzsche claims that events cannot repeat themselves within the span of known history. Despite this suprahistorical view, the idea initially horrified him and he had to struggle severely before he could accept it as the greatest of all thoughts.[16]

The doctrine of eternal recurrence gave rise to the call for the "overman." The terrible doctrine was to inspire men fired by the will-to-power to improve their state of being, to leave the animal herd behind and to join those who embody true humanity—the overmen. Against these self-reliant, brave, and creative men of mastery stand the weak, mediocre, and cowardly, who, aware of their inability for individual achievement on an heroic scale, band together and proclaim the sickly virtues of humility, pity, charity, patience, and forgiveness on which they have to rely in others if their insignificant lives are to be maintained and protected. These virtues make up the slave morality of the great masses; they have found one of their most infectious expressions in the Christian Gospel of the New Testament and in general reflect the will-to-power of the inferior. The transvaluation of all traditional values was, therefore,

---

[12] XV, 154 (emphasis in original).
[13] XIII, 148 (emphasis in original).
[14] Cf. IV, 352.
[15] Cf. XXI, 227.
[16] Cf. XIII, 209.

necessary to give birth to the opposed master morality of the overmen. This master morality would accept as virtues only qualities that enhance the power of the overman. For the great masses, however, slave morality with its glorification of incapacity, mediocrity, and invalidism must be maintained to ensure the continued exploitation of the slaves for the benefit of the "jesuitical" overmen.[17]

Corruption sets in as soon as the aristocrats are tainted by slave morality. Then their true estimate of life can be overthrown by the uprising of the moral slaves as this happened in Buddhism, Socrates, Christianity, and modern humanism; then the great masses are no longer what they should be—the laboring cyclops of the higher, ruling caste.

The mature aristocrat is free and exists only for his own sake. But the master gains his freedom and right to absolute self-determination only through the imposition of strict discipline in his childhood and adolescence. In later years he has to continue this discipline himself.[18] The overman represents true perfection and is different from such human types as "modern" man, "good" man, Christian man, and other "nihilists"; he is master of his emotions, poised, self-contained, and aloof. But he is not to be confused with Prussian Junkers, Carlyle's "counterfeit" heroes, or Darwin's fittest beasts.[19]

Since overmen do not beget overmen, Nietzsche advocated selective breeding to keep the master class constantly supplied. He called for a doctrine great enough to have the effect of breeding so that the strong would be strengthened and the weak and world-weary paralyzed and broken.[20]

Significantly Nietzsche never wavered in his rejection of the powerful state; he remained an ardent individualist; but his heart bled for the high and mighty only. The fate of heroes was significant, that of the little people was not. He called upon philosophical men of power and artist-tyrants to form a vast *international* aristocracy based upon harsh discipline. In this sense he was not a nationalist and more often than not disdained Germany.

He frequently repeated his credo "a good German is no longer German" and described the German "soul" as small and miserable.[21] In his autobiography Nietzsche complained that—with the exception of a few artists—he never spent one good hour with Germans who he considered "*canaille*." It is degrading to associate with them: "The Germans have not the slightest conception of how vile they are—they are not even *ashamed* of being merely Germans."[22]

[17] Cf. XI, 305–308.
[18] Cf. XIX, 290.
[19] Cf. XXI, 214–215.
[20] Cf. XIX, 320.
[21] Cf. XVI, 13, 363.
[22] XXI, 274 (emphasis in original).

For the most part he admired the Jews and hated their enemies; yet at times he revealed that he did not fully overcome the attitudes of anti-Semites, for whom he had otherwise the utmost contempt. His description of East European Jews foreshadows the sick reaction of Hitler—and the German Jews are expected to develop similar feelings so that they may become more "German." They are called upon to accept the German imperative against new Jews: the gates to the east must be barred against further Jewish immigrants.[23] Yet the ambivalence remains: "In Europe the Jews are the oldest and purest race. Therefore, the beauty of Jewish woman is highest."[24]

Nietzsche remained too abstract and upon too unrealistic an intellectual level to advance his fellowmen or to prevent the misuse of his ideas. Bertrand Russell, however, sees his failure psychologically: "It never occurred to Nietzsche that the lust for power, with which he endows his superman, is itself an outcome of fear. Those who do not fear their neighbours see no necessity to tyrannize over them."[25]

The New Equation: Power Equals Truth

Schopenhauer destroyed all metaempirical foundations of reason; for him intellect and reason were products of the will. Yet he retained a belief in the identical structure of reason. He saw the manifestation of this identity in the formal presuppositions of thinking, above all in logic.

Nietzsche destroyed what Schopenhauer had left: faith in the identical structure of reason, in the validity of its formal and logical undergirdings. After the death of God, Nietzsche proceed to bury logic, reason, and truth at His side. Man's conceptual apparatus is reduced to a mere function of biological data. All of reason—content and form—merely manifests the will-to-power which dominates every act of cognition to further its goal: not truth, i.e. the general validity of a judgement, but conquest of things and processes for the intensification of life. The question of truth has become a question of power.[26]

Man's intellect has one function: to serve life. Intellect is a mere instrument, granting the "most unhappy, most delicate, most unenduring beings" their minute of existence.[27]

Our intellect serves the will as a force that seduces us to embrace and maintain life: the intellect is merely an "organ of the will" which does nothing but lust for existence. For the intellect nothingness is no goal:

[23] Cf. XVI, 371.

[24] Ibid., p. 351.

[25] Bertrand Russell, *History of Western Philosophy and Its Connection with Political and Social Circumstances from the Earliest Times to the Present Day*, fifth impression, London: George Allen & Unwin, 1955, p. 795.

[26] Cf. XVIII, 323.

[27] VI, 76.

neither is absolute knowledge since it would be nothingness compared to existence. Each cognitive act is motivated by one purpose only: to support life. This is the "unlogical element" that fathers knowledge and determines its limits.[28]

In this function the intellect derives its strength mainly from the practice of deceit. "The weaker, less robust individuals, unable as they are to struggle for their existence with horn and tooth rely upon deceit as their weapon. The art of deceit reaches its summit in man."[29]

Nietzsche believes that our concern for knowledge and truth is social and he employs the social contract doctrine to explain its origin. "Need and boredom motivate man to desire a social and herdlike existence and because of that he must have a peace treaty and tries to banish from his world at least the worst kind of *bellum omnium contra omnes.*"[30] This peace treaty establishes both society and the concept of truth. Together with the terms of the social contract men determined the meaning of "truth" from thereon in. They invented ". . . a generally valid and binding designation of things and the establishment of rules in language also leads to the first rules of truth: for here the contrast between truth and falsehood arises for the first time."[31]

Man now demands truth and realizes it in the moral context of society: this is the basis of associated living. The dangerous consequences of lies are anticipated. This is how the "duty of truth" originates. Man needs the "belief in truth." Truth is a "social need."[32]

Yet truth starts with language and language does not reflect reality since it is metaphorical and anthropomorphic. From the beginning language is not logical, and everything that man later uses as a researcher or philosopher does not stem from the true nature of things.[33] Language is a mere folly—with it we dance over everything.[34] "The lordly right of giving names goes so far that one should be permitted to view the origin of language itself as an expression of the power of the rulers: they say, 'that *is* that, and that,' they seal off every thing and every event with a sound, and thereby, as it were, take possession of it."[35]

Language introduces into the development of human culture an immediate and erroneous bifurcation of the world: man's conceptual-scientific world is raised above the mute world of animals. Strong motives of power and conquest led man to believe in this allegedly superior world of concepts and names of things as *"aeternae veritates."*

[28] Cf. III, 311. Cf. also XIV, 287; XVI, 272.
[29] VI, 76.
[30] *Ibid.,* pp. 77–78.
[31] *Ibid.,* p. 78.
[32] Cf. VI, 29, 38. Cf. also XI, 28, 164.
[33] Cf. VI, 80.
[34] Cf. XIII, 277.
[35] XV, 284 (emphasis in original).

Logic, as well, rests upon presuppositions to which "nothing corresponds in the real world." Error, then, is the source of logic which assumes that in the real world an object will be identical at different points in time. Similarly, mathematicians share the erroneous belief that an "exactly straight line," a true circle, and "absolute units of measurement" exist in nature.[36]

The activities of our intellect necessarily result in error. Unable to sense the minute gradations of "absolute movement" which are the true quality of everything, we operate with such fictions as substance, form, identity, and being.[37]

Next man invents the notions of meaning and purpose and comes to believe that the world presents him with a goal of some kind which gives meaning to his life. In the final analysis man's belief in the world of being and his failure to accept the world of becoming originates in his *will* to justify his life by talking about its meaning and supra-individual purpose.[38]

Truth emerges as the falsification of reality: we strive for truth to establish permanence and lasting validity; this attempt to abolish the "false character" of reality results, however, in the abolishment of "true" reality which is devoid of everything permanent and lastingly valid. The "true" character of reality manifests itself in the continuous becoming and flowing of autonomous "quanta of will." Truth is not a thing that exists to be discovered. Truth is the name for a process without end, a process that expresses the will to conquer. Truth is another name for the will-to-power.[39]

The application of this definition of truth to the religious sphere leads Nietzsche into the proximity of Helvétius and Holbach: he develops his version of the theory of priestly deceit. What the priests call truths amounts to pathological counterfeits which serve to destroy natural values; their ideas and pronouncements are tools of torture, ingredients of a cruel system which put them into power. The truths of the Church have only one intent: the priest, the most lethal "parasite, the real poison-spider of life" must remain master.[40]

Nietzsche's School of Suspicion

The will-to-power is the metaphysical principle permitting the reduction of organic, psychic, mental, and social life—both in form and content—to mere expressions of this will.

[36] Cf. VIII, 24–25.
[37] Cf. XI, 153.
[38] Cf. XVIII, 15–16.
[39] Cf. XIX, 43.
[40] Cf. XVII, 214–215.

From this vantage point, man's intellectual behavior appears in a completely new light: philosophy is the "art of mistrust," psychology a "theory of evolution" revealing the development of the will-to-power, morality a dishonest "language of signs" expressing drives that originate in this will to motivate the human animal, and religion is either the projection of our feeling of power or its decadent abdication.[41]

Moral pronouncements are especially notorious for covering up their origins in the power nexus; moralists want to be everything but exponents of the will-to-power. Their verbal pomp, their noble, self-sacrificing gestures are designed to prevent the rise of even the slightest suspicion that they are merely the embodiment of the power struggle between individuals, groups, social classes, or nations. Morality is the art of enthroning the great desires: lust of power and avarice as the "protectors of virtue."[42] Ordinary morality is enforced because of the advantages connected with it. With what right do we war against immorality? "According to no right at all: but according to the instinct of self-preservation. The same classes use *immorality*, where it benefits them."[43]

Central to all morality is an "unnatural" conceptual dualism that tears man apart: strong, healthy personalities embody love as well as hatred, gratitude and resentment, benevolence as well as fury. Man cannot be good without the ability to be evil. Morality or the idea that man be exclusively good rests upon the "unnatural" demand to castrate all those instincts that make for hatred, revenge, and fury. The moralist's attack upon man's "natural" ambivalence in thought and feeling reveals a sickness, an ideological perversion: it denies life. "So far there has probably been no more dangerous ideology, no greater nuisance *in psychologicis*, than this will to be good: the most repulsive type, *unfree* man, the bigot was raised; only the bigot, so the teaching went, was on the right way to God . . ."[44]

Critical analysis must penetrate deep enough to reveal the social standpoint of the producers of moral systems. Nietzsche operates with the simplest variant of social stratification theory: all societies develop two social layers; the first of these consists of a small elite of rulers who dominate the mass of the ruled, making up the second layer. The members of each stratum have different interests and embody conflicting versions of the will-to-power. Therefore, they differ in their thinking and moral exhortations. The mass of subjects comes to accept a moral system reflecting its socially determined interests; the ruling elite does likewise. Nietzsche first introduces the distinction between two kinds of morality in *Beyond Good and Evil* and elaborates the conception of

[41] Cf. XIV, 312. XV, 32. XVI, 192. XVII, 185–186.
[42] Cf. XVIII, 224.
[43] *Ibid.*, p. 225 (emphasis in original).
[44] *Ibid.*, pp. 248–249 (emphasis in original).

"master-morality" and "slave-morality" in the *Genealogy of Morals*. The contrast takes into account the morality of groups, not the ethical conduct of individuals. This sociological distinction implies that those who have power develop a master-morality while those who lack in power adhere to a slave-morality. Master-morality expresses the will of the elite, slave-morality that of the mass.[45]

The concept of master-morality was not devised to describe extant conditions; master-morality was envisioned as the ethic of a ruling class that had yet to be formed. The concept was a component of Nietzsche's "philosophy of the future." The society of his own time he believed to be entirely dominated by slave-morality. All classes of modern society are permeated by vice, imbecility, crime, anarchy; modern society is no society at all but ". . . a sick conglomeration of Tschandalas."[46]

The reason for this state of affairs must be seen in the lack of ranks and clear-cut patterns of super- and subordination in modern society. The realization of a healthier society in the future, therefore, depends mainly upon the reintroduction of an order of social ranks that will give full sway to the power of the ruling class of overmen. The morality of the nineteenth century, however, preaches equality and must be destroyed to make room for the new morality admitting of the necessity for inequality, which is the basic law of social life.[47]

Modern decadence originated in the Christian values that had come to dominate all of man's intellectual and moral utterances. The destruction of society began in the Christian teachings of the New Testament —that prime example of "socialism" which glorified the "infamous and condemned, the lepers of all sorts" along with sinners, prostitutes, and stupid fishermen while it denounced the ". . . rich, the learned, the noble, and the virtuous . . ."[48]

The New Testament initiates the cunning strategy of the slaves who lead a new kind of war, the "war of the mind" against the high and the mighty. How is war waged against "manly emotions and values?" The mass of slaves cannot wage war with physical weapons, it can only wage a war of "cunning, enchantment, lies." This ideological warfare consists of six strategical moves: first, the slaves monopolize "virtue as such" and—through a campaign of slander—turn all preceding ideals into the opposite of virtue; second, they establish their ideal of virtue as the absolute criterion of all positive values and project it—as God—into and behind all objects and their fate; third, the slaves mark all enemies of their ideal as enemies of God—they invent the right to have great pathos and power, to curse and to bless; fourth, they blame the enemies

---

[45] Cf. XV, 226–230.
[46] XVIII, 41.
[47] Cf. XV, 82–85.
[48] XVIII, 154–155.

of *their* ideal for all suffering and for everything that is uncanny, terrible, and fatal about existence; fifth, even nature is seen as a force opposing the ideal and everything "natural" becomes a target for disdain taxing the patience of the martyrs; finally, ". . . the victory of the unnatural, of ideal castration, the victory of the world of the pure, good, sinless, blissful is projected into the future as the end, the finale, the great hope as the 'advent of God's kingdom.' "[49]

In the light of Nietzsche's ideological analysis, the New Testament does not reflect the voice of God but only one of the most bottomless forms of slanderous and destructive rage—". . . one of the most dishonest forms of hatred."[50] The teachings of Jesus and his apostle Paulus not only inflated the self-esteem of the little people but also misguided the great and strong minds to take the path toward self-destruction.[51]

Religion is an illusory realm that compensates us for all the things we miss in this world; it is a substitute world that has the function of making life bearable. In correcting the world, religion expresses the will-to-power; but this variant of the will-to-power is sick: this will is so emasculated that it can no longer stand the real world of terrible becoming with its upward and downward movements. The "true" world of religion is a world of decadence: "It is not up to anyone to become a Christian: one is not 'converted' to Christianity—one has to be sick enough for it . . ."[52] This religion is the ally of weaklings, villains, and failures, it idealizes everything that corrodes the desire of the strong to prevail.[53]

The moralistic apotheosis of sacrifice and renunciation expresses the mob's burning *ressentiment* of all that is above its level. The interests of the weak are best served by a decadent social order; the ideology providing the weak with their sharpest weapons is the moral order that has its philosophical roots in Stoic thought and its supranatural sanction in Judaism and Christianity.

The weak combine and form the herdlike mob that wages a "common war on all that is rare, strange, or privileged, on the higher man, the higher soul, the higher duty . . . the wealth of creative power and mastery." Against this onslaught of the mob's *ressentiment* that transforms the "equality of rights" into an "equality in violating rights" Nietzsche pits his concept of "greatness" which entails ". . . being noble, wanting to be by oneself, being capable of being different, standing alone, having to live according to one's own measures . . ."[54]

Today we witness the operation of a particular form of *ressentiment*:

[49] *Ibid.*, pp. 152–153.
[50] *Ibid.*, p. 154.
[51] Cf. *Ibid.*, p. 153, XVII, 226–228.
[52] XVII, 237 (ellipsis in original).
[53] Cf. *Ibid.*, p. 173.
[54] XV, 156 and 295–299.

the resentment of the quantity-minded mass man whose habitat is the bureaucratically regimented world of industrial society is ". . . forever trying to crush, beneath the weight of mass mediocrity, everything private, unadjusted, quality-minded, whether as 'too aristocratic' (in the traditional terminology of resentment) or as 'too leftist' (in the inaccurate terminology—a drugstore 'conservatism'—of the new American right)."[55]

Nietzsche's Theory of Ideology

Although Nietzsche employs the psychological methods of the French *philosophes* and especially Helvétius' sociological reduction of moral concepts to underlying interests, he is in a formal and methodological sense akin to Karl Marx. Like Marx he operates with a two-class theory: all societies are divisible into a minority of rulers and a mass of subjugated people. Again he parallels Marx in assuming a conflict situation: these two groups engage—because of the different development of their respective will-to-power—in social warfare, in class struggle. In their thinking the members of each class reflect this social reality: each class creates an ideological superstructure (law, philosophy, art, religion, morality, etc.) that is totally dependent upon the largely economic life-situation of that class.[56] "Our values correspond to our . . . life conditions: when these change our values also change."[57]

In its God, a people reveres the ". . . conditions which put it on top . . . it projects its pleasure in itself, its feeling of power, into a being whom one can thank for this."[58] Morality is ". . . a fruit in which I recognize the *soil* that it grew out of." Moral judgements are symptoms, components of a "sign language" revealing processes of "physiological development and decay" as well as the realization of "conditions of preservation and growth."[59] In general, any faith or system of beliefs expresses the determining force of the *"conditions of existence,"* our subordination to ". . . the authority of the relations within which a creature *prospers, grows, gains power . . ."*[60]

> The means of the craving for power have changed, but the same volcano is still glowing; impatience and excessive love demand their victims: and what one did before "for God's sake" one does now for the sake of money, that is for the sake of that which gives *now* the highest feeling of power and good conscience.[61]

---

[55] Peter Viereck, *The Unadjusted Man: A New Hero for Americans*, New York: Capricorn Books, 1962, p. 170.
[56] Cf. XV, 130–131.
[57] XVI, 177.
[58] XVII, 185.
[59] XVIII, 190 (emphasis in original).
[60] *Ibid.*, p. 22 (emphasis in original).
[61] X, 189 (emphasis in original).

The existential determination of religion and morality is clearly related to our placement in the social hierarchy: we think as members of a class or caste whenever we employ religious or moral-legal concepts. These concepts are, therefore, components of an ideological superstructure reflecting the fundamental properties of social class reality: having power or seeking power. In the first instance morality serves to justify ". . . its author before others."[62] This is the morality of ruling classes meant to sanction and perpetuate the right to hold power and its fruit. In the second instance, morality serves to "conceal" intentions: the morality of the subjugated classes. In both cases, however, morality is used as a weapon: "all take that for moral which keeps up their class [*Stand*] . . ."[63] The means that keep up and strengthen one social class hurt the interests of another; consequently the different types of morality must clash.[64]

The rulers of a society invent a morality that will lend itself to the preservation and elaboration of the prevailing order of things which has been so beneficial to their interests. All our striving toward moral ideas has its single root in the wish to possess and to retain. Man first calculates the range of accessible booty and, then, proceeds to convince himself that these future possessions are exceedingly valuable to him. Thus, ideas are merely the echo of property. "*We look for the philosophy that fits our property*, that is, gilds it. The great reformers, such as Mohammed, knew this: to lend a new lustre to the habits and the property of men—not to bid them to strive for 'something else' but to see as something higher what they *desire and can have* . . ."[65] Morality begins when the superior and the powerful order others to accept their evaluations, when the rulers announce that their impressions have become the law of the land. "Morality is at first self-glorification of the powerful: and with regard to the powerless contempt."[66] The sociological consequence of morality is the division of society into castes. Moral evaluations are right-away attempts at social differentiation: "the distinction between *higher and lower* men . . ."[67] "Right" means only "the will to perpetuate a given balance of power." The ruling class will, therefore, always invoke all that is commonly considered as venerable. For what purpose? For the single purpose of giving to this order of right and law the appearance of eternity.[68]

The ideology of the subjugated and enslaved masses is, on the other

---

[62] XV, 111.

[63] X, 377.

[64] Cf. XVIII, 223–225.

[65] XI, 216–217 (emphasis in original).

[66] XVI, 187.

[67] *Ibid.*, p. 187 (emphasis in original). For an attempt to empirically verify a similar assumption see Max Weber, *The Religion of India: The Sociology of Hinduism and Buddhism* (translated by Hans Gerth and Don Martindale), New York: The Free Press of Glencoe, 1958.

[68] XVI, 237.

hand, the mother of social change. Even more than that: the ideology of the conquered is revolutionary—this style of thought advocates the overthrow of existing economic and socio-political circumstances.[69] The will-to-power wears many masks: "Striving for *freedom*, independence, also that for balance, peace, *co-ordination*. Also . . . 'freedom of thought.' In its lowest form: the will to exist at all . . ."[70] Behind the glittering verbal facade, Nietzsche detects the scramble of the mass: all the subjugated, the lowly, all the slaves and semislaves are fighting for power.

This struggle for power, this scramble for the top, is a battle which is enacted in four strategic moves. During their first move the slaves free themselves in their imagination: "they recognize each other," they establish themselves as a class. "Second stage: they enter the battle, they want recognition, equal rights, 'justice.' Third stage: they want the privileges (they draw the representatives of power to their side). Fourth stage: they *alone* want power, and they *have* it . . ."[71]

In Nietzsche's theory of ideology all products of the mind lose their autonomy: the claim that moral systems, religious, legal, social, and political theories, are universally and eternally valid is debunked as the propaganda device of men—creatures that follow the will-to-power either by wielding power or by striving for it. The human mind is nothing more than the sum of organic processes of adjustment or seizure; it practices ". . . patience, cunning, simulation, great self-control, and everything that is mimicry . . ."[72] Toward the end of his career, Nietzsche exclaimed: "I do not know what purely mental problems are."[73] Cognition emerges as a process that reflects subjective mental states and class-bound interests: not—as anciently assumed—the essential characteristics of objects. Cognition itself is an act of overpowering.[74] "To know: that is a *joy* to the lion-willed!"[75]

Like Marx and Hegel, Nietzsche claims validity for his own philosophy. Like Marx, he strives to escape the vicious circle of scepticism and relativism; like Marx he has recourse to a personal guarantor of truth: only this time it is not the proletariat that is elected to fulfill this function. In Nietzsche's estimate the downtrodden are too infected by the moral poison of Stoic philosophy and Judeo-Christian religiosity to carry the future. Nietzsche—in striking contrast to Marx—options for the top dogs. His personal guarantor of truth is the aristocratic ruling class of ruthless and bold men—products of a distant, utopian breeding process. For Nietzsche the goal of humanity lies in its highest specimens. Let the

[69] Cf. XVIII, 64.
[70] XIX, 190 (emphasis in original).
[71] XVIII, 158 (emphasis and ellipsis in original).
[72] XVII, 117.
[73] XXI, 81.
[74] Cf. XVI, 191.
[75] XIII, 263 (emphasis in original).

rabble rule and we shall drown in shallow waters. Who can contain the rabble and all that is despotic? Only a new nobility; therefore we need many who are noble and noble men of all kinds, so that there will emerge a nobility: " 'This to be specific is god-like, that there exist gods, but no God.' "[76]

Friedrich Nietzsche, Gesammelte Werke, München: Musarion Verlag, 1920–1929

volume

I.	*Jugendschriften* (Early Writings)	1858–1868
II.	*Kleinere Schriften* (Shorter Essays)	1869–1874
III.	*Die Geburt der Tragödie. Aus dem Gedankenkreise der Geburt der Tragödie* (The Birth of Tragedy. Ideas about the Birth of Tragedy)	1869–1871
IV.	*Vorträge, Schriften und Vorlesungen* (Speeches, Writings, and Lectures)	1871–1876
V.	*Vorlesungen* (Lectures)	1872–1876
VI.	*Philosophenbuch. Unzeitgemässe Betrachtungen* (Philosopher's Book. Untimely Meditations)	1872–1875
VII.	*Unzeitgemässe Betrachtungen* (Untimely Meditations)	1872–1876
VIII.	*Menschliches, Allzumenschliches* I (Human, All-too-Human I)	1876–1878
IX.	*Menschliches, Allzumenschliches* II (Human, All-too-Human II)	1876–1879
X.	*Morgenröthe* (The Dawn)	1880–1881
XI.	*Aus der Zeit der Morgenröthe und der Fröhlichen Wissenschaft* (From the Time of Dawn and the Gay Science)	1880–1882
XII.	*Die Fröhliche Wissenschaft* (The Gay Science)	1882–1886
XIII.	*Also Sprach Zarathustra* (Thus Spoke Zarathustra)	1883–1885
XIV.	*Aus der Zarathustra- und Umwertungszeit* (From the Time of Zarathustra and Revaluation)	1882–1888
XV.	*Jenseits von Gut und Böse. Zur Genealogie der Moral* (Beyond Good and Evil. Toward a Genealogy of Morals)	1885–1887
XVI.	*Studien aus der Umwerthungszeit* (Studies from the Time of Revaluation)	1882–1888
XVII.	*Der Fall Wagner. Götzendämmerung. Der Antichrist. Nietzsche Contra Wagner. Kunst und Künstler* (The Case Wagner. Twilight of Idols. The Antichrist. Nietzsche Contra Wagner, Art and Artist)	1888

---

[76] *Ibid.*, p. 260.

CHAPTER 16

SIGMUND FREUD
A Tortuous Epitaph for the Mind

O<small>N</small> N<small>OVEMBER</small> 11, 1924, the German psychiatrist Hans Prinzhorn received the following letter:

Erlangen, October 20, 1924

Dear P.,

When you receive this letter I am no longer alive. The book is complete; my life has been given the meaning for which I have existed during the last tortured years. . . . Not I, but the spirit of the world, fate, thought within me. I know what satanic task I had to perform. But everything had to be said at this time; this is the beginning of the great despair in occidental culture as it has started with Schopenhauer and Max Weber . . .

Is it treason to leave my work like this? But whoever has read it will tell himself that no man can live with it any longer . . . Work for the publication of the book . . .

I thank you.

Yours,
ALFRED SEIDEL

Meanwhile Seidel had hanged himself; this was no total surprise to his friends who knew that he conceived of his thinking as a form of sublimated, continuous suicide.[1] The author of the book *Consciousness as Fate* was 29 years old when he took his life; he had consummated his compelling desire to "nihilize nihilism."

Dazzled by the enchanting perils of psychoanalysis and Max Weber's vast disenchantment of the world, he set out on that uncharted journey which led to the questioning of the "practical value of cognition," "doubt in the value of consciousness," and ultimately to self-annihilation.[2]

Schopenhauer: Nothing But Nothingness

Seidel viewed megalomania as the only possible rescue from suicide and addressed this *dictum* specifically to Goethe, Nietzsche, and Schopen-

---

[1] For this letter in its complete form see Alfred Seidel, *Bewusstsein als Verhängnis* (posthumously edited by Hans Prinzhorn), Bonn: Verlag Friedrich Cohen, 1927, pp. 45–46 (my translation).

[2] Cf. *Ibid.*, p. 75.

hauer.[3] He probably implied that Alfred Seidel committed suicide because he did not suffer from megalomania. He clearly realized, however, the fateful connection that leads from the crepuscular pessimism of Arthur Schopenhauer to the bizarre realism of Sigmund Freud.

Schopenhauer (1788–1860), a private scholar of independent means, published the first book of his major work *The World as Will and Idea* in 1819, advancing a theory of knowledge which departing from Kantian premises not only claimed the discovery of the thing-in-itself but simultaneously destroyed the traditional belief of occidental philosophers in the supremacy of the human intellect.

He declared: ". . . the will alone is the thing in itself."[4] As willing and striving animals we *are* the thing-in-itself, but the nature of the will as a dark instinctual force explains the ". . . impossibility of attaining lasting satisfaction and the negative nature of all happiness . . . the will, of which human life, like every phenomenon, is the objectification, is a striving without aim or end."[5]

Schopenhauer saw himself as an innovator breaking with all preceding philosophers who had erroneously taught that an intellect had created nature. In contrast, Schopenhauer viewed intellect as the product of nature and proceeded to reduce the world to will; nothing else had any independent existence: "Before us there is certainly only nothingness."[6] Only the will-to-live which is our very nature keeps us from passing into nothingness.

Schopenhauer relegates the intellect to the inferior position of serving the will. In man will becomes identical with the body that strives to live and survive in the endless struggle for continued existence. Thus the function of the intellect is largely biological or, differently worded, the intellect is an instrument "used" by the will in the biological struggle for survival.[7]

Much like Francis Bacon, Schopenhauer debunks our ideas which are rooted in desires and interests as "prejudices." Only a philosophy which is relentlessly dedicated to the service of truth can free man from the power of these prejudices. The attainment of such a philosophy he did not consider impossible; in rare instances of genius man may free himself from the will and bathe in the pure light of distinterested intellect. Such "abnormal" independence from the will is only possible for the few. The

[3] Cf. *Ibid.*, p. 214.

[4] Arthur Schopenhauer, *The World as Will and Idea*, Vol. III (translated by R. B. Haldane and J. Kemp), ninth impression, London: Routledge & Kegan Paul, 1948, p. 225.

[5] Schopenhauer, *Ibid.*, Vol. I, p. 414.

[6] *Ibid.*, p. 530.

[7] Cf. Schopenhauer, *Ibid.*, Vol. III, p. 166.

multitudes of "normal" men remain forever enslaved to the will and never attain to an objective picture of things.[8]

With regard to the mass of mankind Schopenhauer, thus, prepared the pertinent question of the biological determination of knowledge which Freud was to fully develop and "popularize" a hundred years later.[9]

In the work of Sigmund Freud (1856–1939) we find no consolations. Unlike Marx or Nietzsche, he was disinterested in the basic transformation of the human condition; as a "statesman of the inner life" he aimed pragmatically at "shrewd compromises" with reality. "Posterity will revere him as the first prophet of a time that is simply each man's own, the first visionary to look neither forward nor backward except to stare down projections and to penetrate fixations."[10]

An Interpretation of Mental Life

Freud assumes that mental life, instead of being self-sufficient, self-contained, and one, is the function of a psychical apparatus made up of three areas. Freud calls the oldest, the original of these mental regions, the *id*. The id consists of ". . . everything that is inherited, that is present at birth, that is fixed in the constitution—above all, therefore, the instincts, which originate in the somatic organization and which find their first mental expression in the id in forms unknown to us."[11] The second region of our mental life is the *ego*, a transformed portion of the id, which functions as a mediating agent between the outside world and the id. As long as the ego is in connection with the external world, that is during our waking hours, it controls our conscious system. The ego fulfills its task of self-preservation by balancing the demands of the id with those of external reality. During the elaboration of psychoanalysis Freud realized, however, that a third directing force was operative within the psychical apparatus. This third region of mental life stems from the basic childhood experience of dependence upon the parents; the special agency within our ego prolonging this parental influence received the name of *superego*.

In contrast to most philosophers who assumed that consciousness alone

---

[8] Cf. *Ibid.*, p. 139.

[9] Schopenhauer's interpretation of religion was also strikingly similar to Freud's view in *The Future of an Illusion.* Cf. Arthur Schopenhauer, "Religion: A Dialogue," in Schopenhauer, *Essays* (selected and translated by T. Bailey Saunders), New York: A. L. Burt Company, n.d., pp. 213–220.

[10] Philip Rieff, *Freud: The Mind of the Moralist,* New York: The Viking Press, 1959, pp. x–xi.

[11] Sigmund Freud, *An Outline of Psychoanalysis* (translated by James Strachey), New York: W. W. Norton, 1949, p. 14.

is mental, Freud distinguished three mental qualities: the conscious, pre-conscious, and unconscious. The conscious plays a rather insignificant role since it consists only of ideas and feelings, present in immediate awareness or during the conscious perception of our intellective processes, which sometimes persist but which at others merely pass in a flash. The preconscious consists of mental content that is capable of easily entering consciousness. Departing from a long tradition of Western philosophy, Freud described the unconscious as the largest portion of the mind; the mental processes or the mental material of the unconscious have no easy access to consciousness. Relating these mental qualities to the regions of the psychical apparatus, Freud points out that large portions of the ego and the superego are preconscious, while the only quality which governs ". . . in the id is that of being unconscious."[12]

The interchange of energies occasioned by the psychic dynamics of ego, id, and superego is a dangerous process. The ego is caught between the jaws of the id—aflame with boiling energies—and those of the superego that opposes the impulses shooting up from the id with its moral restrictions and icy demands for perfection. Under this pressure, the ego can only escape into the protection provided by neurotic behavior, which becomes understandable as a protective mechanism in a state of im-balance.[13]

Apart from the question of therapy and individual readjustment, Freud's psychoanalytic theory—especially when applied to the wider sphere of culture—climaxes a development which began when the first doubts in the validity of spiritual elements arose. This process of spiritual and mental devaluation proceeded further to undermine the conscious sphere of the mind and reduced all happenings and thoughts to functions of instinctive mechanisms which were entirely divorced from historical and spiritual elements. Somewhat earlier Marx's historical materialism had expressed the distrust in man's consciousness in a generalizing theory which described all reality-transcending idea elements as products of socio-economic group situations. Marx made his probably most viable contribution when he separated social phenomena into a superstructure, oscillating between symbolism and adequate consciousness, and an effective substructure. "The social superstructure relates to the substruc-ture in the same way as the consciousness of the human individual relates to his conduct: just as consciousness can be mere self-vindication, sym-bolic transposition or the inadequate reflection of behavior . . . so the social superstructure will oscillate between ideology and science."[14]

Freud also developed a generalizing theory wherein the idea elements

[12] *Ibid.*, p. 43.

[13] Cf. *Ibid.*, pp. 61–63.

[14] Jean Piaget, *Introduction à l'épistémologie génétique*, Vol. III, Paris: Presses Universitaires de France, 1950, p. 249 (my translation).

became relative to eternal forms in the structure of human impulses—
that is to drives. He, thereby, continued a development that began in
earnest when the British social philosophers of the seventeenth and eighteenth centuries initiated their search for what Hume called the "regular
springs of human action and behavior." We must acknowledge, Hume
argued, in Section VIII of his *Enquiry*, that there exists ". . . a great uniformity among the actions of men . . . passions, mixed in various degrees,
and distributed through society, have been, from the beginning of the
world, and still are, the source of all the actions and enterprises, which
have ever been observed among mankind."[15]

A Theory of Instincts

Whereas Marx stressed the importance of the economy, Freud emphasized biology. Somewhere in the child, somewhere in the adult, he envisioned a hard, irreducible core of biological urgency and necessity. In
Freud's opinion psychoanalytic investigation proved that the core of
human nature is formed by primal instincts striving to satisfy elemental
needs; these instincts, neither good nor evil in themselves, undergo a
lengthy process of development before they are permitted to become
active in the adult and are, furthermore, inhibited and directed towards
other aims. They also become commingled, change their objects, and are
to some extent turned back upon their possessor. An individual's character emerges only after these diverse mutations in his instinctual make-up
have been completed.[16]

In order to explain the dynamic relations in the mind Freud developed
a theory of instincts in his *Beyond the Pleasure Principle* which he enlarged in *The Ego and the Id*. His basic distinction was between sexual
instincts (Eros) and aggressive instincts (death instinct), represented
by sadism. At the beginning of his analytic work Freud furthermore
assumed the independent existence of a self-preservative instinct which
he assigned to the ego and later subsumed under the first class—Eros or
the sexual instincts. While the aggressive or death instinct has the task
of leading "organic matter back into the inorganic state," the sexual instincts aim at the maintenance of life.[17]

Significantly Freud assumed that due to the evolution of unicellular
organisms into multicellular forms of life the death instinct of the single
cell can be successfully diverted away from evolved organisms; through

[15] David Hume, *An Enquiry Concerning Human Understanding*, second edition,
La Salle, Ill.: Open Court Publishing Company, 1966, pp. 89–90.

[16] Cf. Sigmund Freud, "Thoughts for the Times on War and Death," in Freud,
Civilization, War and Death (edited by John Rickman), London: The Hogarth Press
and the Institute of Psycho-Analysis, second edition, 1953, p. 7–8.

[17] Cf. Sigmund Freud, *The Ego and the Id* (translated by Joan Riviere), London:
The Hogarth Press and the Institute of Psycho-Analysis, 1927, p. 55.

the musculature, the destructive energies are redirected to the environment at large. Therefore, the death instinct seems partially to find its expression as an instinct of ". . . destruction directed against the external world and other living organisms."[18]

In the human being, the instincts do not exist in rigid separation; on the contrary, they are always "alloyed"—they intermingle and combine; many instincts are manifest almost from the first in pairs of opposites, giving rise to the "ambivalence of feeling."[19] Thus we frequently harbor such conflicting feelings as intense love and intense hatred for one and the same person.

For Freud's view of man and society, the hypothesis of the blending of instincts is of signal importance. This internal factor, however, can only exercise its influence with the help of the external factor represented by the environment or the learning process. Internally, eroticism or our need for love blends with the egoistic instincts which, then, become social ones. We learn to crave love as a value worthy of sacrifices, and externally the surrounding civilization exercises sufficient pressure to impress this lesson upon us. "Civilization is the fruit of renunciation of instinctual satisfaction, and from each new-comer in turn it exacts the same renunciation."[20]

This transformation of "bad" or primitive instincts into social ones is effected by certain psychological mechanisms, such as conscious restraint that we impose on ourselves for the sake of a self-chosen ideal of conduct or repression of the sexual and aggressive instincts which has its source in the unconscious operation of the superego.

The Sexual Determination of Religion

For the *philosophes* religion had been the invention of deceitful, power-hungry priests, for Marx it was the opium of the people, with Freud it is a derivative of the more primitive instincts, chiefly of the sexual instincts. Again, however, religion is not the only derivative of this kind; religion is part of the entire nonmaterial superstructure that is determined by the—in this case—instinctive substructure. All the elements of nonmaterial culture, such as religion, morality, law, social organization, philosophy, art, etc., are produced by primitive instincts. In more technical language, Freud explains their emergence by reference to those reserves of energy that are built up whenever the instincts are denied an outlet at the primitive, immediate level. These reserves of

---

[18] *Ibid.*, p. 57.

[19] Cf. Sigmund Freud, *Group Psychology and the Analysis of the Ego* (translated by James Strachey), London: The Hogarth Press and the Institute of Psycho-Analysis, 1921. Cf. also, Sigmund Freud, "Why War?" in Freud, *Civilization, War and Death*, pp. 90–93.

[20] Freud, "Thoughts for the Times on War and Death," p. 9.

energy man has employed in the course of history to create the refined and complex expressions of civilized living.

Much like Durkheim, Freud traces the origin of religion back to its primitive beginnings in totemism: the totem feast—perhaps mankind's first celebration—is ". . . the repetition and commemoration of this memorable, criminal act with which so many things began, social organization, moral restrictions and religion."[21]

Freud establishes his hypothesis by associating the psychoanalytic interpretation of the totem with both the meaning of the totem feast and the Darwinian assumption of a primal state of human society: history began with the primal horde ruled by a violent, jealous father who kept all the women for himself and expelled the growing sons. The expelled brothers banded together; they killed and ate the father thereby terminating the father horde and acquiring each a part of his strength.

Totemism as the first attempt at the establishment of a religion connects anciently with the taboo protecting the life of the totem animal which provided the murderous sons emotionally with a natural and appropriate substitute for the father. The compulsory treatment of the totem animal seems to indicate that this father substitute served the sons' attempt to assuage their deep guilt feelings and to effect a kind of reconciliation with their victim. The system of totemism represents a form of agreement with the father whereby he belatedly fulfills the desire of his children for care, protection, and forbearance. In return for this wish fulfillment, the sons pledge themselves to honor the father's life, that is to say, not to repeat the criminal act against the totem through which the real father had perished. In this way some psychological elements originated which henceforth determined the character of all later religions which also attempt to palliate the sense of guilt and to conciliate the father through subsequent obedience.

The ambivalence of feelings, however, attached to the father complex is still another characteristic that began with totemism and continues in religions in general. The totemic religion was ambivalent in its feeling tones from the onset; it was not only the manifestation of remorse and reconciliatory strivings but also the commemoration of the sons' triumph over the father: the totem feast repeats the killing of the father through the symbolic slaying of the totem animal and reinforces the privileged position and power of the sons in the face of changing life situations. At times ". . . the son's defiance also reappears, often in the most remarkable disguises and inversions, in the formation of later religions."[22]

[21] Sigmund Freud, *Totem and Taboo: Resemblances between the Psychic Lives of Savages and Neurotics* (translated with an introduction by A. A. Brill), New York: Moffat, Yard, 1918, p. 234.
[22] *Ibid.*, p. 240.

On the basis of this analysis of totemism, Freud establishes the thesis that society, as an outgrowth of the brother horde (which introduced safeguards to preclude a repetition of the fate of the father amongst themselves) is based on complicity in the common crime.

Christianity, too, is the fruit of murder: the Christian myth of man's original sin points to an offense against God the Father. Christ redeemed mankind from the weight of original sin by sacrificing his own life; the conclusion must be that this sin was murder: "the self-sacrifice points to a blood-guilt."[23]

Christians acknowledge the crime of primordial times and atone for it by the sacrificial death of the son. The Christian reconciliation with the father is completed by the total renunciation of the female, which caused man's rebellion against the father.

The Jews who did not participate in the "progress which this confession to the murder of God betokened" were accused by the Christian community with the murder of God: "'They will not admit that they killed God, whereas we do and are cleansed from the guilt of it.'"[24] But also in Christianity the ambivalence of feelings makes its appearance. When the son sacrificed his life he not only atoned his crime against the father but fulfilled his wrath against him by rivaling his place as God. "The religion of the son succeeds the religion of the father."[25] In this light different elements of the Christian ritual assume deeper and more sinister features. The practice of holy communion is a case in point. As a sign of the father's replacement by the son, communion brings back the totem feast—only now the brothers join in consuming the son's flesh and blood instead of eating that of the father. The brothers identify in this manner with the son ". . . becoming holy themselves."[26]

The Violent Roots of Civilization

The superego arises from an act of identification with the father viewed as a model. The nature of this identification is that of a desexualization or even of a sublimation. This dissolution of the Oedipus complex is accompanied by an instinctual defusion, i.e. by a breaking apart of the fusion of the two classes of instincts—sexual and aggressive instincts separate: as soon as sublimation has occurred eroticism loses its hold over the primitive instincts and these are unleashed in the shape of destructive and aggressive tendencies. "This defusion would be the

---

[23] *Ibid.*, p. 254.

[24] Sigmund Freud, *Moses and Monotheism* (translated by Katherine Jones), New York: Alfred A. Knopf, 1939, p. 216.

[25] Freud, *Totem and Taboo*, p. 254.

[26] *Ibid.*, p. 255.

source of the general character of harshness and cruelty exhibited by the ideal—its dictatorial 'Thou shalt.' "[27]

Without strict cultural demands, the universal inclination to aggression and destruction would run amok destroying civilized social life. The pressures of culture call forth reaction-formations in the minds' of men which keep their aggressive instincts in check. But even so civilization is constantly threatened by the violence boiling beneath the thin veneer which cultural striving has laid over human primitivism. The achievements of culture are still insufficient and soon in life we all become disillusioned with our fellowmen, realizing ". . . how much hardship and suffering we have been caused . . . through their ill-will."[28]

Men are ill at ease when they cannot satisfy their tendency to aggression. But they have, nevertheless, renounced this satisfaction to a great extent along with their primitive sexuality. In exchange for some part of his chances for happiness man has attained civilized life, that is to say, a measure of security. But the price for this measure of security is high and it is not surprising that individuals find it difficult to be happy in such a restrictive civilization.

Compared with civilized man, his primitive forebear was better off in this respect, for ". . . he knew nothing of any restrictions on his instincts."[29] On the other hand, primitive man's chances of enjoying his happiness for any length of time were very slight. His price for the unrestrained satisfaction of aggressive and sexual instincts was insecurity, oppression, and an early death.

Modern man shares an important psychic trait with his primitive ancestors: a deep sense of guilt and remorse which results from the earliest primal ambivalence of emotions towards the father, whom the sons hated and loved at the same time. Once the sons had satisfied their hate by killing the father, their love for him manifested itself as remorse about the aggressive act and established the superego by identification with the father. Thus the superego was invested with the father's power to punish, as he would have done, the sons' criminal deed and created the restrictions which should prevent a recurrence of the destructive act. But aggression continued and feelings of guilt accumulated from generation to generation, burdening even the innocent, for guilt expresses the unavoidable struggle of ambivalence, the never-ending conflict between the sexual and destructive instincts—between the forces of life and the cohorts of death. Civilization will, therefore, never overcome its nervous rhythm; it can only reach an equilibrium of discontents.

[27] *Freud, The Ego and the Id,* p. 80.
[28] Sigmund Freud, *Civilization and Its Discontents* (translated by Joan Riviere), New York: Jonathan Cape and Harrison Smith, 1930, p. 87.
[29] *Ibid.,* p. 91.

Man is not unhappy because of his frustrations, but frustration is his fate inasmuch as he is an unhappy synthesis of incompatible drives.

This conflict expresses itself in the Oedipus complex as long as man's social life is restricted to the family and thus causes the development of conscience and the first feelings of guilt. The conflict continues through man's attempts at wider forms of social life, is intensified, and leads to a further reinforcement of the sense of guilt. Since culture follows an inner erotic impulse leading to social cohesion, it can maintain this social unity only by answering growing tendencies to aggression with a steady increase in guilt feelings. If civilization is a process leading from the family to community, then the sense of guilt will mount until it may reach ". . . a magnitude that individuals can hardly support."[30]

It is important to realize that aggression is not just a response to the frustration of some social or sexual need. If this were the case aggression could be resolved, or at least ameliorated, by a specifically social reform of the conditions of frustration. But ". . . an aggression that is built in, due to the presence of a 'death instinct,' cannot be entirely manipulated, let alone abolished."[31]

Thus, Freud did not subscribe to the comforting notion that aggression is a secondary emotion, a result of the frustration of love. Aggression is permanent—part of man, and our destructive tendencies are entirely natural. Ironically, men become more aggressive when the demands for virtuous conduct are sharpened—a lowering of our exaggerated moral standards would decrease human aggressiveness.

Our civilized, humanistic view of man as expressed in ethics, religion, and philosophy is not reality-adequate. Commenting upon the horrors of the First World War that shattered the faith of most intellectuals in human perfectibility and progress, Freud pointed out that their mortification and grievous disillusionment regarding the uncivilized behavior of men were unjustified. These feelings were based ". . . on an illusion to which we had abandoned ourselves. In reality our fellow-citizens have not sunk so low as we feared, because they had never risen so high as we believed . . ."[32]

Still, Freud was aware of the existence and ugly consequences of social injustice; his pessimistic—now outmoded—view of man as a creature chained by its own instinctive mechanism prevented the further development of this thought potential. He remained aloof to all progressive ideologies and was always on guard against the thought that civilization is destined to become perfect.[33] He considered the fact that men are divided into leaders and the led as proof of their innate and incurable

---

[30] *Ibid.*, p. 122.
[31] Rieff, *op. cit.*, p. 343.
[32] Freud, "Thoughts for the Times on War and Death," p. 11.
[33] Cf. Freud, *Civilization and Its Discontents*, p. 61.

inequality. The masses need their leaders and the best solution to this "natural" inequality would be the formation of a superior class of independent thinkers to ensure responsible leadership. This first prerequisite for progress Freud dismissed by pointing out ". . . how little the rule of politicians and the Church's ban on liberty of thought encourage such a new creation." The other necessary condition of progress he saw in the establishment of an ideal community where reason would govern instinctive life. "But surely such a hope is utterly utopian, as things are."[34]

Arguing from the static, conservative position of an "instinct theorist," the Austrian claimed that man's development needs ". . . no different explanation from that of animals. What appears in a minority of human individuals as an untiring impulsion towards further perfection can easily be understood as a result of the instinctual repression upon which is based all that is most precious in human civilization."[35] We must become accustomed to the notion that culture is circumscribed by factors defying all efforts at reform. Foreshadowing the concept of the "lonely crowd" Freud even suspected a turn for the worse brought about by the "psychological misery" of intensified group living. In his *Group Psychology and the Analysis of the Ego,* he practically spoke in terms of "other-direction" when pointing to the disastrous consequences of egalitarian leveling. With an eye upon American civilization he sees us ". . . imminently threatened with the dangers of a state one may call *'la misère psychologique'* of groups."[36] This misery befalls us as soon as group formation results mainly from identifications of group members with one another while outstanding personalities are ignored.

Beyond History

In the late nineteenth century, history loomed large as the central concept and interpretative principle. History was the spirit that man had invoked to resolve the riddles of the universe. For Hegel, private psychological motives were nothing, the world spirit fulfilling its own immanent purposes was everything. Behind historical development and social change ground the collective wheels of large public contexts providing the universal spirit with the changing sceneries that his fateful metamorphoses demanded. In this world theater individual personalities performed no roles other than those of puppets dangling from their strings.

The next script for this antipsychological stage originated with Marx, who described the drama of capitalism as a phase in the unfolding of the inexorable historical process. Capitalism came and will disappear

[34] Freud, "Why War?" pp. 94–95.
[35] Sigmund Freud, *Beyond the Pleasure Principle* (translated by James Strachey), New York: Liveright Publishing Corporation, 1950, p. 56.
[36] Freud, *Civilization and Its Discontents,* p. 93.

as part of the march of history, not as a consequence of the activity of certain personality types. The capitalist personality does not make capitalism, capitalism makes the capitalist personality.

The attack upon the dictatorship of history was largely initiated by Nietzsche. Freud delivered the final thrust that toppled history and replaced it with the new master science: psychology. Following the pioneer trail that Nietzsche had left behind on his way to the night of unreason, Freud journeyed beyond history and discovered mass psychology. Where formerly historical processes had been extolled because they were characterized by change, Freud now proclaimed: the more things change, the more they stay constant. Society, as a psychic process always remained the same and the history of mankind is repeated in the development of individual men. Freud reassured his contemporaries—dizzied as they were by the speed of social change—that history possessed stability after all. The sophisticated youth, Rieff points out, turned away from both Christian and Marxist doctrines because modern men had become disillusioned with all attempts to keep nature and the naturalness of human needs suppressed by history. "It is in this sense that the sociologist Karl Mannheim understood both Christianity and Marxism as utopian doctrines. Indeed, Mannheim awarded Marxism the honor of having been the last utopianism of Western culture, before the sociogenetic analysis of sociology and psychoanalysis together closed off the future to all illusions."[37]

While the advocates of grand history had deflated the private and hypostatized the social context, Freud's psychologistic social theory devaluated the public sphere with its diverse social acts by viewing it as the superstructural layer of manifest content that was determined by the substructural layer of latent psychological motive. The public and the social emerged as mere "reflections" of the private and pathological. This interpretation of the public as a consequence of the private, this transformation of history into mass psychology, is at the center of Freud's social theory; its operation may be illustrated by the conclusion of *Totem and Taboo:* neurosis constitutes private religion, religion is mass obsessional neurosis.

Freud does not consider this analogy between the mental life of individuals and the social processes in groups as startling but "rather in the nature of an axiom."[38] Consequently, all historical and social phenomena become suspect as expressions of this parallel relation between individual neurosis and group life. All historical events appear as functions of human drives that are totally divorced from historical and spiritual elements. The Viennese physician is cast into the role of the executioner of all illusions—a role that enacts a generalizing theory which sees all reality-

[37] Rieff, *op. cit.*, p. 214.
[38] Freud, *Moses and Monotheism*, p. 114.

transcending elements such as ideologies and utopias as relative to drives, that is to say, to eternal forms in the structure of human impulses. This approach involves a distinction between two layers of experience and alleges that one of them is ontologically more real than the other—a methodological device also to be found in the social theories of Montesquieu, Feuerbach, Marx, Durkheim, Pareto, and other exponents of cognitive relationism; it distinguishes between the ontologically "more real" substructure and the "less real" superstructure that is somehow erected over the substructure which figures as the nonmental basis emanating all that is mental. The particular orientation of a researcher determines which substructural factor will be singled out.

Montesquieu emphasized climatological factors; Ludwig Feuerbach saw the determining substructural factor in the potato diet when confronted with different degrees of political success among nations; Marx pointed to economic interests and the relations of production as the main substructural content; Pareto found the basis of the "derivational" superstructure in certain sentiments manifested by "residues," while Freud in similar fashion declared that latent psychological motive of an instinctual nature determines the manifest content of a superstructural layer consisting of the rationalization, sublimation, or projection of the substructural instincts.[39]

In this perspective the ideals of a culture, that is, its judgements of what are its "loftiest and its most ambitious accomplishments," emerge as by-products of a "narcissistic" satisfaction that counteracts the "hostility to culture within the cultural group"—a hostility caused by the pressure culture exercises and by the instinctual renunciations which it demands.

Art, to be more specific, not only subserves a narcissistic gratification but also provides the privileged leisured members of a cultural group with "substitutive gratifications for the oldest cultural renunciations." Therefore, art ". . . serves like nothing else to reconcile men to the sacrifices they have made on culture's behalf."[40] Aesthetics, to further illustrate, conceals its lack of results in the study of the origin and nature of beauty under a ". . . flood of resounding and meaningless words." We know very little about beauty with its lack of evident use; the only thing that seems certain is its derivation from the spheres of sexual sensation. The aesthetic attitude, that is to say, the love of beauty, ". . . is a perfect example of a feeling with an inhibited aim." Beauty and attraction are ". . . first of all the attributes of a sexual object."[41]

[39] Cf. Gerard L. DeGré, Society and Ideology: An Inquiry into the Sociology of Knowledge (Ph.D. Thesis), New York: Columbia University Bookstore, 1943, p. 70.
[40] Cf. Sigmund Freud, The Future of an Illusion (translated by W. D. Robson-Scott), 4th impression, London: Hogarth Press and Institute of Psycho-Analysis, 1949, pp. 21–23.
[41] Cf. Freud, Civilization and Its Discontents, pp. 38–39.

Religious ideas, finally, are neither the residue of experience nor the final outcome of reflection; "they are illusions, fulfilments of the oldest, strongest, and most insistent wishes of mankind; the secret of their strength is the strength of these wishes."[42]

The entire process of cultural development shows a striking similarity to the process of the libidinal development in an individual. Such cultural demands as thriftiness, orderliness, and cleanliness exemplify this observation. Their necessity for survival is not particularly apparent— neither is their suitability as sources of pleasure. Their origin is to be found in the anal eroticism of young humans: their primary interest in the ". . . excretory function, its organs and products, is changed in the course of their growth into a group of traits that we know well— thriftiness, orderliness, and cleanliness." These character traits may be intensified till they ". . . visibly dominate the personality and produce . . . the anal character."[43] The tight-fisted businessman emerges as an elaboration of the anal character.[44]

As in the case of the individual, so also in the instance of humanity as a whole, cultural evolution advances as primitive impulses become subject to sublimation. Anal erotism and eventually the whole of sexuality are victimized by the "organic repression" that became operative after man adopted the erect posture and lowered the value of the sense of smell.[45] Freud speculates that the family—which he views as the fundament of human culture—results from the replacement of olfactory by visual stimuli of mental sexual excitation. In this evolution the organic periodicity of the sexual process has, of course, persisted, but its effect on the male has been reversed.

At first, the menstrual process with its olfactory stimuli aroused the male sexually; the desire for intercourse occurred, therefore, only from time to time. Then, the human animal erected himself from the ground and developed an upright gait. As a consequence the genitals became visible and sexual excitement was produced by visual stimuli which operated permanently. Therefore man, in his ape-like prehistory, adopted the habit of forming families when the need for genital satisfaction no longer appeared on and off but had settled "like a permanent lodger." It was then that the male ". . . acquired a motive for keeping . . . his sexual objects near him; while the female, who wanted not to be separated from her helpless young . . . too, had to stay by the stronger male."[46]

Since man experienced sexual (genital) love as the source of his

[42] Freud, *The Future of an Illusion*, p. 52.

[43] Freud, *Civilization and Its Discontents*, p. 62.

[44] Cf. Sigmund Freud, "Character and Anal Erotism," in S. Freud, *Collected Papers*, Vol. 2 (authorized translation under the supervision of Joan Riviere), New York: Basic Books, 1959, pp. 45–50.

[45] Cf. Freud, *Civilization and Its Discontents*, p. 78.

[46] *Ibid.*, pp. 65–66.

greatest satisfaction, he was driven to seek his happiness further along the path of sexual relations, to make genital erotism the core of his existence. This, however, made man to a very dangerous degree dependent on a part of the outer world, that is to say, on his chosen love-object, and exposed him to great suffering if he was rejected by it or lost it "through death or defection."

Only a few are able to find happiness through love; "but far-reaching mental transformations of the erotic function are necessary before this is possible." These individuals protect themselves by transferring the main value from the fact of being loved to their own act of loving; they do not have to fear the loss of their object since they attach their love ". . . not to individual objects but to all men equally." In this manner a minority avoids the uncertainties and disappointments that accompany genital love by renouncing its sexual intent. The instinct is transformed into an impulse with an inhibited aim—another procedure by which the pleasure principle fulfills itself; its operation can best be observed in the field of religion where saintly individuals have used love in this diluted form to develop an unchangeable, tender attitude and inner feeling of happiness. This is "religious love," love of the world at large; it is rather meaningless because of its lack of discrimination and deluded because of its failure to realize that not all men are worthy of love.[47]

Religious ideas, however, are also prized by the majority as the most precious part of culture. Most men assume that ". . . life would be intolerable if they did not accord these ideas the value that is claimed for them."[48]

The "ordinary man" encounters his religion as a system of doctrines explaining the enigmatic universe and an array of pledges assuring him that a solicitous Providence is guarding his steps in this life, as well as in the next, where all his earthly renunciations and shortcomings will find their compensations. He imagines this Providence as ". . . a greatly exalted father, for only such a one could understand the needs of the sons of men, or be softened by their prayers and placated by the signs of their remorse."[49]

For this, man must pay an exorbitant price, for religion systematically devalues life and deliberately offers a picture of reality which is ·as distorted as a delusion. This is also the chief method of religion; its success stems from the preliminary intimidation of intelligence. "At such a cost —by the forcible imposition of mental infantilism and inducing a mass-delusion—religion succeeds in saving many people from individual neuroses. But little more."[50]

[47] Cf. Ibid., pp. 69–71.
[48] Freud, The Future of an Illusion, p. 35.
[49] Freud, Civilization and Its Discontents, p. 23.
[50] Ibid., p. 42.

In the manner of Karl Marx, Freud views religion as a narcotic, as a "sleeping draught" upon which the believer has become dependent. Turning to the United States of the 1920's, he grimly tackles the champions of Prohibition and Momism which provide him with a contemporary illustration for his suspicion that religion is essentially what Marx made it out to be. "That the effect of the consolations of religion may be compared to that of a narcotic is prettily illustrated by what is happening in America. There they are now trying—plainly under the influence of petticoat government—to deprive men of all stimulants, intoxicants and luxuries, and to satiate them with piety by way of compensation."[51]

Mistrust of the Intellectual Attitude

Freud's legacy is a fundamental mistrust of the intellectual attitude. Having unmasked the aesthetic attitude as nonsensical, the moral and religious as illusory, he proceeds to debunk human thought as the distorted product of instinctive mechanisms: our intellectual utterances and judgements are shaped by "hidden" fantasies derived from the repressed sex and aggressive instincts in their various stages of development. These fantasies are controlled by the pleasure principle, aim at wish fulfillment, and produce wishful thinking, that is to say, thinking directed by wishes that are either unconscious or wishes whose connection with the thinking is unconscious. The wishful thinker does not objectively appraise facts; he favors statements corresponding to his wishes and dismisses others opposing them; his intellectual activity violates the reality-principle since it springs from the fantasies of the unconscious, selecting and using only such knowledge as it requires to satisfy the unconscious wishes of the thinker. "Man is a creature of weak intelligence who is governed by his instinctual wishes."[52]

Human life has the pursuit of happiness for its purpose and object; it is dominated by the pleasure principle which aims negatively at the avoidance of pain and positively at the experience of intense pleasures. The operation of our mental apparatus is entirely subject to the program drawn up by this principle which conflicts with the whole universe, since ". . . the intention that man should be 'happy' is not included in the scheme of 'Creation.' "[53]

The possibilities for happiness are limited ". . . from the start by our very constitution." On the other hand, it is much less difficult to be unhappy. "Suffering comes from three quarters: from our own body, which is destined to decay and dissolution, and cannot even dispense

---

[51] Freud, *The Future of an Illusion*, pp. 84–85.
[52] *Ibid.*, p. 84.
[53] Freud, *Civilization and Its Discontents*, p. 27.

with anxiety and pain as danger-signals; from the outer world, which can rage against us with the most powerful and pitiless forces of destruction; and finally from our relations with other men."[54]

It is, therefore, *la condition humaine* that turns us into "ideologists" offending the reality principle. This discrepancy between the real world and the intellectual universe is especially glaring when the most vital and cherished possessions of a culture are at stake. It is in this context that the human intellect produces judgements of value. The value judgements made by men are "immediately determined by their desires for happiness" and not by facts discovered in the world of reality. In other words, the value judgements that men make ". . . are attempts to prop up their illusions with arguments."[55] Even the best intellects are easily motivated to display "narrowmindedness," "obduracy" and ". . . uncritical credulity for the most disputable assertions."[56] We are mistaken to consider our intelligence as an independent force and to ignore its dependence upon the emotional life. Psychoanalytic experience shows daily that the ". . . shrewdest persons will all of a sudden behave like imbeciles as soon as the needful insight is confronted by an emotional resistance . . ." Similarly nations, those greater units of the human race, still obey their ". . . immediate passions far more readily than their interests." As a matter of fact, their ". . . interests serve them, at most, as rationalizations for their passions; they parade their interests as their justification for satisfying their passions. Actually why the national units should disdain, detest, abhor one another, and that even when they are at peace, is indeed a mystery . . ."[57] The same applies to the passionate and often deadly battles that are carried out within a nation. The stimulation of the aggressive instincts by "appeals to idealism and the erotic instinct" leads to the ". . . innumerable cruelties of history and man's daily life . . ."[58]

The dilemma of the human intellect is a direct result of two pernicious factors in man's early development: religious indoctrination and sexual thought-inhibition. Freud was distressed by the sad contrast between the "radiant intelligence" of a healthy child and the "feeble mentality" of the average grown-up. Religious up-bringing is largely responsible for this degeneration of our mental capacities. Without the influence of religious indoctrination the child would ignore God and other-worldly phenomena for a long time. But instead of granting the child unencumbered development adults introduce him to religious doctrines ". . . at a time when he is neither interested in them nor capable of grasping their

[54] *Ibid.*, p. 28.
[55] *Ibid.*, p. 143.
[56] Freud, "Thoughts for the Times on War and Death," p. 13.
[57] *Ibid.*, pp. 13–14.
[58] Freud, *"Why War?"* pp. 91–92.

import. Is it not true that the two main points in the modern educational programme are the retardation of sexual development and the early application of religious influence?"[59]

Our religious contemporaries follow the behavior of ". . . paranoiacs, who draw conclusions from insignificant signs which others give them . . ." Religion arose in this paranoid atmosphere when "the dim perception . . . of psychic factors and relations of the unconscious was taken as a model in the construction of a *transcendental reality* . . ." This mythological conception of the universe which is psychology projected into the outer world is ". . . destined to be changed again by science into *psychology of the unconscious.*"[60]

Thus, Freud came to embrace a vague belief in progress and meaningful change. The human intellect is weak in comparison with instincts, but they cannot muffle the soft voice of intellect forever. Despite his contempt for Marx's utopian scheme—which he dismissed as a violation of the reality principle—Freud, in the end, sought solace himself in the uncharted future to ease the burden of a present that had yielded too many depressing facts to the scientific investigator. He welcomed the anticipated victory of the human intellect as ". . . one of the few points in which one may be optimistic about the future of mankind . . ." The primacy of the human intellect "certainly lies in the far, far, but still probably not infinite, distance" and represents a "starting-point for yet other hopes."[61] Among these other hopes Freud counts the brotherhood of man and the reduction of suffering, that is, aims which Marx before him sought in the unrevealed future. These aims will only be realized very gradually, "only in the incalculable future and for other children of men." There will be no compensation for us who suffer grievously from life and "religious doctrines will have to be discarded" on the way to the distant goal.

Turning against the defenders of religion, Freud rests his case on science: scientists hold the key to the future, they can discover something about the reality of the world through which men can increase their power and according to which they can regulate their life. "If this belief is an illusion," then Freud recognizes his position to be no different from that taken by his religious opponents. But science, he thinks, has shown men "by numerous and significant successes that it is no illusion."[62] On the other hand, ". . . it would be an illusion to suppose that we could get anywhere else what it cannot give us."[63]

[59] Freud, *The Future of an Illusion*, p. 82.

[60] Cf. Sigmund Freud, *Psychopathology of Everyday Life* (translated and with introduction by A. A. Brill), New York: Macmillan Company, 1929, pp. 309–310 (emphasis in original).

[61] Freud, *The Future of an Illusion*, p. 93.

[62] Cf. *Ibid.*, pp. 94–95.

[63] *Ibid.*, p. 98.

CHAPTER 17

Epilogue

THE MODERN MENTALITY does not have one dimension as did the medieval; the people of the Middle Ages accepted a system of beliefs and values which they never felt seriously threatened. The system assured to everybody a "natural" place in life; an authoritarian hierarchy of official interpreters guarded its survival and effectively coped with the few dissenters who criticized or denied the beliefs and values cherished by the majority.

The system perished not because of its lack of inner consistency or because of its failure to establish a rather general sense of well-being. The system disappeared along with the people who desired it: when the agrarian order became an industrial society the serf turned factory worker, the feudal lord suffered annihilation or joined the rising class of businessmen, the spiritual masters became salesmen of sectarian creeds competing in a market, the guardians of ideas changed into ideological technicians providing the legitimation for the power of diverse ruling groups.

Fundamental changes in the structure of society replaced the one-dimensional mentality of the past and introduced the multidimensional mentality characteristic of modern people who are urban in their orientation, industrial in their way of making a living, commercial in their striving, technological in their training, and scientific in their allegiances.

The modern mentality has its dominant themes and is apparently as capable as the medieval to provide men with common values, shared purposes, and a general sense of well-being: yet we live in an age haunted by much individual anxiety and more social malaise.

Why?

Among the contributing factors three stand out. First, modern men have not made a clean break with the past. Medieval formulae find a ghostly afterlife in quite a few solutions offered for the handling of contemporary problems. In the international balance, Catholicism is still medieval; for a long time Protestantism remained so in its value emphasis, and many of its varieties have never connected with modern times. What Luther and Calvin changed was merely the locale—asceticism and self-negation moved from the monastery to the factory; both no longer fitted. Men became bewildered and faltered; a few became successful—and neurotic. In this fashion the population was unevenly distributed between hell and heaven and paid the consequences on earth. Medieval guilds find their spectral afterglow in the glorification of the group and work team which attracts many modern social scientists and their clients. The closely knit medieval community is revived in the neighborliness of suburbia where it lacks the saving grace of naturalness. There together-ness is perhaps even more tyrannical than in the original setting. The political and military anarchy of the Middle Ages survives almost un-challenged into contemporary foreign policy.

Second, modern men were never granted a respite from social changes. Once the basis for medieval life had been destroyed, funda-mental alterations in the structure of society continued at increasing speed, compounding the original problems of transition. Protestantism and industrialism joined forces to give us the early type of modern man: ceaselessly working, struggling hard against the natural and social envi-ronments. He served his God by asserting himself, and the most ruthless servants of a ruthless deity were rewarded with spectacular material success. The second type of modern man—now in the ascendancy—favors his acceptance by the group and the prerequisite virtues of cooperation and adjustment over the older ones of competitive, selfish individualism. Yet, again there has been no clear-cut, general break with the past and the rugged values of eighteenth- and nineteenth-cen-tury individualism reappear either in the form of confused speech-making or as inconsistencies in the life of group-centered societies, where democracy and authoritarianism, freedom and thought-control, love of peace and militarism, egalitarian leveling and the desire to be different, are precariously juxtaposed.

Third, and as a consequence of these structural antagonisms, the modern mentality encounters its greatest difficulties in its relations with values. Among our contemporaries we find many whose lives are domi-nated by a sense of crisis because they fear for the survival of the values they depend on; a few panic, convinced that all their values are doomed. A growing number of people exist indifferently without any awareness of either values or threat. Another segment of the population experiences an undefined anxiety: among them there is no awareness of values; there is only an awareness of danger.

Nowhere do we find unity. The value-conscious cannot agree on a common set of tenets, the anxious cannot agree on the nature of the threat, and the indifferent follow their private, isolated paths into apathy. But all are suspicious of the motives of the others; they are also eager to doubt and scandalize the premises of opposite positions. The exhaus-tion of the ethical attitude, therefore, goes hand in hand with the exhaustion of the intellectual attitude which began when the first doubt was cast upon the efficacy of man's cognitive apparatus; from there it grew into the ideological suspicion of all thought products. With the recent disintegration of the world into incompatible and separate universes of discourse, the very notion of "truth" took on the appearance of an empty, ritualistic postulate that retained little or no practical significance.

The mental sets of doubt and suspicion gave rise to an area of socio-logical specialization, known as the sociology of knowledge, which simul-taneously provided them with documented and systematic formulations. Émile Durkheim and his school were mainly responsible for the early establishment of the discipline as a research method which made it possible to reveal and describe the differences in thought and worldview setting apart human groups and historical periods. These French re-searchers found the real basis determining the forms and the practices of intellectual life in the various factors constituting the structure of society; as they implied a social genesis of the categories of the under-standing, they expressed an—at least well-documented—rejection of Kant's belief in the universality and timelessness of human reason.

Bouglé's and Halbwachs' social psychological approach helped the acculturation of a sociology of knowledge derived from Durkheim in the United States, where the emphasis shifted—via Znaniecki and Merton —into the direction of audience and public communications research.

What was needed to complete the sociology of knowledge was an exact theory of the relation of ideas and reality. Karl Marx provided a starting point when he asserted the primacy of economic reality, proclaiming that it determined ideas. Following the later scientistic Marx-Engels tradition, the "vulgar Marxists" hardened this theory into an empiricist dogmatism, stressing the all-importance of matter which exhibits its stubborn factness in the social world by economic relationships. Opposing these "positivist," as well as the Neo-Kantian, interpretations of Marxism, the Hungarian Georg Lukács returned to the Hegelian strand in Marx's earlier writings and used historical materialism as a method leading to a universal understanding of historical reality. He held that the bourgeois class is condemned to think falsely by its very position in the objective socio-economic structure. Only the proletariat has "right" consciousness, because in that class the historical process attains self-consciousness: history is the genesis of "proletarian" class-consciousness.

Lukács represents a partial relativism, mitigated by his belief in the utopia of proletarian world revolution which is to make the reign of truth universal. A, formally, similar faith in an imaginary world of time-less and universally valid essences led the renegade Catholic Max Scheler to establish a moderate sociology of knowledge which solves the question concerning the social determination of knowledge in a different fashion: social factors influence the selection of ideas; they accelerate or impede their dissemination—but they do not determine their content or validity.

As the protagonist of a radical sociology of knowledge, Karl Mannheim was perturbed by Scheler's solution of the relativism problem which rests upon the assumption that there is a mental realm with an immanent logic of meaning in relation to which the empirical realm with its social factors plays a merely selective role. Mannheim critically confronted the "static conception" of his opponent with his own "dynamic position" where the sociology of knowledge is possible only in the shape of an extrinsic interpretation of mental products. As such, the discipline is based upon the understanding of manifestations; the sociological observer views knowledge as the expression or manifestation of an absolute stratum: social reality evolving around its core of socio-economic orders and their transformations. Mannheim's concept of a "socio-existential determination of knowledge" expresses the conviction of a total sociology of knowledge, namely, that social life does not only have importance for the realization of thoughts and ideas, but that it also finds its expression in the content, form, and structure of intellectual utterances.

With Mannheim, the existentially determined standpoint of thinking extends into the content of ideas, leaving its imprint on the entire utterance since it exerts a decisive influence even upon the categorical apparatus. In time, Mannheim came to a basic doubt regarding man's intellectual behavior; he eventually arrived at the question of the basic meaning of mind and culture—a question to which he never found a satisfactory answer within the framework of his radical theory.

Presently sociologists of knowledge experiment with the concept "image," which promises to release them from the obligation of finding a satisfactory relation between thought and reality which has been bracketed off; according to its proponents it is the image and not reality which determines the current behavior of all individuals and groups.

Modern men take their clues from images structured around value systems that are usually the expression of yesterday's wisdom. Images, therefore, are easily corroded by the rapid spread of the scientific information relative to the immediate present. This precarious balance on the instantaneity of the knife-edge present makes value-oriented images poor guides of human behavior.

Images are consequently in need of a different normative structure capable of withstanding the heavy flow of scientific messages and this structure can be provided by the same quantitative conceptions forming the core of science itself. Value conceptions have proven incapable of bridging the chasms separating the world's warring universes of discourse —the potential objectivity of quantitative conceptions may overcome the communication blackout.

This suggestion points to a new, possible practicality; it also reveals the frontier of the sociology of knowledge as the locale where values found their liquidation. This event announces, moreover, another grey dawn in the inexorable process of mental entropy.

Significantly the sociology of knowledge represents one of the end products of a chain of developments in intellectual and social history. Premonitory rumblings, forecasting these developments, could be heard already during earlier periods of history, when the view of mind that makes it sovereign, complete, and self-sustaining remained in the main unchallenged. It was essentially the dissolution of the medieval order, however, that started the movement of philosophy toward a view that makes mind reflective of time and circumstance: a view that is suspicious of the sovereignty of mind and of the independence of truth.

This modern view—progressively formulated by sociologists of knowl-edge—has important presuppositions in undercurrents and often un-expected consequences of major European thought systems. Among the more general, philosophical presuppositions we first encountered John Locke's insistence that all our concepts were derived from experience and David Hume's scepticism which relegated the cause-and-effect rela-tion to the same empiricist context. Technically, Kant overcame the scepticism of Hume, who had maintained that we could not arrive at general and necessary laws about empirical facts: Kant argued that statements derived neither from experience (judgements *a priori*) nor from logical inference, (analytic judgements) could attain the status of objective knowledge (synthetic judgements).

But his argument implied that such statements could only attain objective validity as long as reason itself "created" the objects about which the statements were made: reason knew objects *a priori* as long as it created the objects. Apart from the wider epistemological doubt in the cognitive powers of human reason, which originated in Kant's limitation of knowledge to things as they appear in our experience (phenomena), it was especially his emphasis on the object-constituting function of cognition that supplied later theorists with an important presupposition: the sociologist of knowledge, for example, claims that knowledge depends on social reality. This premise would be meaning-less, were it posited in the context of those pre-Kantian varieties of realism that pictured the mind as confronted by an autonomous object which had merely to be registered in photographic fashion. In this context, perceiving man could never exert any influence upon the object of cog-nition. Such influence is conceivable only if we assume with Kant that the object of cognition is constituted by a "creative" act of the perceiving individual. Reality for Kant was no alien object facing us; it was our personal activity—it was a short step from here to equate reality with social and economic activity.

Among the first who took this step was Hegel, who worked out the equation: history is life and life is history. Hegel and the members of the historical school also began with the assumption that the world is a unity and conceivable only with reference to a knowing subject. But they significantly augmented this Kantian premise when they concluded that this unity is caught up in a process of continued historical transformation. Philosophy now assumed a much higher degree of concreteness; philosophy began to absorb historical-political events and thoughts —a change brought about mainly by the new intellectual generation's intense concern for ideas arising from social life and conflict.

Kant's central question was based on the mathematical physics of Kepler, Galilei, and Newton—Hegel, on the contrary, was interested in life, history, and the solution of the contradistinctions besetting his time. His question was: How is life, how is history, possible, and where is the Archimedean lever that will unhinge the manifest contradictions of existence? Hegel's philosophy was, from the start, philosophy of life, philosophy of history, social philosophy. At the dawn of the social question, dialectic changed into the logic making possible the analysis of the social process and of a world which the historical struggle involving men and their institutions denied stability.

Hegel came to measure the pace of history in temporal progress: only consequential events count in world history; all happenings must be evaluated by their success. Whatever is successful has proven its higher right over whatever is unsuccessful—the most successful is simultaneously the most legitimate. Like Darwin, Hegel inferred from the fact of success that the victors' triumph was necessary and justified. But the criterion of success is fraught with relativistic ramifications, and a philosophy worshipping success throws the doors to relativism and cynicism wide open: history was all too often a circus, providing the fat cats with amusements and the masses with sweat and blood; success was all too often bestowed upon the vile and stupid, the vicious and insane.

Hegel's notion of the dynamic reason pervading men's historical creations provided the link to Dilthey's approach to history which was to result in the philosophical interpretation of ideas in their total sociocultural setting. Dilthey discovered the integrity of meaning in a complex historical situation and succeeded in rejuvenating not only the thoughts and personalities of individuals but the spirit of entire eras. In the course of his thinking, however, Dilthey came to abolish all eternal criteria of truth: Kant's transcendental apperception and timeless a priori as well as Hegel's personal guarantee of supertemporal knowledge. Dilthey had no use for metaphysics; he was determined to establish that experience was the sole basis of knowledge. Experience or life moved to the center of his philosophy; but life, Dilthey believed, was fragmentary, manifesting itself differently at each moment in history. Dilthey, then, arrived at the historicist formula: each worldview, that is, each organized, evaluative expression of lived experience, is historically determined, limited, relative.

Thus, reason, the element that supposedly linked all men, suffered a

drastic loss of status: thought became functionalized; it was interpreted
as a function of life. Life as lived, expressed, and understood by men
became the center of philosophy and, significantly, changeability—man's
supreme characteristic—remained as the only constant factor. Furthermore, the atheoretical manifestations of life were considered more relevant to the understanding of empirical reality than thought. Ultimately,
the worldviews were atheoretical units—not products of thinking; they
did not result from the mere will to perceive. Dilthey's emphasis on the
atheoretical elements, his attempt to approach thought from life, must
be understood as an important preparation of the idea that thoughts are
existentially determined: this idea is the principal girder, supporting the
platform of the sociologist of knowledge.

Life, Dilthey argued, cannot be grasped in its totality: the knower can
only perceive life and, thereby truth, in its perspective variations. Only
some of life's aspects are visible from a given worldview position.
Whereas Dilthey was too preoccupied with the development of his theory
of worldviews to further explore these limitations of reason, Edmund
Husserl made this very problem one of his central concerns.

In the reestablished tradition of ontological realism, Husserl developed
his realistic phenomenology and claimed—in opposition to the then
dominant Neo-Kantian schools—that our consciousness merely approaches objects; it does not constitute objects as Kant had maintained.
Husserl's unintended contribution to the further development of epistemological uncertainty and doubt stems mainly from his notion that the
spatial thing can never be entirely comprehended. The particular physical
object, for instance, can only be intended in partial aspects or in perspective; there is, therefore, a large amount of uncertainty and error in
the intention of particulars. The contention that the spatial thing could
only be perceived in perspective variations was of special importance
for the development of the radical sociology of knowledge: Husserl
established the idea that our perception of physical objects is bound to
certain spatial standpoints and Mannheim applied this notion to the
research method intending historical-mental objects.

Furthermore, Husserl's radicalism of method demanded the abolition
of all presuppositions: all principles had to be clarified, all things had to
be constituted on the basis of pure consciousness—a realm purged of
all beliefs in transcendent existence. Husserl endeavored to give epistemology a basis which would not be open to doubt; since no statement
about reality is beyond doubt, he withdrew in his phenomenological
reduction to the only certain fact, namely, that we have experiences.
Philosophy, therefore, must begin with a dismissal from consideration
of everything except the observable character of our experiences, purely
as experiences. Ironically, Husserl felt that he had checkmated error and
doubt when his phenomenology of knowledge defined the objective

world as something which neither exists nor does not exist, but which we believe to exist.

The intellectual development leading to the sociology of knowledge was spurred, furthermore, by certain conceptual presuppositions which were, because of their directive power, even more significant than the philosophical ones. Some of these conceptual presuppositions reflect the dynamics of entire thought movements; others connect more intimately with the labors of individual thinkers.

Historicism is a concept essentially derived from a forceful intellectual current; it is attuned to the ability to experience every segment of the spiritual-intellectual universe as in a state of flux and growth and, as such, it became feasible after the transcendently anchored medieval picture of the world had fallen apart—historicism grew from a rivulet into a stream after the Enlightenment, with its static idea of a supratemporal Reason, had lost its persuasive power.

Historicism in the idealist tradition (earlier historicism) has its root in the original growth of historical consciousness which, in turn, had its beginning in the work of Vico, attaining perfection in the thoughts of Goethe and Hegel, where the historic process moved in the luminous glow of its own deeper meaning. Earlier historicism reached its full bloom in the thoughtful climate created by German idealist philosophy and social science: the founders and exponents of the historical schools revealed the leading ideas behind the diversity of historic phenomena which a pantheistic spirit wove into a many-spangled, yet coherent, tapestry.

The fabric of this tapestry was torn asunder by the men who established historicism in the positivist mood (later historicism), which reached its maturity in the 1870's. The positivist onslaught not only killed the remnants of the pantheistic and universalistic spirit of Goethe's era, where history had been understood as the unfolding of God in time, but all metaphysical presuppositions and in the end—moving far beyond Comte's position—even corroded the will to arrive at any kind of theoretical decision. The meaning of history lay buried beneath a mountain of empirical facts.

Again, reason had suffered a remarkable loss of status: the earlier historicists had organically related the diverse manifestations of history to a transcendent unity, thereby finding reason and meaning in the plurality of absolutes. The mechanistic thinkers of positivism renounced the idea of a universal, cosmic reason and experienced the same pluralism as a meaningless aggregate of factual phenomena, as a mere chaos of worldviews that only statisticians and aestheticians could bear.

Twentieth-century historicism (extreme historicism) found its most forceful expression in the work of Karl Mannheim, who gave it a central position in his sociology of knowledge. The last form of historicism expressed a new attitude to the world leading to the sociological reconstruction of an intellectual cosmos centered around such supratheoretical realities as biological generation, social class, historical time, economic striving, religious outlook, and political commitment. In contrast to the positivists, Mannheim demanded of historicism that it should derive an ordering principle from the seeming anarchy of change; he did not overcome the relativistic consequences of the theory, but he, at least, restored the muscular vitality of the concept, when he answered the challenge of relativism with a call to action.

Epistemological doubt reached a climax in the historicist fragmentation of the world into a bewildering succession of gliding standpoints. An even deadlier threat to truth arose when the suspicion of ideology invaded the intellectual universe. The psychological theories of ideology —mainly represented by the French Enlightenment—viewed ideological distortion of thought as a psychological problem: idols, interests, and priestly fraud were presented as the causal determinants creating a psychic sphere of error that clouds man's understanding of reality. These deceptive mechanisms, however, could be eliminated, and man was pictured as basically equipped to grasp truth. The French philosophers of the Enlightenment transformed the naive distrust and suspicion which men everywhere and at all times showed toward their opponents into a systematic, but particular, notion of ideology which did not discredit the total structure of the adversary's consciousness.

The historical theories of ideology brought a further advance: error and deception became inevitable and irremovable. In this tradition, which anciently connects with Christian and Hegelian determinism, Marx fashioned the total concept of ideology: he accused the entire mind of being ideological; he sensed in man's total behavior an unreliability which he regarded as a function of the social situation in which man found himself. Yet, Marx's concept was limited or special since it exempted the thought of the proletarian class from the charge of ideology.

Finally, Mannheim advanced the total and general concept of ideology: he saw the thought of all groups as ideological. He elaborated this view into an all-inclusive principle which pictures the thought of every group as arising out of its life conditions. Mannheim ascribed to the sociological history of thought the task to analyze without regard for party biases all the factors in the existing social situation which may influence thought. Despite various efforts he never found a satisfactory answer to the question "How is it possible for man to go on thinking and living, once the problem of ideology has been radically raised?"

The first philosopher who systematically explored problems that would later lead to Mannheim's question was Francis Bacon. In the course of his investigations concerning the proper method of inductive research, Bacon discovered obstacles in the path of true knowledge: these he called idols of the mind. He distinguished four species of idols besetting the mind: Idols of the Tribe, the Cave, the Market, the Theater. The first species of idols inheres in the very tribe or nature of man, the second arises from the fact that we are particular kinds of beings who interpret nature from given points of view, the third results from associated living and problems of communication, the fourth species of idols stems from the influence of traditional theories and schools of thought. Bacon considered these idols as the main obstacles in the path of true knowledge; yet he believed that a thorough analysis of their origin and mode of functioning would free the human mind from their distorting influence.

Bacon claimed that the four species of idols are joined by superstition, which is nothing else but perverted religion. Superstition, he felt, resulted from the vested interests of the clergy, which opposes itself as a social class to the rest of society. This thought and his analysis of the psychological preconditions of intellectual operations explain why Bacon is to be considered an immediate precursor of the French Enlightenment.

With Bacon, all science came to rest upon experience, which Hobbes transformed into the abstract understanding of matter as an aggregate of mechanical and mathematical processes. Locke, who provided these notions with a firmer basis, gave the signal for the attack of the French philosophers upon all metaphysics and the resulting battle against extant political institutions and their supposed ally: religion.

The philosophers who developed the most radical stand were Holbach and Helvétius; in the epistemological and ethical realm they adopted a totally materialistic position: man's intellectual capacities were simply an outgrowth of his basic ability to register sensations; everything that caused pain was bad, everything that caused pleasure was good. These simple relations were subject to distortions caused by the operation of three prejudices: interests (man has, essentially, politico-economic interests in deception and evil deeds), idols (in the Baconian sense), and priestly deceit (the clergy in alliance with worldly rulers deceive the masses by spreading a cover of superstitious darkness over true reality to further their own selfish politico-economic interests).

In this climate of opinion the notion that ideas are socially determined found its early formulation: our ideas, argued Helvétius, are of necessity the consequences of the societies we live in. And Holbach saw man as a creature enslaved by his passions and desires which in turn reflected the social environment—that powerful determinant of all cerebral, volitional, and emotional functions.

Finally, the philosophers declared that both the unwitting and the deliberate distortion of true reality could be eliminated: they would educate the masses to achieve the first objective and destroy the power of the Church to realize the second.

Karl Marx accepted and expanded the antireligious program of the philosophers, especially the militantly atheistic version which Holbach and Helvétius had developed. In Marx's criticism religion stood revealed as the opium of the people, paralyzing their revolutionary will. Since Marx's historical materialism was a theory of social revolution, the destruction of religion assumed the rank of a central strategic principle.

Marx transformed the ideological theory of the Enlightenment, however, from a particular one—operating on the psychological plane—into a total theory that invades the entire structure of human consciousness. This new concept made short work of man's intellectual achievements, which were all debunked as distorted expressions of the general self-alienation in social life which originates in economic relations. Truth, finally, was dead and the only thing that still separated Marx from the position of a radical sociologist of knowledge was his utopian faith in the proletarian restoration of truth.

Friedrich Nietzsche was the first philosopher who tried to live with the notion that truth was dead. The falsest judgements, he claimed, are the most necessary for man. Nietzsche's philosophy embraced untruth and made the lie into a life necessity. His revaluation of the intellectual situation elevated error and illusion to life-enhancing factors: it opened the door to the irrationalistic theory of ideology as continued by Pareto and Sorel.

Nietzsche's critique of logic culminated in the reduction of man's conceptual apparatus to a mere function of biological data. All of reason merely manifests the will-to-power which dominates every act of cognition to advance its goal: not truth, but conquest of things and events for the intensification of life. The question of truth had become a question of power.

Nietzsche dismissed modern society as decadent; for this he mainly blamed Christianity—that physiological regression resulting from the decline of the will-to-power, which is a weakness parading under the name of "good." Like Marx, Nietzsche construed his utopia: a distant breeding process would create an aristocratic ruling class of ruthless, bold men who would restore nobility to the world and a measure of truth—daring to live with the naked and unconcealed will-to-power.

The philosopher with the hammer also made sociological imputations and unmasked ideologies, using as his main categories aristocratic and democratic cultures, to each of which he ascribed certain modes of thought. From Nietzsche, the lines of development led to the Freudian and Paretian theories of original impulses and to the methods they developed for viewing man's thoughts as distortions and products of instinctive mechanisms.

Bringing to perfection one of Schopenhauer's flashes of insight, Sigmund Freud elaborated the theory of the biological determination of knowledge. The Viennese physician accepted the devaluation of reason with frightening calm: he had no message, he simply accepted contradiction and error and built his psychology of the absurd on it.

In contrast to most philosophers who assumed that consciousness alone is mental, Freud divided mental life into three parts: the conscious, preconscious, and unconscious. Departing from a long tradition of Western philosophy, he described the unconscious as the largest portion of the mind and climaxed a development which began when the first doubts in the validity of spiritual elements arose. The process of spiritual-mental devaluation had now proceeded far enough to undermine and debunk the conscious sphere by reducing all thought products to functions of instinctive mechanisms, which were entirely divorced from historical and spiritual elements. In essence, Freud taught that all the elements of the nonmaterial superstructure, such as religion, morality, law, social organization, philosophy, art, etc., were determined by the instinctive substructure.

Renouncing their sexual and aggressive tendencies, men attain civilization, and it is not difficult to understand why they find it so hard to feel happy in it. We are not unhappy because we are frustrated, we are frustrated because we are unhappy combinations of conflicting desires. Civilization, Freud concluded, can, at best, reach a balance of discontents.

Freud's legacy is a fundamental mistrust of the intellectual attitude: he unmasked the aesthetic attitude as nonsensical, the moral and religious as illusory, and proceeded to debunk all intellectual utterances as the distorted products of "hidden" fantasies, derived from the repressed sex and aggressive instincts in their various stages of development. Yet, somewhere in the distant future, Freud hoped, scientists would discover something about the reality of the world through which men could increase their power and according to which they could regulate their lives. With the fragmentation of the world into warring universes of discourse, however, we have lost the last illusion which Freud still left us.

Index